Ten Journeys
on a
Fragile Planet

Rod Taylor

Published by Odyssey Books in 2020
www.odysseybooks.com.au

ISBN: 978-1925652789 (paperback)
ISBN: 978-1922311269 (ebook)

NATIONAL LIBRARY LIBRARY OF AUSTRALIA

A catalogue record for this book is available from the National Library of Australia

For Anne, who makes it all worthwhile.

Contents

Preface: Houston, we have a problem   1

Foreword   5

Introduction   11

The Activist: Simon Sheikh   15

The Solar Pioneer: Professor Andrew Blakers   37

The Maggot Farmer: Olympia Yarger   65

The Accidental Activist: Charlie Prell   91

The Thoughtful Salesman: Leonard Cohen   119

The Politician: Susan Jeanes   145

The Climate Game Changer: Inez Harker-Schuch   170

The Advocate: Professor Kate Auty   191

The Lady with a Laser: Monica Oliphant   221

A Question of Hope: Dr Siwan Lovett   243

Epilogue: Houston, I Have a Plan   273

Afterword   281

Acknowledgments   283

About the Author   287

Preface
Houston, we have a problem

In a classic moment of understatement, the crew of Apollo 13 announced they were in trouble. It's easy to imagine them bottled up in that tiny, fragile spaceship. Back on Earth, the ground crew worked frantically, trying to figure out how to save the three astronauts. In the movie, you see them ask what equipment they have on board. Rolls of tapes, pipe, assorted bits and pieces. They have only what they took with them, and to survive they'd need to cobble it together without blowing their meagre energy budget.

The Apollo spacecraft was obviously a closed system bound within its thin shell. The only things entering or leaving was energy and a small amount of gas. Getting them home took a deep understanding of all the parts, the humans, and the machinery.

Now the same phrase applies to our entire planet. Houston, the Earth has a problem. Sadly, there is no home base we can call for help. We're going to have to fix this on our own, and it's not going to be easy.

In a fundamental way, humans are no different to yeast. Put a gram of yeast into warm, sugary water and it'll happily double its population every 90 minutes. At that rate, it'll exceed the mass of the entire Earth within a week. Clearly, that can't happen because other forces intervene, and pretty soon it's eaten all the sugar and is stewing in its own juices. It feels as though we're set up to fail because it's in our nature to consume as much as we can, as fast as we can, until we hit the limits of our ecosystem. I imagine some sort of creature living on, say, Kepler-452b that, like us, has evolved to be extremely successful at exploiting its environment. It'll grow out of control until it hits catastrophe. Or perhaps it also has intelligence, in which case it has some ability to predict the future. That makes us very different from yeast because we can see it coming and, hopefully, alter our course.

In my lifetime, the world's population has grown by over three billion people, and I'm not that old. When you hear that equates to just over 1% per year, that doesn't sound like much, but this is compound interest, with year-on-year growth. What looks like a modest percentage has doubled the population since 1959.

It's a simple statistic, but what's alarming are the people who say nothing's wrong. On its own, we might say it's fine, nothing we can't handle, but what we're seeing is the collision of large forces we seem unable to control. We're depleting natural resources as fast as we can plunder them. We're polluting our ocean, our rivers, and our air.

If that's not enough, on our current path, we are headed for uncontrolled global warming. The recent Paris Agreement aims to keep warming to under two degrees, but if we're going to meet that, we'd better quick-sticks because time is running out. Two degrees doesn't sound like much if you're boiling the kettle or heating dinner. It isn't much until you compare it with the scale of the entire planet. Given the vast size of our oceans and our atmosphere, two degrees is actually a big number.

The global climate system is vastly more complicated than a spaceship, and we only dimly understand it. There are many moving parts in this system, and they are deeply interconnected. Change one and it affects others, often in unpredictable ways. We humans are giving the Earth System a good hard kick, and when it bucks we become passengers. The Kraken, Godzilla, or whatever you want to call it, awakens.

What we do know is that on our current path, sooner or later the system will flip, and then all bets are off. I get an idea of what this is like as I learn to ride a unicycle. It's all good for a while, as I rock back and forth, but when I lose the plot, it's arms, legs, and unicycle in all directions. If I let it get that far, I have no chance. The only way to avoid the catastrophic moment is to keep the system in balance. Heaven help us all if the planet goes that way, because it won't be pretty.

When I started this project, we'd just seen the election of Donald Trump. This is a win for the denialist camp. Science, which provides the hard evidence, is under attack. It's being replaced by emotional, gut feelings, which are the opposite of science. It embraces ignorance, which is not an option. The reasons why Americans voted for such a man are beyond the scope of this book, but it is a deep warning. When a population is unhappy, irrational beliefs take over, and despots take advantage. As global warming and other problems kick in, things will get ugly, not just on the streets, but between nations.

The remarkable thing is that this is a problem entirely of our own making. This is caused by humans, not some malevolent external force. World wars? The Global Financial Crisis and the Great Depression? All human-managed systems. Or perhaps "managed" is not the right word, because clearly we're not in control. It's said that governments don't "manage" the economy. They meddle in it.

So what to do? Social researcher Hugh Mackay makes an interesting observation. We feel so overwhelmed we give up. We can't control the planet, but we can control our backyard. We retreat into the backyard blitz. Fix the pergola, plant some flowers. I don't mind a bit of that, nobody can cope with relentless doom. Another response is disaster euphoria. You see this in the harrowing movie, *Downfall*. It takes place in the bunker in Berlin during the final days of the Third Reich. The Allies are approaching from the west, and the Soviets tanks are rolling in from the east. They're screwed, and they know it. What do they do? Party! They drink, they have an orgy. Nothing matters so they let loose.

It's a bleak, depressing situation, but to me there is only one choice. The musicians played beautifully as the ship sank beneath the waves. This book is my catharsis, my own sense of hope. In the midst of crisis, there are people doing great things, things that make a difference. They are my inspiration, and I hope yours.

We're going over the waterfall, but I'm paddling my little boat upstream.

Foreword

At 4pm on Saturday 4 January, I stood at my front gate. It was pitch black. Only the headlights of slowly moving cars on my street provided any light. The next morning, the sun rose but the world had lost its colour. A thick layer of soot covered everything, including the car. I hosed the windows so I could see through them and drove along deserted streets. "Welcome to the apocalypse," said my friend.

And yet cleaning up after this ash fall was trivial compared to the trauma other Australians endured over the horrendous summer of 2019-2020. Temperature records not just broken, but shattered. Annual rainfall at a record low, caused in part by a record positive Indian Ocean Dipole. The country ravaged by fire "from sea to sea" following, in many regions, the worst drought on record. Towns out of water, rivers dry and, in places, massive fish kills. Over a billion animals perished in the fires; indeed, many firemen sought counselling after hearing the screams of burning koalas. Thousands of people stranded on beaches, sometimes for days, before being rescued by boat. Over 2,000 homes lost and countless outbuildings. Rainforest, previously considered unburnable, burned. Sydney blanketed by smoke for weeks on end, with still unknown health consequences. Canberra was hit by a hailstorm with golf ball-sized hailstones causing widespread damage. And then came the rains that quenched the fires but heavy enough in places to cause flooding.

This is "climate change playing out in real time", as leading climate scientist Michael Mann said at the Climate Emergency Summit in Melbourne in February. "This is what we have had with one-degree warming; imagine what it will be like with four degrees … Dangerous climate change has arrived now."

"There is urgency, but there is also agency. There is still time to act," says Mann. "We have the solutions that will make the shift away from fossil fuels to renewable energy." Leaving it to market forces alone will not be enough to avert dangerous climate change.

Yet for the past decade at the federal level, we have faced a vacuum when it comes to climate action. The one exception was the Private Member's Bill introduced by Zali Steggall and three fellow cross-benchers to provide a regulatory mechanism for achieving zero net emissions by 2050. Amongst the Coalition government, there is even an unwillingness to accept that we are facing a climate crisis. Yet, if there is no action at both national and international levels to radically bring down emissions, we may render the world uninhabitable.

As David Spratt, co-author of *Climate Code Red*, reminded us at this same Climate Summit, meeting Paris emission reduction targets will not be enough to keep within so-called safe levels of warming. Paris agreed that two degrees was the upper limit. We are, instead, heading for three to five degrees warming. And yet four degrees is inconsistent with civilisation as we know it and the proper functioning of ecosystems.

"The nation must go onto a war footing," singer and former Cabinet Minister Peter Garrett said at the Summit, as he called on the federal government to declare a climate emergency and set up mechanisms to achieve a reduction in emissions.

One of the mechanisms that he mentioned was to "restore

our waterways". And this is exactly what Siwan Lovett is doing, as described in this book. Messing up rivers, slowing them down, will restore carbon to our waterways. The beauty of this is that there are a host of other benefits, not least maintaining biodiversity in the rivers and along the riparian zones.

Other Australians in this book whom I have admired over the years include Professor Andrew Blakers, a world leader in solar cell development and inventor of the sliver cells. I have heard his upbeat talks—talks that provided a much-needed antidote to my growing despair over climate change. "Andrew Blakers is the only reason I get up in the morning," I joke.

And Charlie Prell. With the exception of the Lock the Gate movement, which brought environmentalists and farmers together with a common cause, the divisions between the two groups have run deep. Now Farmers for Climate Action has helped break down those barriers. By example, Charlie has shown that farmers can supplement their incomes—in drought years possibly their only income—by installing wind turbines or solar panels on their properties.

Farmers for Climate Action, incidentally, is lucky enough to have Simon Sheik's wife Anna Rose working for them. She came to fame with her book and TV program *Madlands*, in which she tried to persuade climate sceptic Nick Minchin of the reality of climate change. Simon and Anna are a remarkable couple who have achieved a great deal. Simon's collapse on *Q&A* is seared into memory for many of us. It prompted his move away from the public arena to being CEO of the superannuation fund Future Super. It has no fossil fuel funds in its portfolio and instead invests in renewables.

Professor Kate Auty well understands how such ethical superannuation funds can be used as a climate action vehicle. Indeed, at the 2020 Climate Update in Canberra, she was urging the 500-strong audience to look at how their superannuation funds were invested and change their fund if necessary. Kate is a remarkable leader, not only in her work for the Aboriginal community but for sustainability. A "force of nature" you could say.

Climate action is not just about shifting our energy sources away from fossil fuels to renewables. Olympia Yargar has demonstrated how the larvae of the black soldier fly can help convert mountains of food or agricultural waste (that would otherwise emit carbon when decomposing) into animal feed. Two problems solved: reduce waste and provide food for pets, chickens, pigs, and fish.

And then there's Leonard Cohen, not the singer, but a man of Jewish-Maori descent who loved the Kauri trees of his youth in New Zealand and saw the need to sequester carbon through planting trees, thousands of them. He set up the business Canopy, which now has 15 carbon sinks in South Australia and many more around Australia.

The political left does not necessarily have a monopoly on environmental action. Former federal Liberal MP Susan Jeanes turned out to be a champion of renewable energy. Two decades ago, she was instrumental in getting the Mandatory Renewable Energy Target (MRET) through parliament.

Legislation is critical to achieving change, but there must be community understanding of the underlying problem. What better way than to start with 12-year-olds? Create a computer game that helps them take in new information and yet is fun; a game that can be played in the classroom or at home. This is exactly what Inez Harker-Schuch has done.

Invention, development, and investment in renewables, repairing waterways, reducing waste, tree planting, legislation, education—they are all part of the solution. Sometimes it takes someone to combine technical skills with social solutions and Monica Oliphant, daughter-in-law of the late, great Australian scientist Sir Mark Oliphant, did just that. A laser specialist, she saw it was not only necessary to supply renewables, but also address demand, and in doing so, improve energy efficiency.

While climate change looms as an almost overwhelming existential threat, nevertheless, it is but one manifestation of a bigger environmental problem. As Rod Taylor writes: "We're depleting natural resources as fast as we can plunder them. We're polluting our ocean, our rivers and our air." In other words, there are too many people using too many resources and producing too much waste. The natural world is being destroyed by human activities. Biodiversity is being lost at an alarming rate. Populations of wild animals have more than halved since 1970, while the human population has more than doubled from 3.7 to 7.7 billion. Indeed, a 2019 report by the Intergovernmental Science-Policy Platform on Biodiversity and Ecosystem Services (IPBES) found that more than one million species are at risk of extinction.

Some of these ten environmental heroes described in this book have had difficult backgrounds so their achievements are all the more remarkable. My admiration and thanks go to all of these Australians who have made such a difference, and to Rod for bringing their stories to a wider audience.

Jenny Goldie
February 2020

Introduction

The situation reads like a B-grade movie script. A rapidly growing world population collides with environmental destruction while our priority is to grow as fast as possible. The more we consume, the happier we are according to this logic. Combine that with denial from an influential minority that global warming is real, and we have an unholy brew. Clearly, this can't go on, something has to give.

Politics is failing at a time when we need it most. It's miserable, depressing stuff, but I am by nature a problem solver and so I started this book. Where, I wondered, are the glimmers of hope in all this? I wanted to focus less on the dysfunctional mob in parliament and more on what real people are doing. People with talent, people with motivation. People who are making a difference. There are many out there who aren't sitting around waiting for leadership. The people I write about *are* leaders.

Everybody I asked said, *now is the time for this book*. We need some positive stories that inspire and lift us out of the pit of gloom. Okay, I thought, I guess I'd better. So I spent the next 18 months travelling across south-eastern Australia to write about the people you'll meet here.

The central question is why do some people succeed and others fail? Why do some try while others give up?

This book, then, is the story of ten Australians who are not sitting on their hands, waiting for someone else to act. They're a diverse, fascinating bunch of people and each of them has found tangible ways to improve our environment. Whether it's waste, energy, or water, they are steering us toward a more sustainable future. And more importantly, perhaps, they are changing the way our communities think about the environment.

Sometimes when I'm reading back over the manuscript, I think *Wow, these people are amazing.* I feel motivated. Maybe we can do this. There is my glimmer of hope.

This is also the story of a supporting cast of people who popped up as I was writing. I learned about them because they're associated with the people I was writing about. They serve to remind us that we're not talking about lone heroes because each one belongs to a network of others with similar goals.

There's also another group of people whose presence I felt while writing these stories, but who remain in the background. These are the indigenous Australians who still have much to tell us about how to live on—or I should say *in*—this land. Although I didn't find any Aboriginal people to interview, their stories are central to Kate Auty and Leonard Cohen. Perhaps that's an omission that I should address in a future book.

In a small way, this is also my story, if only as an observer on your behalf. I have been given a glimpse into what makes these people special while in other ways they are very ordinary, just like you and me.

There are also people you don't meet directly because they are behind the scenes, helping me write this book. They, too, are leaders. Why? Because in a project like this you flip between the highs and the lows. Occasionally they grab me by the scruff and tell me, *get back in there and finish the job.* They, too, exemplify the spirit that I want to celebrate. You can read about them in the Acknowledgements.

More importantly, you are also part of this story because I'm guessing you too have fears and hopes. Perhaps you feel powerless in the face of daunting odds.

But what would you rather do: die trying, or go down giving fate a good hard kick?

If nothing else, I hope you feel motivated by the people in this book. I do.

The Activist
Simon Sheikh

In the rough neighbourhood of his youth, Simon Sheikh would sleep with an axe next to his bed after being threatened by a local gang. Suffering from mental illness, his mother nearly burned the kitchen down. Then his father had a massive heart attack, leaving Simon with the care of both parents.

After a chance encounter with Justice Michael Kirby, Sheikh realised he could be an activist. He saw how Australian voters have become disaffected, grumpy, and generally turned off politics.

He was only 22 when he became director of GetUp, taking it from a fringe organisation into one that no political party can ignore.

Sheikh found early success, but he was to learn that a public profile has a price.

Outside it was beautiful and sunny, but it was a bleak day. Donald Trump had just delivered his inauguration address and already he was attacking climate science. The world had just broken temperature records for the third year running, while then Prime Minister Turnbull was blaming renewable energy for blackouts in South Australia. All this was just as the nation was about to record mean temperatures for the month (0.77°C above average) and eastern Australia would be hit by a run of heatwaves.

After reading all this grim news I met Simon Sheikh, but he was cheerful, friendly, and upbeat. We were about to record a live interview, but it was he who started asking me questions. How long had I done radio? How did I start writing for the newspaper? What were my plans for *Fragile Planet*? I could see he's a good operator because of his genuine interest in other people and it was hard not to be carried along by his enthusiasm. It gave me a glimpse of how he's been able to stir people out of their complacency to get them active with groups such as GetUp.

Like anyone I don't mind talking about myself, but we were about to go on-air and I needed to get ready, so after a few minutes I had to cut in, "Hey, I'm supposed to be interviewing you."

Transcribing the interview later, I was struck by his use of language, which was peppered with words like "passionate" and "enthusiastic". I made a note to learn about how a person could stay hopeful in the face of relentless bad news.

Simon's father was born in India and spent time in Pakistan. Somewhere in his heritage is Saudi Arabian, which is where he gets his surname. On arriving in Australia, his father quickly detached himself from his ethnic background and assimilated. He's even largely forgotten his native Urdu. Sheikh, who was born in Sydney, says he doesn't think too much about this, but sometimes wishes he knew more about his mixed background. He thinks of himself as Australian and was surprised one day when his wife Anna Rose told him most people don't think of him as a "white Australian".

Simon is tallish with soft features and breaks into an easy smile. His Indian heritage is visible but not dominant. If you meet him on the street, you'll see he's obviously not "full blood white", but with the ethnic mix in Australia, it's hardly noticeable. What stands out more is his surname, which, with his public profile, has made him a target for online racist attacks. Even in a multicultural, relatively progressive nation, some of these forces are just below the surface. Still, he's prosaic and shrugs it off. "That's the nature of modern-day engagement on things like social media."

His sister Belinda died before he was born and his mother had a bout of encephalitis when she was much younger. Later she suffered mental health issues, which left Simon's father the job of looking after him. Sheikh describes those times in a *Sydney Morning Herald* article. His mother's mental health worsened during her pregnancy, and by the time he was born, Simon's parents were living apart. His mother was becoming increasingly delusional with psychotic episodes.

Simon had to deal with his mother's instability such as the day she set fire to the kitchen while cooking chips. It wasn't made easier living in the inner-Sydney neighbourhood. Enmore was a rough neighbourhood back then and drug and alcohol abuse was common. It was an unsettling start to life as he recalls, "I'd often hear huge fights as I lay awake at night. I remember being scared a lot."

"I slept with an axe next to my bed after being threatened for not paying enough protection money to a local gang."

When Simon was 10 or 11, his father had a major heart attack leading to a quintuple bypass. Now the young Sheikh found himself caring for his father as well as his mother. He says his father "really didn't recover full strength for quite some time" and at various times both parents were dependent on welfare.

For Simon, it was a formative moment that could have gone either way. In an ABC interview, he told Richard Aedy:

[His father] would come back from work, in those years that he was working, cook dinner, ensure that I was studying, and then go back home again. Every single day. And that put in place for me a regimen that was very helpful in keeping me grounded and particularly in keeping me away from a lot of the troublemakers that I grew up around.

I had a year or two there where things could have gone wrong.

By Year 7, Simon was showing glimpses of his future life and the energy that would propel him into national prominence. Already he had an emerging political awareness and a sense of social justice. His first rally was against the rise of Pauline Hanson. It was, he says, something he did with encouragement. "I was lucky in high school to have teachers help propel that along."

Simon's impressions from the "fairly poor" community of his childhood have stayed with him. "I got to see a few challenges faced by the people around me." There were sole-parent families and most parents didn't manage the finances very well. There were high levels of drug and gambling addiction. His parents had other problems, but he's grateful for the strong grounding they gave him. "I owe a lot to my dad," he says.

After a day at school, he would go off to private tuition, which was something few other parents could manage. Today he can see that it was the commitment of his parents and their focus on education that got him into university. "They were always putting every dollar they could into education," he recalls. "Growing up the way I did meant I learned to be self-sufficient and to navigate systems to achieve the best outcomes."

It was also central to the skills that would be part of his future life in activism. "I learned how to read people, to be alert to the smallest signs of a changing mood, and to diffuse tense situations. I saw first-hand the inequality that exists in our society. It breaks my heart that this inequality is worsening."

By age 16, the regimen his father established was showing

results and he was accepted into Fort Street High School. It was an early success, but he says he was "very much embarrassed" by his background.

It was something he preferred to keep secret until a couple of events changed his mind. In 2002, Senator Bill Heffernan used parliamentary privilege to attack High Court judge Justice Michael Kirby on the basis of his sexuality. The next day, ABC reporter Fran Kelly described his allegations as "sensational and highly defamatory". Heffernan was suggesting that Justice Kirby had committed child sex offences with male prostitutes. It had a strong effect on Sheikh who says, "I saw him do those horrible things, making those horrible suggestions about Justice Kirby."

Kirby had himself been a pupil at Fort Street High School. He made a speech to the assembly, describing he'd been in this same hall, hiding his homosexuality. It was a pivotal moment for Sheikh, helping him to realise he didn't need to be ashamed of his home life.

It was a great moment of validation when some years later, Justice Kirby came back to his school to give a speech and Sheikh was able to introduce him onstage. Being recognised at such a young age helped confirm to Sheikh that he should pursue his future in activism.

It didn't take long for Sheikh to move beyond writing letters to the editor. Already in 2006 he was the convener of the Australian United Nations Youth Association and was able to introduce the keynote closing speech by Governor-General Michael Jeffery. That led him to get involved with the Australian Youth Climate Coalition movement that now has a membership of over 120,000 young people.

It was here that he met his future wife Anna Rose. By coincidence, they'd both seen an ABC *Four Corners* special about coal, which had focused their attention on global warming and became a trigger for further activism. Later their paths converged during the formation of the Youth Climate Coalition and in November 2011 they were married.

If rise to prominence through activism was swift, the backlash was not far behind. They would soon learn what life can be like in the public sphere. One blogger described the AYCC as a "hard left movement". Andrew Bolt already had Sheikh in his sights, writing, "I don't consider Sheikh a man of any great integrity, to put it mildly. And that's without even considering what he says about global warming."

Other News Limited columnists seemed to enjoy the sport. One referred to Sheikh as "the former madam of left-wing cause bordello GetUp!"

Then another writer in the online magazine *Quadrant* didn't hold back with an extended ad hominem, which he called "March of the Climate Cult Kiddies".

> Perhaps because of the koala costumes and elephant suits, the Australian Youth Climate Coalition's zealots seem no more worthy of adult attention than any other noisy assembly of adolescent public nuisances. Dopey as the rank and file may be, their leaders are a lesson in slick marketing.

The writer went on to pull apart the AYCC's membership claims with phrases such as "dedicated lobbyists determined to see the imposition of economy-busting carbon dioxide controls".

The online trolls soon emerged on various websites, launching often juvenile personal insults. One referred to "Gullible Warming" and there was page after page of vitriol.

> *Sheikh is a puppet stooge …*
> *A very thick Sheikh …*
> *Just another mongrel trying to get on board the gravy train with the Stupid Club in Canberra …*
> *That poor misled, over-educated boy needs serious medical help.*

For many people, such sustained online attack would be unbearable, but Sheikh shrugs it off. "The negative reaction hasn't affected me too much and I have been able to ignore them. The Internet is full of crazy people."

Even the blast from columnist Andrew Bolt made almost no impression. "I must say I never thought about the article since. It rings a bell, but I think that says it all. For some reason, I have a strange ability to not remember it."

Public attacks of this sort must be hard to weather, so it seemed there must be either an excessively robust ego or the ability to switch off. Or perhaps a bit of both. "I think there is no logic to this," he says. "It's a subconscious protective mechanism that has been formed so much over the years. It might have been that the difficult, violent, and highly confronting situations in my childhood literally changed the way my brain functions."

As he said this he waved his hands cheerfully, but what, I wondered, if the criticism is valid? Does this make him impervious to good advice? Sheikh rejects the idea. "When you have staff telling you constantly you're making mistakes, that leads you to reflect. But Andrew Bolt's article seems so absurd that it's hard to find a grain of truth."

Clearly, Sheikh has a thick skin. But as I was soon to learn, not that thick.

GetUp and AYCC draw fire for their slender online signup process. For critics, it has little value because it's too easy. Some have registered themselves multiple times and even their pet dog.

By February 2017, GetUp claimed to be "a movement of 1,077,615 Australians". It takes only a minute or two to provide an email address and there's no fee. To join the Liberal or the Labor party takes a little longer, and does not require a membership fee. With each party having only 40–50,000 members, they are dwarfed by GetUp.

It was a deliberate strategy by Sheikh and the GetUp leadership to boost numbers as fast as possible. That is reflected in their use of social media, with rapid-fire interactions. They wanted to minimise the barriers to participation. This rankles in traditional circles who see it as one-click activism, but in many ways, it mirrors other online interactions where you can purchase a book with a single click. Firing up a GetUp campaign takes just a few moments on the website, which suits the connected generation who expect to do almost everything on their mobile devices and doesn't require tedious meetings. That led GetUp to say in their 2014-15 annual report that there'd been "959 community-run petitions, 1,175,437 signatures, and 141,210 emails to members of parliament."

This approach by GetUp opens it up to criticism that they inflate their membership count by targeting people who care but don't really care. Their concern is enough to click, but that's all. Some call it "slacktivism", a term that technology commentator Clay Shirky describes as "ridiculously easy group forming".

Sheikh counters, saying in a 2012 interview: "In the last 12 months about 80,000 people have made a financial donation." That number is roughly equivalent to the *combined* membership of the Liberal and Labor parties.

Even with that caveat, over a million GetUp members in 2017 is a formidable number, and one a marketing executive would envy. During Sheikh's tenure, the number rose to 600,000, but their real influence is harder to judge. Former finance minister Lindsay Tanner suggested that GetUp is "a battle between Labor and the Greens", which means he could ignore them because they're not an election decider.

Another Labor MP, Steve Gibbons told online magazine *Crikey*: "I've long held the view that these bloody lobby groups, even if I'm sympathetic to their causes, are a fucking nuisance. Because what it does is it just crams our inbox with crap." Others quoted in the

Crikey call them "those fucking GetUp! pricks", "armchair activists", and "remorseless self-promoters".

Their expletives underlie the political establishment's irritation, but it clearly shows GetUp had made it past first base. GetUp now had the attention of federal politicians. They may have found it irritating, but they couldn't ignore such a large support base. What then did Sheikh do with this sort of influence?

One difference they introduced was to flip the usual activist method. Most organisations set up a campaign then enlist supporters. But GetUp allows any member to initiate one. Broadly, it pitches a progressive-left agenda with their signature themes being Social Justice, Economic Fairness, and Environmental Sustainability.

Sometimes the activism was a show for the media. In 2011, they paid $16,000 for an Afghan asylum seeker's surfing lesson with prime minister Tony Abbott. Riz Wakil had arrived by boat, but Abbott told reporters, "He's an Australian now." It didn't change the government's policy, but Sheikh still believes it had an impact. He told the ABC: "Well, those people who went along were given, suddenly, overnight media prominence."

Other GetUp campaigns were more substantial. In 2010, they took a case to the High Court, saying the Electoral Act violated the constitution. The Act blocked voters who had not enrolled at the time the election was called, excluding a large number of voters. It particularly affected younger, first-time voters. By winning the case, they gave access to registration for 100,000 people who otherwise could not have voted. After winning the case, 58,000 voters actually registered.

Sheikh and the GetUp movement had long been concerned about global warming. "Runaway global warming is reaching scary tipping points—we are reaching 1.5°C now, hurtling toward 2°C," he says. They were galvanised by the rise of Tony Abbott, who is quoted as saying that science is "crap". Abbott was quick with the slogans, describing the Gillard government's carbon pricing as a "big new tax" and with the help of conservative media, succeeded in turning public opinion against it.

In an attempt to counter the conservative views, GetUp ran an extensive campaign during the 2013 election that demonstrated the potential of their huge membership base and on a single day they raised $100,000 for advertising.

One prominent billboard played on Abbott's catholic background: *Tony, abstinence is not a climate option!*

Nevertheless, the Liberal-National Party won the election and on the first day of the new parliament, Abbott introduced legislation to repeal the "Carbon Tax".

Even then, it wasn't just Abbott who was the target of GetUp's climate campaigns. Earlier, the Kevin Rudd government had lost its nerve and failed to introduce a price on carbon. Then during Julia Gillard's reign, the government was wavering. Under Sheikh, GetUp paid for a slick TV advertisement with an actor portraying Gillard talking to an unnamed person. The comic script skewers the convoluted responses to climate change, with subtle jibes about asylum seekers. It went (in part):

> **Gillard**: *Climate change is our greatest challenge.*
> **Gillard**: *We could move our country to East Timor … scratch that … Papua New Guinea.*
> **Gillard**: [speaks on the mobile phone] *Do you have room for 20 million people?*
> **Gillard**: [hands over snorkel and flippers] *You may need these.*
> **Gillard**: *Tony Abbott is about Direct Action. We're about Acting Directly.*
> **2nd Character**: *Why don't you just put a price on pollution?*

During Sheik's time at GetUp, they ran a series of similar campaigns. In each case, they were giving voice to Australians who were otherwise disengaged. This is perhaps the most significant achievement of GetUp, regardless of any particular issue. Membership of the major political parties has dwindled to a level where they're almost insignificant. There are ten times more members of golf clubs in Australia than there are in the Labor party.

Post-Traumatic Stress

At 7.30pm, it was the end of a long day at the Melbourne Town Hall. Many of the 600-odd participants at the Community Energy Congress had drifted away, but a sizable number were still there for the announcement that had been promised.

The video screen lit up and was filled with Simon Sheikh's earnest visage, describing his newest foray. The Future Energy Fund is for people who want to make ethical investments, but don't want to shift their superannuation. It promises to channel money into what it called "Australia's clean energy future".

It seemed odd that Sheikh, a naturally articulate speaker, had not shown up earlier. For most of the event, he was nowhere to be seen. Participants might have been expecting to see the high-profile figure presenting a talk or taking part in the panel discussions, but there was no sign of him. Instead, I found him in the lower level among the trade displays, peering into his laptop. Surely he'd be up and about, mixing with the other speakers?

The video clip ended, and then there he was. He bounded onto the platform, his grin as wide as the stage. "We are so excited about the Future Energy Fund and we need your help," he enthused. "Please sign the forms we're passing around and we'll keep you in touch when the prospectus is issued."

This was more like the bouncy character we expected, but a

moment later he was gone. I gave him a cheery wave as he trotted past, but for the rest of the event, he was almost invisible.

What was not obvious to the audience was that he found this simple occasion extremely difficult. Nobody in the auditorium was aware that Sheikh was suffering from trauma. Simon Sheikh has PTSD.

The term "shell shock" appeared during World War I, which morphed into "combat fatigue" during World War II. It's an evocative expression that captures the ongoing impact of stress. Today we have the more complicated but nuanced version: Post-Traumatic Stress Disorder.

People with PTSD aren't necessarily the victims of war. It can be any sort of violence or even the result of repeated bullying in a toxic work environment. In Sheikh's case, the cause is unusual because it was public, but in other ways, it's not that remarkable.

The cause? Simon Sheikh fainted on live national television. That's certainly uncommon, but to me it did not look like a big deal. You can easily make yourself faint by hyperventilating then standing up suddenly.

A web search for Simon Sheikh brings up on the first page articles such as this one from the *Sydney Morning Herald*: "Coalition frontbencher Sophie Mirabella says she was in shock when GetUp! director Simon Sheikh collapsed next to her on live TV."

Footage shows him leaning forward, clutching at a glass of water. Slowly his head slumps until his forehead bumps the table, and beside him Mirabella leans back, looking startled. Watching the footage now, Sheikh says, "At first, she thought I was just being an over-dramatic," but he wasn't faking it. Sheikh had just collapsed, on live national television.

Sheikh is only out for a few seconds and studio staff rush to assist. One puts his hand on Sheikh's chest, presumably to feel his heart. As he sits up, Mirabella reaches across and touches his shoulder. Her reaction was soon mercilessly trolled in social media, with things they'd never say directly to another person.

Fucking useless bitch next to him.
Look at how she leaned away from him, almost in disgust.
Only the men in the room came to his aid.

Predictably, Sheikh also came under attack, but in some ways, Mirabella came off worse. Even though they are politically opposed, GetUp felt obliged to defend her, tweeting: "Folks, please don't criticise @SMirabellaMP—it was an extraordinary circumstance and everyone was shocked." Sheikh was sympathetic, commenting, "If I was her, I probably would have reacted in the same way."

The entire incident lasts only a few seconds before Sheikh is helped offstage. He gestures with his hands, mumbling, "Sorry, I just fainted." Now his memory of the event is hazy. The next thing he could remember is only what he's seen on TV. "I got up and apologised—which was a strange reaction, but is very me—a natural thing that I would feel apologetic. I left the stage feeling woozy. I had lots of water being poured on me, to try and keep me awake until the ambulance came."

The ambulance took Sheikh to Sydney's Liverpool Hospital where he again apologised, this time on Twitter. "For those watching *Q&A*, sorry I couldn't stay—I'm in hospital, thanks for all your support." He didn't stay long, checking himself out after a few hours because there was no doctor available.

The *Q&A* session had been about the carbon price, which he used to make light of the incident, saying he'd suffered a carbon dioxide overload. It wasn't obvious to the public, but this was his way to cope with a difficult situation.

Sheikh was accustomed to media attention, but he was not prepared for the intensity this would generate. Fainting on national television was enough, but now it was amplified by the barrage that followed. Sheikh describes what happened next:

> It was a simple thing, but unfortunately, this particular one went viral. The challenge for me was my phone went bananas right away, with messages flooding in, phone calls flooding in, voicemails flooding in, emails flooding in, and calls flooding in from journalists from all over the world trying to get in touch with me to see if I was okay, to see what was going on, and it didn't stop for a week.

Meanwhile, a war raged on *Wikipedia*. In the world of quantum Internet weirdness, Simon Sheikh was alive and Simon Sheikh was dead. His wiki entry played out a sort of *Schrödinger's Sheikh*, where one moment his entry said he'd died and the next he'd only fainted. Sheikh's friend stayed up late correcting the entry while somewhere an unseen person was killing him off again. *Wikipedia* is supposed to trap these events, but for some reason it didn't, and it left a trail of flip-flopping entries before finally subsiding.

The Australian newspaper also got it wrong and for a while they exaggerated news of his death. One source of the rumour couldn't even spell the name of his supposed condition, saying, "At 10:12pm AEST, Sheikh was pronounced dead at St Vincent's Hospital, Sydney. Doctors attributed the cause of death to excessive carbon consumption exacerbated by bouts of 'tosseritis.'"

In hindsight, Sheikh can see he'd been pushing himself hard and it wasn't surprising that something had to give. He told the ABC: "The last four years in this job have been pretty intense. I've been feeling pretty tired for the last three or four months and probably should have taken a break earlier." Sheikh did have a mild flu, but there was more than that. He'd been campaigning relentlessly with GetUp and the signs were starting to show.

Using the influence of GetUp, he'd been asked by the parliament to participate in multiparty meetings on carbon pricing. That was a demanding commitment on top of his already heavy workload and it brought things to a head. The night before *Q&A*, he'd decided it was time to quit the organisation. "I had come to the view that I was so in the weeds, I had to remove myself." He spent a sleepless night worrying over his decision and by the time he arrived at the ABC studio, he was exhausted.

Sheikh felt his role had become too managerial when what was needed was an innovator. An organisation, he says, should reinvent itself every five years if it's going to succeed. In fact, it's a willingness to take risks that he says is a key part of his own success. He says GetUp's 2010 High Court challenge to the Electoral Act "cost about as much money as they had in the bank". They literally bet the bank on this campaign and it was fortunate they won.

At this point in our conversation, I diverted him to get a better understanding of what GetUp was doing in the multiparty carbon pricing meetings. What was their goal? What were they contributing? For a while, we talked at cross-purposes until another side of him emerged. "You're not following me," he said. It was a mild rebuke, but it revealed something that often occurs in highly intelligent people. It's obvious, why don't you get it? I got the sense he could be hard work when he's agitated.

Carbon pricing was a core issue for GetUp, who was campaigning for action on climate change. They were pushing the Clean Energy Finance Corporation and ARENA (the research funding body). "We wanted to make sure Australia's carbon pricing regime actually supports a transition to renewables," he says.

Sheikh says this was a membership-led campaign. It's the members who were saying this is what they wanted and it was for the GetUp management to make it happen. The role of GetUp is to amplify the voices of people who would otherwise be left out. This is part of GetUp's progressive-left agenda of Social Justice, Economic Fairness, and Environmental Sustainability. On the GetUp website, there's a constantly updating scroll from members. The rapid-fire messages convey a sense of urgency, a sense of action.

> **17 sec ago** *Callum called on Jay Weatherill to back 24-hour clean power for SA*
> **52 sec ago** *Zoran called on Jay Weatherill to back 24-hour clean power for SA*
> **2 min ago***Nic called on Jay Weatherill to back 24-hour clean power for SA*
> **5 min ago** *Phoenix called on Jay Weatherill to back 24-hour clean power for SA*
> … and so on.

Sheikh has the useful ability to ignore national newspaper columnists and streams of internet abuse, but the *Q&A* incident let him know that he too can be vulnerable and perhaps he needed help. He sought counselling from a psychologist who suggested that being able to filter the negativity was linked to his childhood. Perversely, perhaps the toughening of his early years was good preparation for his later public life. As he says, "When you're exposed to a trauma, you become really good at forgetting things. It's an adaptive reaction and when I have a difficult situation for me I can't recall. I genuinely can't remember."

He's able to filter the words of loud people, but he can't ignore his strongest critic—himself. He feels that in the *Q&A* incident he let himself down, that he let his supporters down, and he failed at a time when a critical public needed him. "My father told me from an early age to be quite a proud person, which isn't necessarily the greatest of traits and I think this is a challenge. Also this sense of embarrassment."

The incident on *Q&A* has left him anxious and speaking in public—even before a friendly audience—is something he avoids. This is from a person who was still young when he introduced a nationally prominent figure—Justice Michael Kirby—to his high school assembly.

The events on *Q&A* were traumatic.

I couldn't even complete an episode. Mid-sentence I started to lose my train of thought. I've never had anything like that happen before. I remember thinking, how am I going to get out of this situation?

It felt really slow. The whole process felt like forever, but it was probably five minutes, maybe less.

As soon as the first question was asked of someone else, I started to feel really bad. Right at the start of the program I thought, how am I going to get out of this?

Sheikh's determination had been part of his success, but now it was a liability.

I thought, you know what, Simon, you just have to stay here. Until that time I never felt anything other than almost invincible, full of young bravado. Everything I've tried has been successful. For the first time in my life, I had a spectacular failure.

Or at least what felt like a spectacular failure.

The words *spectacular failure* resonate and now Sheikh feels it is unlikely he will ever return to high-profile public life. Or at least, a life where public speaking is crucial and almost certainly not politics. He exhibits the classic symptoms of PTSD, which revolve around endless replays of those traumatic moments. "Even as I talk to you about it now, it brings it all back. It was such a difficult process. It was an extremely difficult thing trying to push through."

He remembers *Q&A* host Tony Jones asking his view on a particular question and he says, "In my head, I knew exactly what answer I wanted to give, but I couldn't get the words out." And now the experience is still with him. "Over the years I've noticed that if I get up in a room where I plan to speak, I just play it in my head over and over again and it kind of becomes a self-fulfilling prophecy. I'm playing the possibility of feeling anxiety."

Perhaps as much as anything, it surprised him. "This has never happened before. I know it sounds strange, but I've never found myself lost for words."

Sheikh is a confident speaker and forceful when he wants to be, which makes his experience particularly difficult for him. As he spoke I was reminded that the way we appear on the outside is often very different to how we feel on the inside, and even the most resilient people can be more vulnerable than they seem.

It didn't take long for Sheikh's determination to kick in, and in July he decided he should return to *Q&A*. "I thought the best thing to do is get back on the program," he says. He did a couple of weeks later, but it was difficult and he remembers, "I really just wanted to rip the Band-Aid off. I got a bit of a joke at the start, which I really needed just to loosen up. It was excruciating because already by that point I had developed anxiety, replaying the moment."

Tilting at Politics

After GetUp, Sheikh made the final jump into politics. Inevitably it would entail almost daily confrontations with his demons and he couldn't shake the *Q&A* incident. "I felt like people started to think I might be unhealthy," he says.

He launched himself into the 2013 federal election, winning preselection for the Greens Senate ticket in Canberra. The Greens were a natural fit for his environmental progressive views, but some people saw him as a celebrity ring-in. Sheikh didn't even live in Canberra, so that meant moving with his wife Anna Rose.

Politics, he says, has become particularly tribal and unpleasant. Around this time Tony Abbott was proving to be a brutal opposition leader. He ruthlessly attacked Kevin Rudd, but was even more savage when Julia Gillard became prime minister. It shifted the political culture toward the negative, making it a game of winners and losers where the best result for the nation is secondary. Fuelled by the media, the public saw political debate that seemed unable to shift beyond insults.

There were occasions when Sheikh's public profile intruded into his private life and his family. At one point he recalls, "A large man turned up angrily at my door. My mother-in-law was moved to tears when an aggressive journalist came to my home. It's a shocking thing to be involved with."

The nasty style infected the public debate, but it was also projected by the media—in particular, the Murdoch press. Sheikh remembers, "I had journalists from *The Australian* newspaper parked outside my home and outside my office. To get through either one, I had to push past them. There was a lot of venom from *The Australian*."

Ultimately Sheikh came close to knocking the Liberal incumbent Zed Seselja off his seat. It was a near success, but laid on top of his disastrous *Q&A* experience it became too much and he retired from politics.

In all, Sheikh is pragmatic about the media. He says, "You have to play the game. Take it as it comes, and don't be surprised." He might have been a target himself, but he could still dish it out in return. During the election I heard him on local radio, playing on the Liberal party leader's unpopularity. He looked bemused when I reminded him of how he'd said that Zed Seselja "is nothing more than Tony Abbott lite".

Still, in the scheme of things it was fairly mild, nothing like the treatment dished out by others on Julia Gillard. Anyway, who wants a bland politician? I didn't know Simon back then, but I remember thinking, "Who is this guy?"

Sheikh laments the impact of Tony Abbott, but he thinks it's also a product of the 24-hour news cycle. The media needs a constant stream of input so it feeds on the negativity that gets attention. He's also concerned about the impact of political donations and lobbyists, who've skewed the balance of power away from ordinary people.

Hearing Sheikh tell his story, it's hard to imagine why anybody with talent and determination would want to put themselves into such a toxic environment. Why would anybody punish themselves trying to do something they believe in? We've built a system that is ideally tuned to selecting the self-serving narcissist and then complain we don't like them.

Tilting at Finance

In 2011, a *Crikey* online columnist made an observation that hinted at Sheikh's future thinking.

> The activist outfit [GetUp], while talented at fundraising, also lacks the financial muscle to go toe-to-toe with cashed-up vested interest groups like the mining industry.

After leaving GetUp and missing a seat in parliament, Sheikh moved onto the next lever—money. The divestment movement hopes to pull the financial rug out from under fossil fuel industries. The aim is to direct investment toward ethical causes instead of projects such as the giant Adani Carmichael coal mine. The principle is simple, but it relies on informed investors taking the time to do it. Given the complexity of which companies own what and how they earn their money, it's not easy. You might invest in a bank or a supermarket, but a few layers down the money goes into coal.

In 2014, a group of ethical investors including Sheikh eyed the vast $2 trillion superannuation industry. That amount of money would be a powerful force to steer money away from environment-damaging industries. By early 2017, the results were showing. "Money talks when it walks, and that's certainly what we found. Now we manage over $200 million, and some of that is invested in renewable energy projects," he says.

GetUp was about disrupting the political establishment, and now Sheikh aims to do something similar to the finance business. "Our theory is that there is more than $2 trillion in a sector that can be disrupted," he says. He doesn't imagine that Future Super will take over the superannuation business, but it can be a catalyst that changes where money goes.

In many ways, Future Super is the ideal choice for Sheikh. It's taken him away from the hurtful public life to a place where he can still exert an influence. It builds on his skills in the finance business, but he says, "I don't think the PTSD will ever really resolve itself. I have avoided it and instead I'm running a social enterprise."

"I spend my days in spreadsheets looking at general ledgers and answering accounting questions. I really enjoy it and I can make an impact helping renewable energy. It's been really great to be able to transform myself from a political activist to a market activist."

"I can't see myself going back into politics."

Americans are fascinated by extroverts, but in Australia we're not so sure. The smooth talker, the self-promoter, the square jaw with the easy smile don't always sit with what we imagine as the laconic character. Sheikh's public persona might suggest an extrovert, but it's misleading. He claims, "I've always been a natural introvert. Even though it doesn't come across, I've always needed a push to do public speaking. Representing people's voices in the media has only ever been a means to an end."

He attributes his success to being able to connect with other people who are "deeply concerned about our fellow humans". He's learned from behavioural economics and from social psychology about how people form groups. Being a good communicator, he says, is not just listening, but "being able to think logically and turn people's sporadic thoughts into a set of logical thoughts and say it back to them".

He says his ability to negotiate has been a critical skill, especially in the tough world of politics. Part of that was taking a proposal to a politician, but having another plan. "We could agree to X, Y, and Z, but if you don't I got this great alternative and I'm going to this party."

I arranged to meet Sheikh so we could do an interview at the Future Super office. Planning my schedule carefully, I trotted up the stairs in a run-down office building and along a dingy corridor to where the office should be. When I saw the lights were out, I realised it was the old address. After a few text messages, I soon arrived at the new location. There, I was met by a cheery staff member who let me in. Inside I found a much brighter, more modern room with about a dozen people bustling around desks. Future Super is a long way from taking over the superannuation industry, but their presence will be felt.

I couldn't finish my conversation with Sheikh without an inadvertent reference to Pauline Hanson. I asked him if he'd ever thought it was too hard, that maybe he should give up and just work in a fish and chip shop?

"No. No, I don't think I have."

The Solar Pioneer
Professor Andrew Blakers

It's odd when a prominent person tells you they're proud their parents were locked up, but that's how Andrew Blakers described his reaction to the arrest of his parents during the Franklin Dam protests.

Realising the perils of global warming, Blakers committed himself to developing solar energy. Back then, solar cells were little more than a novelty only found in labs and fringe applications such as space satellites.

It didn't take long to notice that Professor Andrew Blakers is a physicist. We were sitting at an outdoor coffee shop on a wintry Canberra morning, and the proprietors had placed gas heaters beside the tables. They were like small beach umbrellas with burners positioned on tall posts while the heat was focused down toward the patrons. It's a nice gesture, but we were only there a few minutes before Blakers pointed upward and remarked, "Very inefficient."

Indeed. With the heaters placed up high, the great majority is wasted because the warm air simply wafts away. Add a slight breeze, and a lot of gas is burned for little benefit.

It's the kind of calculation that comes naturally to the engineering mind of a physicist. Blakers is one of the key brains behind the development of photovoltaics—the silicon cells used in a vast number of solar panels around the world today. Look out your window and if you see any solar panels, there's a good chance they use technology developed by Professor Blakers and his colleagues. (Technically these are PV—photovoltaic cells—but "solar" is simpler.)

Blakers embodies the physicist engineer mindset. It's a dogged approach: try, fail, try again, succeed a little, analyse what might work, why something didn't work, and then hopefully why it did work. In the early 1980s, the best solar laboratory cells could manage less than 18% efficiency and generating a useful amount of power required a large surface area. With that sort of output, they were never going to be viable for the mass market. They were also exceedingly expensive, putting them out of reach for all but the most specialised applications, such as in remote areas or on satellites.

The first demonstration of a solar panel was back in 1954 at Bell labs in the USA, but the idea goes back much further. The first person to make a solar cell of any kind was Edmond Becquerel. He was only 19 in 1839, working in his father's laboratory when he coated electrodes with light-sensitive substances such as silver chloride. He couldn't explain why, but he noticed it produced a small electric current.

The first solar cell was made in 1883 by American inventor Charles Fritts, using selenium. The best it could achieve was only 1% efficiency, but it was the primitive precursor to the solar cells used today. The first useful application of a solar cell was the Vanguard satellite, launched in 1958. It had six square solar cells covering 30 square centimetres. Each produced only one watt of power at 10% efficiency. Even though Vanguard was a tiny 1.46-kilogram aluminium sphere, the panels didn't produce enough power, so it also carried a set of mercury batteries. These lasted three months while the solar cells soldiered on for another six years.

Today Vanguard is still spinning around the Earth. It's now the oldest satellite still in space and expected to stay up there for about another 240 years.

Protest

It seemed almost strange to hear an otherwise conservative university professor say, "My father and mother both ended up in gaol," but that's what happened when they were protesting against the Franklin dam in Tasmania. In the late 1960s and early 1970s, the Tasmanian Hydro-Electric Commission set about constructing dams on environmentally sensitive rivers. They dammed Lake Pedder and in 1978 announced their intention to dam the Franklin River. It was a divisive move that created political turmoil not just in Tasmania, but on the mainland.

The Lake Pedder dam had already drowned 242 square kilometres of pristine wilderness, and now the Tasmanian government was determined to build another. The dream was a grand project in the same vein as the Snowy Mountains Scheme.[1] Industry would flock to Tasmania, which would be transformed by cheap, abundant electricity. The majority of Tasmanians supported the scheme, and in 1963 the *Hobart Mercury* wrote "The imagination of thinking Tasmanians will be excited" when they learned about an access road toward the remote and almost inaccessible south-west region where the dam was to be built. The article continued: "With a high element of romance, the hydro-electric potential has a significance equal to the mammoth and costly Snowy Mountains scheme."

Ultimately the project to build the Franklin dam was defeated, but in the process it mobilised the Blakers family. Andrew now says that protest is a "family business". His sister is prominent in the

---

1   A key difference, however, is that the Snowy scheme is primarily about redirecting water to the west of the Great Divide and electricity is a secondary benefit.

environmental movement. His brother is a wilderness photographer inspired by pioneers such as Peter Dombrovski, whose iconic photographs were instrumental in swaying public opinion toward the Tasmania wilderness.

The dam proposals triggered a wave of environmental protests as big as any in Australia's history. Andrew's parents sat down in front of bulldozers at the Franklin until they were arrested. They spent the next few days in prison where it was so crowded with protesters, the police didn't know what to do with them. The sight of overflowing gaols, offenders queuing through the courts, and 10,000 protesters on the streets of Hobart moved the nation.

It had the desired effect, and in March 1983, the Australian Labor Party won the federal election, with the new prime minister Bob Hawke vowing to stop the dam construction.

It was also a key moment for Blakers. He'd developed a great love of the Australian landscape while bushwalking in the alps near Canberra, and could see the imminent danger of global warming. "I took up bushwalking as a teenager and it was not possible for me to go into the Brindabellas and other lovely places without realising that there are an awful lot of threats out there. Way back in the seventies it was quite obvious to any physicist that if you put more carbon dioxide into the atmosphere then the world is going to warm up."

Global warming is much in the news today, but the idea is not new. Joseph Fourier first proposed the idea in 1824 that carbon dioxide absorbs infrared radiation, trapping heat at the surface of the Earth. Later, the Swedish scientist Svante Arrhenius (1859-1927) and Thomas Chamberlin (1843-1928) calculated doubling the Earth's CO_2 concentration would lead to a 5°C temperature rise. They saw that increases in CO_2 concentration were correlated with the end of the great Ice Ages. It's basic physics, but there those who still don't believe the science.

Most greenhouse gas emissions are now caused by the burning of fossil fuels, with land clearing contributing most of the rest. To make a serious dent in this, Blakers could see the need to find sources of energy that do not involve pumping CO2 into the air.

In his youth, Blakers' first career choice was astronomy, but it was his growing awareness of the looming environmental crisis that pushed him down a different path. He decided his future lay in renewable energy. In some ways, he says, astronomy and solar energy are similar. "Solar energy is astronomy except using the light from the nearest star."

Renewable energy offered a practical way to reduce the amount of greenhouse gasses, but it was also attractive because the goal is peaceful. As he puts it:

No country will ever go to war over solar. It's almost totally benign. This is one of the very few technologies that can't be used for military applications. It's very hard to kill someone with PV. You could hit them over the head with a module, but they weigh 20 kilograms.

I could've worked in a field where I was making more compact nuclear weapons with a higher yield that could be put in a howitzer rather than dropped from a bomber. That would be really interesting technically, but appalling from every other point of view.

He studied physics and maths in his undergraduate degree at the Australian National University, but at the time, ground-breaking research was being done at the University of New South Wales. The Solar Photovoltaics Group had been set up by Professor Martin Green and they needed talented people. The decision was easy and in 1979 Blakers started his PhD, guided by Professor Green. He launched himself into his doctoral research and spent the next 10 years working on high-performance silicon solar cells.

It was, he says, "rudimentary, but solid science". He was sure from the beginning that silicon photovoltaics was the future, but "never imagined that the price would come down so far that the cheapest way to make hot water is by running solar PV electricity through a resistance heater in a water storage tank."

Solar cells are complicated devices, but the principle is simple. The key is that a photon of light kicks an electron out of its orbit, which is then steered through a gate that forces it to travel through a circuit. The flow of electrons is, of course, electricity. Blakers describes how it works:[2]

A solar cell is a thin wafer of silicon, about 156 millimetres square and one-tenth of a millimetre thick—twice as thick as a human hair.

In a solar cell, a ray of light knocks an electron away from its host silicon atom. The electron wanders through the silicon crystal. Just under the top surface of the wafer is a one-way membrane called a p-n junction.

When the electron crosses the junction, it can't easily return. This makes the top surface of the wafer negatively charged, and the bottom surface positively charged (because it is missing electrons).

We connect the top and bottom surfaces with a wire that passes through an electrical load. The electrons travel

---

2   Or if you prefer, a metaphor: Imagine an atom sitting at the bottom of an apartment block and around it are electrons. When a photon hits, it knocks an electron out of orbit and up to the top floor. On the way back down we make the energy do useful work. It's as though the electron is water pumped to an upper reservoir and as it falls back, it turns a wheel. To stop the electron from taking a shortcut straight back to the atom there's a "p-n junction" at the base of the cell. This is a kind of trapdoor that forces it to take the long way round so we can make it do some work.

through the wire and do useful work in the load before re-entering the wafer at the rear surface.

As long as the sun keeps shining then there will be a continuous supply of electrons to do work.

Full sunlight has an intensity of about 1,000 watts per square metre, which is about enough to power an electric heater in your home. A commercial silicon PV module has an efficiency of about 19%, which means it can produce about 190 watts of electricity per square metre. The best laboratory silicon cells have an efficiency of 26% and the best cells (made from a complicated mixture of materials) reach an efficiency of nearly 50%, but they are far too expensive for ordinary applications.

The trick then for researchers is to generate the most electricity for the lowest possible cost. About 95% of all solar cells are made using silicon, and in an effort to reduce cost, scientists are working with a range of other materials with intimidating names like "perovskite", "quantum dot", and "silicon heterostructures".

The Lab

When I visited Blakers' lab at the ANU, it looked like the sort of place you'd expect at a high-tech research facility. Students were peering into complicated pieces of equipment, surrounded by banks of dials, flashing lights, and mysterious looking electronics. They wore white lab coats and protective glasses. Around the room were polished stainless steel pipes and vessels. One was chipping the crusted ice off a tall steel container. I'd be fibbing if I said I saw puffs of mist wafting around the room, but it wouldn't have been out of place.

Making a silicon solar cell is a long, laborious process. I'm pretty sure the instruction manual begins with: *Before you start, here's a handy list of expletives.*

For his PhD, Blakers would slice the silicon into 10x10-centimetre squares, then subject them to a long, complicated series of steps. It involved baking it multiple times in a furnace. He'd "screen-print" a metal paste to make contacts onto the rear surface, then dry it in an oven. Then he'd put the batch into another furnace so that the contacts would melt into the silicon. The front side of the cell needs a similar process. He'd apply some more metal and then put it back into the furnace. Once that's done, he'd take the cell and encapsulate it into a module.

It could take as long as a month to go through the full cycle to produce a single batch. A single mistake and all that effort would be wasted. Time to check that list of expletives.

In the popular imagination, scientists struggle for years to solve a difficult problem and then emerge to announce a breakthrough. It makes for a good story, which is what research organisations and the media need. The "struggle for years" part is true, but breakthroughs are rare because most advances are really just incremental steps. Nobody really wants to read," Today the lab succeeded in producing a batch of solar cells." So media departments hoard announcements until they can be released with a bang. It's a necessary part of the process to generate some excitement for the public, and hopefully the funding bodies.

For Blakers there was no single "Ah-ha!" moment, no flash of inspiration when the answer became clear in a burst of clarity. The key was more dogged persistence than great leap, and during his PhD research he says he spent most days in the lab "failing".

> A lot of the time you're fumbling around not really understanding what you're doing. Sometimes it's good, but most of the time it's a failure. Then maybe come up with something new and publish the result.

He'd experiment with different ways to make the solar cells, different materials, different times, sequences of the fabrication process, and different temperatures. The fabrication process could take anywhere from a day to a month and lots of things can go wrong along the way. And when it did go wrong, he had to decide whether it was fundamental or just an error in the process.

In a clean room, he'd take the wafers out of the packet and wash them in acid, then put them in a furnace at 1,000°C, then selectively etch them to remove the surface, then back into the furnace at 900-1,000°C to diffuse phosphorus into that window, then he'd open another window and put boron in. Finally, he'd remove all the oxide and regrow the oxide, and deposit and pattern the metal.

It's complicated, which means juggling the length of the process against the decreasing chance of success. The process might be perfect, but the chance of getting through it without a problem is low. It was slow work, but he is pragmatic. "It's very frustrating and you can go for a long time then suddenly it would work."

Still, there were moments where luck intervened. As Edison said, "Fortune favours the prepared mind."

One day I put my silicon wafers into a furnace that had been running a phosphorus infusion. I didn't realise at the time, but the results were much better. It took a while to work out what went right, but when we did, it was obvious and very quickly we transitioned to using that.

Blakers' moment of solar luck had been preceded by Russell Ohl who, in 1940, chanced upon a way to make a p-n junction. The p-n junction acts as a kind of trapdoor, allowing electrons to flow out of the silicon but not back again. Ohl was investigating semiconductors at Bell Labs when he noticed one of his silicon samples had a crack down the middle. Rather than binning it, he tested it and found it generated a current when it was exposed to light. The design has changed, but the p-n junction is now fundamental to all solar cells.

For Blakers the years working in Professor Martin Green's lab at UNSW were highly productive, with a steady improvement in cell efficiency. One by one they knocked over the records: 18%, 19% and 20%. By 1988, the team had made substantial gains, but still it was not enough. Too much energy was lost when the sunlight wasn't captured. Some sunlight would bounce off or shine straight through. And of the electricity that was generated, some was lost as it leaked back into the cell instead of doing useful work.

By changing the front and rear surfaces they pushed efficiency to nearly 23%. It was a significant improvement and today PERC cells are predicted to become a dominant feature of solar cells produced globally. That equates to US$9 billion in sales a year, but Blakers laments, "Sadly, the property rights have long since expired."

Still, he takes comfort in the fact that the efficiency alone will probably save $750 million in Australia's electricity generation over the next 10 years. It's innovations such as these that are drastically cutting the price of PV electricity and driving the renewable energy revolution.

CHAPS

In 1997, not many homes had solar panels on their roof, but many did have solar hot water. Why not combine the two? Blakers led research that took this angle. CHAPS (Combined Heat and Power Solar) used a trough-shaped reflector with a high-efficiency PV cell along the axis. On the back was a heat exchanger to drive hot water.

It sat on a circular track while the reflectors would rotate toward the sun. The swivelling and tilting was similar to the way radar dishes are aimed at stars. A larger version was installed on the roof of Bruce Hall at the ANU in 2004, with eight 24-metre long concentrating collectors. A microprocessor was used to keep the reflectors pointed at the sun. The idea was that with this system they could supply 25% of the hot water and space heating and 30% of the electricity for the 90 residents.

That was about as far as the ANU CHAPS progressed. It looked promising, but what happened? Blakers was sanguine as he explained, "CHAPS was predicated on the fact that at the time solar cells were fairly expensive and the idea was to replace most of the solar cells, buying cheap parabolic mirrors, and focus a lot onto a line of fairly expensive but efficient silicon solar cells. We completed the project, the technology looked good …"

And then the kicker, "… but then the price of solar cells came down by a factor of four."

The irony was that his project was killed by the very innovations that he'd helped create. "Over the years, several of my pet topics have been killed off by progress in silicon photovoltaics," he says.

Blakers shrugged when he told me how he'd learn to accept the nature of innovation as long as it drives toward the bigger goal of renewable energy. "I'm very sad to see that happen, but also very happy to see that happen."

It's not just in his own work, because solar technology is disrupting the power industry everywhere. He says, "People who have invested in coal mines and coal-powered stations and nuclear power stations and carbon capture and storage and solar thermal and ocean energy and bioenergy are all finding that their business models are being destroyed as we watch, by photovoltaics and wind energy."

PV and wind are now the dominant technologies installed worldwide, pushing coal into third spot, simply because they are cheaper.

Sliver

PERC solar cells proved a success, but they were still too expensive. To drive them into the consumer market, they needed to be cheaper without sacrificing efficiency. In 2000, Blakers and Dr Klaus Weber were attending a conference in Scotland when they turned their attention to one of the most expensive components: ultra-pure silicon.

Silicon is a good raw material because it's cheap, but that's just the starting point. To get sand into 99.99999% pure silicon requires a series of energy-intensive steps. Unfortunately, after all that processing, cheap sand becomes expensive silicon—and that adds up to about half the cost of a solar panel.

It would be a train ride between Glasgow to Edinburgh that brought together all the ingredients for a spark of inspiration. The two highly skilled specialists mulled over the problem, rocking back and forth as their rail car rattled across the Scottish countryside. It was then that Blakers and Weber came up with a way to make solar cells use less silicon by making them thinner. They reasoned that if they could cut tiny grooves into the silicon, they'd greatly reduce the amount used. And better still, they could also increase the surface area, giving the panel more room to catch light.

They'd take a one-millimetre thick wafer and cut it vertically into thousands of narrow strips. Blakers describes how it works:

"Imagine a standard solar cell is a loaf of bread. When you put it out in the sun it generates energy based on its surface area. Now imagine you cut that loaf up into slices and lay them horizontally. You get a lot more surface area." Using chemical etching along lines put down by a laser, they made thousands of extremely fine cuts.

By 2008, the rewards were evident. Testing compared the sliver panels alongside conventional panels, which showed that a sliver cell needs only a tenth the amount of hyper-pure silicon and produces a better yield.

The super-thin sliver construction proved to have other advantages. They're about as thick as a sheet of paper and deliver an energy-to-weight ratio of more than 200 watts per kilogram. That makes them flexible enough to be used in novel places like roll-up solar panels. They've even found their way into the "Soldier Integrated Power System".

For their work, Blakers and Weber were awarded the Walsh Medal from the Australian Institute of Physics.

Commercialisation and Back Again
With the initial excitement of the sliver advances came the announcement that sliver cells would be built in Australia. In March 2007, the ABC *Catalyst* program ran a feature story about a company that was to set up a manufacturing plant. Origin Energy teamed up with Micron to form a venture they called Transform Solar, and with much optimism they announced plans to build a pilot plant in Adelaide. The jobs, profit, and know-how would stay onshore.

It was, says Blakers, "an exciting $240 million adventure". It included the construction of a large pilot production facility in Boise, Idaho. However, other forces intervened, and in 2012 the worldwide PV industry was hit by a severe downturn following the GFC. No one was going to invest in new plants now, and

Transform had to decide whether to grow the pilot plant to full size or get out.

It was an unfortunate turn for Australia, which has a remarkable reputation for clever ideas but frequently struggles to turn them into profitable ventures. Transform Solar would have been a step toward changing that, but it couldn't control international events.

Moving from the lab to full production is always difficult. Consumers and investors expect predictable quality and price. If you buy a solar panel, it should come without cracks or scratches. It should generate what it says on the label. In the lab, each piece is handcrafted and if one part is not right, an expert is on hand to fix it. Or it might be binned and replaced by another piece. On a factory floor you need a worker of average skill to produce pretty much the same product every time, and when a batch fails it directly hits the bottom line.

Fabricating a cell is a long, complicated sequence of steps and it takes only a single mistake to ruin an entire batch. That translates to lower profits and higher cost to the consumer. And worse, if a defective product is released to the market, the reputation of the company is damaged. It's difficult to recover once confidence is lost.

The culture, too, is different. In science, the sharing of discoveries is essential. Scientists rely on worldwide collaboration and open sharing to develop their ideas. In the corporate world, information is an asset to be protected and they will go to great lengths to avoid sharing it.

For a scientist, managing a budget means balancing grant money with costs. In a business, there's nothing without profit. Blakers makes no apologies about the need to make a profit. For some in the environment movement, profit is seen as a dirty compromise. Even some of his colleagues in the academic world share that view. "Some look down at me because of my involvement with commercialisation," he says.

It's a theme that also appears in the book *Following the Sun*, by Robin Tennant-Wood, which chronicles the struggle to establish renewable energy research at the ANU. One researcher commented that others at the ANU thought the solar research group were "hackers and hobbyists", while many in the broader scientific community had, at best, a lukewarm attitude toward solar research. The book quotes ANU solar researcher Bob Wheeler, saying:

> We weren't in the same echelon as the high intellectual endeavours that they were pursuing. In a couple of the reviews, it's implied that there was no place for this sort of work in the ANU, which was a bit disheartening because we had people at the forefront of control technology, we were right into catalyst reaction rates and things like that.

Blakers is a committed environmentalist, but he says that doesn't make him "anti-capitalist". There's no point in making the best solar cells in the lab if nobody uses them. To really make a difference, science and industry must be part of what he calls a "virtuous circle". He feels vindicated to see the economics of solar changing, and now there are real profits to be made, saying, "The people who manufacture these machines and install them are our hard-headed businessmen and women who are not interested in going broke."

Baseload Funding

As with any innovative industry, the renewable energy field is going through stages of maturity. *Following the Sun* charts its origin at the ANU in the 1970s. It began as a tottering child, driven by the energy and the vision of a few key people; then staying in the game required persistence through the highs and lows, especially the flip-flop funding. Since then, the solar industry has matured considerably but remains a slightly uncertain adolescent that still needs parental support.

Sometimes it's been pushed along by circumstance. In October 1973, the OPEC oil cartel triggered global economic shock by proclaiming an oil embargo. By March 1974, the price of oil had shot up from US$3 to nearly $12 per barrel, and even higher in the US.

That oil is a finite resource should never have been in doubt, but developed nations were shaken when they realised how vulnerable they are. Then, as now, oil is the foundation of the economy and when the cost goes up, everything goes up. Fuel shortages and higher prices smacked into the economy, rippling into every sector, and the world slid into recession. It was a painful moment, but it was a critical event that sparked the birth of alternative energy.

In Australia, the benefits for research into renewable energy were immediate, and the ANU received major funding for a concentrating solar project at White Cliffs in far western NSW. Dr Roger Gammon, who was involved, remarked, "Our total budget for one year was close to a million dollars. I know some of the projects right over the life of the funding."

For the first 30 years, funding of solar research was an erratic game. The money would come and go with the political climate and in 2016 there was another spin on the merry-go-round. Critics of renewable energy point to the intermittent supply, but there's a parallel in science funding. The on again, off again supply makes it difficult to build long-term capacity, which can take years to develop. When the money disappears, so do the skilled people and they might never return. Australia loses its edge when those people and opportunities leave.

In August 2016, Blakers heard news that would threaten ANU's solar research. Under pressure to balance the budget, the federal government intended to slash $1.3 billion from the solar research funding body ARENA. It was, he feared, "an existential threat".[3] The Clean Energy Council said it would be "plunging into the clean energy valley of death".

Blakers was mystified and alarmed. At the very time when the planet is facing the dire threats of global warming, the government spends billions of dollars on weapons while cutting Australia's world-leading renewable energy research. If we're concerned about security, we need to address climate change because it will—and arguably already is—destabilising nations. Funding cuts are not just about the science, because winding down solar research would also be a lost financial opportunity. PERC solar cells have global sales worth about $9 billion per year, and Sliver cell technology attracted $240 million in commercialisation, with $11 million in royalties paid to the ANU.

The announcement triggered a flurry of commentary and political manoeuvring, and an agreement was struck. In September, ARENA was given a reprieve with a lifeline of $800 million over five years. It was a near-death experience, but the agency survived.

Staying on the Grid

On 28 September 2016, an event occurred that is revealing for both politics and in the way power generation works. Australia saw the interplay between the weather, the grid, and ideology.

During the afternoon, a "once-in-50-year" storm hit South Australia, with gale-force winds across a large part of the state. There were at least two tornadoes. Some areas experienced winds as high as 190–260 km/h.

At around 4pm, almost the entire state's power was blacked out. Without waiting for detailed reports, then Prime Minister Malcolm

---

3   Professor Andrew Blakers, "Margaret Throsby interview", 13 June 2016, www.abc.net.au/radionational/programs/archived/throsby/professor-andrew-blakers/7501326.

Turnbull jumped in,[4] saying, "Energy security should always be the key priority. Now, I regret to say that a number of the state Labor governments have over the years set priorities and renewable targets that are extremely aggressive, extremely unrealistic, and have paid little or no attention to energy security."

He and other commentators claimed the problems were caused by the state's drive toward renewable energy. For the next few weeks, the media was full of chatter about whether this was caused by reliance on wind power. It was almost pure speculation until the Australian Energy Market Operator released a report in December into what they called a "Black System Event".

As is usually the case, the problem turned out to be more complicated. It began when three transmission lines were taken down by tornadoes. The grid would've survived that, but then protection circuits tripped on several wind farms when their voltage dropped a pre-set number of times within two minutes.

When they lost power, South Australia overloaded the Heywood interconnector to Victoria, and within 700 milliseconds it tripped a safety feature. It cut off the state, and most South Australians were without power until midnight.

The incident inevitably sparked calls to build more coal power stations for "baseload power". Treasurer Scott Morrison took a lump of coal into parliamentary question time, saying, "This is coal, don't be afraid." Behind him, Barnaby Joyce could be seen smirking while Morrison praised the virtues of coal.

The stunt earned Morrison some attention, but coal has become a fossil thinking as much as it is a fossil fuel. Even so-called "clean" coal isn't viable, despite now being loaded with superlatives such as

---

4   This contrasts with successive governments' attitude toward fuel security. The Australian Strategic Policy Institute describes the current situation: "A series of reports on Australia's liquid fuel security published in 2013 and 2014 by the NRMA are frightening."

"ultra", "super", and "critical". Carbon capture and storage is another hope for fossil fuels, but it's unproven and adds yet more cost when coal is already too expensive to compete with. Blakers' former research supervisor Dr Martin Green stressed this point when he told the online magazine *RenewEconomy*[5] that he could see the price of solar PV halving within the next few years and "there's no way coal can match that".

In May 2016, the coal furnaces at Alinta Energy's Port Augusta power station were shut down, followed soon after by the Hazelwood power station in Victoria. Around the world, coal is being replaced, and half of all new electricity generation everywhere is wind and solar.

In 2016, India announced in its electricity plan[6] that they'll complete coal power stations currently under construction, but after that there'll be no new coal-fired power stations. In the first half of 2017, the amount of new solar PV installed in China was roughly equivalent to Australia's entire coal-fired capacity. This suggests that Blakers is right when he says there will never be a new coal-fired power station built in Australia without massive government subsidies, not least because it's too expensive.

In some parts of the world, electricity is a luxury, and where it is available, supply is flaky. Locals shrug when the power drops out, and blackouts are a normal part of the day. Meanwhile, in Australia, we've grown used to reliable 24x7 power, and if the grid goes out for a few hours, voters get angry. With the rapid growth of renewable energy, Blakers has turned his attention to the problem of how to feed the grid when renewables can't keep up.

---

5   Giles Parkinson, "Super cheap solar – and why that's good for Australia's mining sector", *Renew Economy*, 22 August 2017, www.reneweconomy. com.au/super-cheap-solar-and-why-thats-good-for-australias-mining-sector-55652/.

6   Tim Buckley, "No new coal fired power plants for India", *Renew Economy*, 20 December 2016, www.reneweconomy.com.au/no-new-coal-fired-power-plants-india-80026/.

Part of the solution is the grid, which we've already paid for and is proven to work. The grid spreads generators across the country so that if it's cloudy in one place, it's probably windy in another. Or if the air is still around one wind farm, it'll be blowing at another a hundred kilometres away. Or it could be cloudy in Adelaide, but sunny in Queensland. It makes the grid into a sort of giant battery where renewable sources are always generating somewhere.

If the grid is part of the renewable solution, it also offers an intriguing possibility. Australia is blessed with vast areas of land and lots of sunlight. To the near north are the densely populated islands of Indonesia. In a presidential decree in 2006, Indonesia announced its intention to build four nuclear power plants by 2025. The region is prone to earthquakes, and the disaster at Fukushima in 2011 is a warning of what can go wrong. The announcement was unpopular with many Indonesians, who showed their displeasure by launching street protests.

If Indonesia has a power problem, Australia has an abundance of sun. Blakers sees this as an opportunity because electricity could be generated in Australia's northwest, and exported to Indonesia using a high-efficiency DC (Direct Current) connector.[7]

Blakers points to this as another opportunity where Australia could use its natural assets to make a profit. A report suggested that a 1500-kilometre undersea cable could run from the Dampier Peninsula to East Java, sending power from three one-gigawatt solar farms.

Running that length of cable across oceans with a seismically active seabed presents a few formidable challenges on top of the $9.5 billion estimated cost. But Blakers the engineering optimist is unfazed as ever, saying, "The political issues are much tougher than

---

7   Sophie Vorrath ,"WA mulls three gigawatt-scale PV plants to export solar to Asia", *Renew Economy*, 28 August 2017, www.reneweconomy.com.au/ wa-mulls-three-gigawatt-scale-pv-plants-to-export-solar-to-asia-93596/.

the technology issues. How do you convince Indonesia to rely on Australian electricity?"

Even if it turns out that the plan isn't viable, the deeper message is that a good environmental solution can make a profit. Blakers insists that environmental solutions should make economic sense. Renewable energy isn't an ideological movement that wants to see the end of capitalism.

Meanwhile, the world is not waiting, and international grids are already underway. In October 2016, Japan, South Korea, China, and Russia signed an agreement to build a grid linking vast parts of Asia. Supply will come from locations such as Mongolia, which has huge wind resources. Large parts of Europe are interconnected, and more is planned.

Nothing to Invent Here

Blakers has no doubt that coal power is disappearing, but that leaves the question of how to provide reliable electricity when intermittent renewables can't meet demand. To solve that problem he turned his attention to grid-scale storage, and contrary to the popular image of engineers, the answer isn't waiting for ground-breaking research. It's easy to imagine that engineering has to be complicated boxes and wires, computers, and mysterious machinery. Sometimes that's true, but a good engineer always favours simplicity, and if something's already there, use it.

The history of electricity generation doesn't go back that far, and it wasn't long before ways to store energy were invented. In Michigan, USA in 1880, a water-driven dynamo was used to provide arc lighting to a theatre and shopfront. It was only about a decade later that the first pumped hydro systems were built in the alpine regions of Switzerland, Austria, and Italy. This makes pumped hydro is one of the oldest and simplest methods ever devised.

The shopping list for a pumped hydro storage system couldn't be more basic. Take a pair of dams—one high and one low; a pump and a generator—often combined; some water to kick it off; and plug it into the grid. It's rudimentary stuff, and today 99% of storage around the world uses it. Its simplicity means that it's low risk and it's cheap. "Nothing to invent here," as Blakers puts it.

A pumped hydro system is not much more than a couple of oversized farm dams and some hardware that fits neatly into the variable generation from wind and solar farms. When there's spare, cheap electricity, pump water up to the top dam, and when demand peaks and the price is high, let it run down again through a generator. Round and round it goes, in a closed loop. There's no need to dam any rivers since the water is endlessly reused. All it needs is water to fill the dam, and then top up the small amounts lost through evaporation.

In Australia, there already are three pumped hydro systems, one built in 1971 for the Snowy Mountains scheme, another in Kangaroo Valley, and a third at Wivenhoe in Queensland. In Talbingo, they dammed the Tumut River and a smaller lower reservoir below where it flows into Blowering Dam.

Blakers was describing this to me, but he'd already seen that I was about to object—this was coming from the same Andrew Blakers who'd boasted that his parents had been gaoled for protesting against the Franklin Dam! He didn't wait for me to ask, cutting in with: "We don't need to dam any rivers for this, it's not necessary. If someone did suggest that, I'd be the first one chaining myself to bulldozers." An off-river system can sit anywhere there's enough height difference and they're not too far apart.

Pumped hydro would have helped during the South Australia blackout because they can kick into the grid with about a minute's notice. They could have been ready when the wind farms went offline and may have held off the surge that cut the state's grid connection to Victoria.

In a flat, dry land like Australia, it might not look like there are many places where pumped hydro would work, but it turns out that's not the case. All it needs is a location where a pair of dams a few kilometres apart, with the upper one about 400 metres higher up, close enough to a grid connection, and not in a national park or sensitive area. Blakers and his colleagues have been using computer algorithms to find potential sites, and already they've found 22,000.

If the archetypal engineer is a boffin with a clipboard and calculator, it's easy to overlook their immense creativity. Solving problems often involves lateral thinking such as the realisation that a pumped hydro pair of dams doesn't even have to be a "pair" of dams. Why build a lower dam when nature has provided one? That's what they did in Okinawa where the upper dam is a "turkey nest" at the top of a seaside cliff, and the lower dam is the sea itself. Blakers doesn't think this will be significant in Australia, but there might be places such as the coast of the Eyre Peninsula in South Australia where it would work.

Meanwhile, 400 kilometres south-west of Cairns, a pumped hydro scheme is taking shape. Startup Genex is working with Entura and HydroChina to convert a disused gold mine. It's expected to be able to produce up to 450 megawatts for five to six hours—about a quarter of the Hazelwood coal power station's 1,600-megawatt capacity. Hopes are that this will become a model for other plants around Australia.

Blakers has been busy working with colleagues to find where storage schemes might be viable, but that's largely the backroom, engineering side. Scientists and technical people love the intellectual challenge, but it is wasted effort if their ideas sit on the shelf. Blakers recognises this, and spends 10% of his time with media, publicity, and promoting the possibilities with politicians from all sides. I saw that myself when he worked with me to produce pieces for the radio and newspaper—and this book. He's now become a familiar figure in the national media where he's the go-to guy for topics such as pumped hydro.

Politics vs Physics

In 2016, speculation emerged that the Turnbull government would offer a "concessional" (i.e. cheap) loan of up to $1 billion to the Carmichael coal mine in Queensland. This is from the same Malcolm Turnbull who in 2010 said, "I believe our long-term global goal is to very substantially reduce our emissions, a goal that will require almost all of our energy to be produced from zero or very near-zero emission sources …"

If physics is difficult, people are infuriating. Blakers is scathing. "I cannot tolerate people who lie or don't follow evidence. In science, evidence is everything, but to some people it means nothing. Some of these people don't really believe climate change is happening despite a mountain of evidence. In Australia and the US, there has been a right-wing backlash against the newcomer—renewable energy."

The logic of MP Barnaby Joyce is hard to follow. On one hand, Joyce claims to represent the interests of rural and farming communities, while on the other, he denigrates renewable energy, which is bringing thousands of jobs to regional areas, while advocating a huge coal mine on agricultural land that has been granted unlimited access to water for 60 years. If it were developed fully, the mine would include two huge open-cut mines, five underground pits, and export millions of tonnes of coal.

Blakers finds the logic of climate denial hard to fathom. "… where so-called conservatives were resisting to the end, similar to getting lead out of petrol, similar to getting CFCs out of refrigerators where they were damaging the ozone layer." Conservatives would usually be thought of as resisting change, and yet climate change will cause vast changes to Earth.

He laments that personal belief has muddled the evidence that humans are disrupting the climate. "For some reason that escapes me, these people go to the doctor when they are sick and follow her evidence-based advice, but they refuse to do anything for a sick planet. That works in the political sphere, but nature doesn't care what your ideology is."

I didn't have to dig far to see his pent-up irritation when I asked what are the top three hurdles. He didn't hesitate:

The Liberal Party
the National Party
and the Murdoch press.

Then he added, "None of these follow the evidence in anything to do with climate change. Individual members are appalled, but they are in the minority."

Blakers has come to the view that we can't wait for leadership from parliament. Now he devotes a considerable portion of his time to promoting the benefits of renewable energy. This does include "hardcore" politicians, but he says gloomily, "You'll never change their mind. These people sit in echo chambers and hear what they want to hear. A good scientist abandons precepts in the face of evidence, but these people don't do that."

Showing the same dogged determination from his lab days he persists, devoting his scarce time to promote the cause, but sometimes he says, "They are quite aggressive." They still haven't caught up with the PV revolution."Until recently, many would say that PV and wind are only 1% of electricity production, which makes them a trivial, boutique, latte-sipping solution."

He says renewables are the future, regardless of whether conservatives want it. The question is how much they can delay it. "In short order, they are going to demolish the fossil fuel industry.

The argument is not over whether it can be done, but whether change can be pushed back a decade and more damage can be caused."

Is there any way to change their opinions? "I fear not. Many are at the end of their career, and there's no motivation to change tack. But *who* would have any respect for a tobacco executive? *Who* would have any respect for a coal executive?"

In mid 2016, not long after I interviewed Andrew Blakers, Radio National's *Science Show* broadcast a panel discussion about renewable energy. It was engaging and informative, but the speakers didn't seem to know about pumped hydro. That prompted Blakers and I to produce a story about pumped hydro, which the *Science Show* host Robyn Williams broadcast soon after. It was a small step, but it helped to change the national conversation.

Pumped hydro will be part of the transition to larger-scale renewable energy, but in the national media it was invisible. After the South Australia blackout event, a public stoush blew up between the state and federal governments as to who was to blame, and who had a plan to fix the electricity system. State Premier Jay Weatherill unleashed a TV-broadcasted tirade against federal energy minister Josh Frydenberg. The next day, Prime Minister Malcolm Turnbull spun into damage control by announcing plans for a "$2 billion expansion" of the Snowy Hydro scheme.

Somebody gave it the catchy name "Snowy 2.0", which was primarily about adding pumped hydro storage. It soon transpired that the commitment was only for a feasibility study and arguably not much more than a thought bubble. Overnight, the idea of pumped hydro went from unknown to part of the national vocabulary. Getting it there was the work of dedicated researchers from people such as Blakers and his colleagues at the ANU and the Melbourne Energy Institute.

About a year after meeting Andrew Blakers, I finally got my own home on track. It'd been bugging me that all the time I was writing *Fragile Planet*, we were still connected to the old-fashioned, polluting grid. Now that the prices have plummeted, we were able to install a chunky 6-kilowatt system for just over $6,300. Just 10 years ago, a system of that size would have been unthinkable. And that's not just our house, because even though Malcolm Turnbull is still attached to his predecessor's climate and energy policies, renewable energy is relentlessly driving out fossil fuels. The uptake of rooftop solar in Australia has more than doubled, and for that we are in debt to Andrew Blakers and the other inspiring scientists who have made it possible.

Andrew Blakers still has a lot of commitment to drive Australia toward its energy future, but his career has been long enough for him to now look back and reflect. What was the skill that got through?

"Hard work, long hours, persistence, and a belief that technology and the material I was using was the best, and the field I was in was the best."

Later, I thought about the mind-numbing steps it would've taken to develop a new type of solar cell. Step one, step two … step 15 … fail. Start again. Step twenty … fail, start again. It was not just persistence, but a near obsessive attention to detail that is key to his success. That might make science sound like a dull plod through endless, mindless detail, but it misses the creative spark.

Somehow, deep in our brains, an idea emerges. And somehow, we can make it come true. That is the sort of spark we need to renew Australia.

The Maggot Farmer
Olympia Yarger

Maggots. It's one of those special words that evokes a strong response, usually revulsion. It seems a rude way to start a chapter, but Olympia Yarger is, well, a maggot farmer. Her words, not mine. But then Olympia doesn't look like the sort of person who'd worry about such things.

Launching an innovative business such as this is always complicated and involves taking a few risks. It also needs money, and to calm herself before delivering a funding pitch, she once jumped in front of a mirror in her hotel room. Naked.

If that was what she needed to do, she didn't hesitate. But I was to learn that quirky self-therapy in hotel rooms was probably the easiest part of Olympia Yarger's story.

Olympia's grand plan is to reshape the animal feed industry. It revolves—literally—around using maggots to recycle food waste. Given her somewhat chaotic journey, how she got to this point is far from obvious. Even she says her career looks very much like she has ADHD. There's a frenetic energy to Olympia. She's done so much and she's not even old.

When we met to record an interview, I told her how I was fretting about *Fragile Planet* and whether the people I wrote about would like their chapters.

"Artists," she harrumphed, "get over it."

Right then.

I wondered how she'd managed to channel that energy into launching into a field that few people have done before. To kick off an innovative business from scratch is such a daunting job. It involves assembling many moving parts such as finance, science, marketing, and managing people. There are the pragmatic things like collecting material, paying the rent, shovelling waste into the feed bins, harvesting the maggots. Talking to the media. It's almost overwhelming; how does she do all that?

Looking at Olympia's early life, it's hard to know. She was born in Canberra in 1975 when the city was not much more than a large country town. The population was 170,000 and there were maybe a dozen traffic lights. Her Greek-born father was what she calls "not a nice person". When she was only nine he returned to Greece and they never met again. Later, her mother Louise remarried to Kim who was a sign-writer. If Olympia's two sisters and two brothers needed a stabilising influence, they didn't find it in their new stepfather. Olympia says he was more fun, but he proved to be a tortured artist and an alcoholic. Kim died in 2015.

Olympia was aged just 13 when her school class was shown a documentary about what was then called "the Greenhouse Effect". The film showed chimney stacks billowing dark smoke, mostly from burning coal that had been buried for millions of years. It told of how global temperatures could easily rise by three degrees or more if we don't act soon. It described how we are converting carbon from the ground into a giant gassy blanket that is trapping heat, and continuing on our current path will have grim consequences. It might not sound like much, but if sea level rises by just one metre, it will be a disaster for the 56 million people now living on the Bangladesh delta.

You don't have to be 13 years old to find this disturbing. It certainly had an impact on Olympia. "It was horrifying," she says.

"I remember having a panic attack. I went into the toilet and I was deep breathing."

Fear was her immediate response but, I wondered, had she been through the stages of grieving: denial, anger, bargaining, depression, acceptance? "No," she says. "I'm still angry. There was disbelief and shock, but I don't think I've been through all the stages."

"I don't want to. If I'm not getting angry then I might get complacent. We might just drop the rubbish in the recycling bin and think we've done enough."

The fact that global warming operates on a scale far above us as individuals doesn't mean we do nothing. The anti-global warming refrain goes that Australia emits only 2% of global greenhouse gasses, which makes us too small to matter. Apparently, that means it's up to others to be the leaders and we can do whatever the hell we want. Or we'll look at the other people in the dinghy as it fills with water and say, "They're not bailing, why should we?"

At first, Olympia would try to talk to the people she calls climate deniers, and try to explain how it's real. She'd show them the facts, but found that it was usually fruitless, so now she rarely bothers.

"When you're talking to climate deniers you're not talking to people who are logically thinking through their idea. They are purposefully and unashamedly refusing to change. If an engineer told you the bridge was broken you wouldn't drive on it, but that's what we're doing when we ignore climate science."

"Now I laugh at the climate deniers because that's all they deserve. They're ignorant, so I'm not going to validate their opinion with discussion. I don't respect them. And then they get angry— which is hilarious."

Teenage Pregnancy

Olympia's life took what was to be the first of many sudden turns when in her final year of high school, aged 17, she discovered she was pregnant. It wasn't deliberate, it wasn't planned, and she says it wasn't an act of rebellion. It was more that she was just doing what young people do. "At that time of life, everything is racy," she says, "and our culture tells you that if you want boys to like you, that's what you do."

At her conservative Catholic school, no one talked about sex and there definitely wasn't any contraception. The potent mix of emerging sexuality, ignorance, and no birth control means that girls are going to get pregnant, she says.

Hearing Olympia's story about the lack of support from people around her, it's hard to know where she gets her determination. Determined and, as she was telling her story, she seemed so unflustered, unfazed. Or maybe that's just with hindsight. At age 18 she was a single mother with no support, but she had an ambition to build a life in agriculture. She might not have been quite so calm back then, but now she says it was just one of those things she had to do.

"When I found out I was pregnant, it wasn't what I wanted. I was frustrated that it was going to stop me going to uni."

"I thought, okay, I'll just make that work."

Olympia graduated from school while she was pregnant and the next year her son Jeremy was born. Her family had owned a farm in Canberra, and she knew she liked being around animals and watching things grow. She loved being hands-on, doing things. She enjoyed working on fences and being in the shearing shed, which, she says, people either love or hate. Her ambition was to go to an agricultural college, but then the school careers counsellor told her, "St Clare's girls don't become farmers."

"And I said that's great, but I will be applying." That was the plan, but it wasn't possible when she was soon to be a single mother. Instead, she went to Cooma to complete a wool classing certificate. She did rouseabout jobs, then moved to Goulburn to do a traineeship in agriculture.

"And then my son drowned."

She said it in a matter-of-fact way, but it was an event that would haunt her. "My boy was amazing. He spoke at seven months, he walked at nine, and he was having full conversations by the age of two. He was very smart and very fun. He rode horses and he could ride a four-wheel motorbike—it was hilarious watching this tiny boy because he was short. His father was short."

Jeremy was aged two when he died. Olympia was hanging clothes on the line and went back into the laundry, and when she came back out, he was gone. He'd climbed the fence into the paddock in the backyard and drowned in a creek. "It took us about an hour before I found him. He had sunk, then risen back to the top. I was walking back down the creek looking for him and saw his gumboot on the bottom of the creek. I jumped in trying to grab it."

Even the death of her son didn't elicit support from Olympia's family and she was left pretty much to her own devices. She and the boy's father Geoff moved to Darwin. "I wasn't really in a good place and I was not happy in the relationship." So they parted.

In Darwin, Olympia took up what was to be the first of her unconventional jobs when she started working nights in a sex shop. I was a bit surprised when she told me, but she couldn't see what the fuss was about. "You laughed, but it was a job and I really enjoyed it," she said. "It was like an anthropological study. I loved working there; it was the most interesting study of humanity. In a good way really."

I guess I shouldn't have been surprised. Olympia has a blunt way, so you're not usually left wondering what she thinks. She's not easily distracted by superficial attitudes to things like sex. I like that—you might need a thick skin, but think of how much energy we waste dancing around people who think one thing while saying another.

"You remind me of people like nurses," I suggested. "They have a no-nonsense approach to life. They don't have time. 'I have a patient here who's just soiled himself and you want ... what?'"

It wasn't just men who were going into the sex shop. She estimated it was a 50-50 split of women and men. Often they were having problems, and in the sex shop people felt they could talk about things they probably wouldn't normally discuss with other people. I could imagine people talking about such private matters with Olympia because her no-nonsense but empathetic character would put them at ease.

She says we think that people that go into sex shops are not like us, "but to me it was just normal life". It was instructive, but it also proved to be another step toward building her business skills. Back then she couldn't have known, but this would become essential in her future. "I learned better customer skills there than in any other company I worked for. Doing that sort of work, you develop an innate ability to truly serve your customers' needs."

The move to Darwin had provided a change, but she needed a clean break "to start again and not be around people who'd had any idea what happened." Now aged 24, she travelled to the US to start a traineeship in training horses where she was paid $175 a week. "It was interesting," she says. "I worked for an arsehole." She didn't elaborate on what she meant by that so we moved on.

In 2000, she moved to Texas where she worked as a horse groomer on a family farm. The family had a different attitude to religion, but she remembers they were kind and caring at a time when she was still disturbed by the death of her son. "Jeremy had been dead for four years and I was mentally unwell," she recalls. They accepted her "warts and all" when she had been at her worst. "The extraordinary thing was an evangelical family accepting a swearing, smoking, tattooed person into their home and giving her honest sympathy. It was unusual and a gift, of sorts."

One night she went to a bar, where someone spiked her drink. "Roofied," she says. By the time she got home, she was looking unwell and the family thought she was hungover. Olympia's self-assessment is typically prosaic. "I just made a shit choice. The end."

"I could see how far removed they were from my way of thinking. I was probably the least likely person to live in their home and yet they decided to embrace me. There was a lot of compassion and thoughtfulness, but there were things I did that were challenging, given their religion. They just absorbed it and let it keep going. There's a beautiful lesson in having empathy."

By this stage, I was already having trouble keeping up with all the jobs she'd had, but it was about to get a whole lot more complicated. She got a job as a manager of an up-market tanning salon. Every day they'd see about 300 customers who paid a monthly subscription. They were long days, starting at 9am and not finishing until 10pm. "It was pretty insane," she remembers. Even stranger, perhaps, were the customers.

It was no surprise that Olympia is not the sort of person who'd be interested in tanning. Not just because she's part-Greek and already quite tanned, but because of the lengths some people go to change their looks. "I couldn't see how anybody could be that interested in it, but it makes some people feel skinnier. We had a lot of really weird and curious traits around tanning; it was hard to understand." Some customers were addicted to tanning and couldn't stop. There are real health risks with excessive exposure to UV light and customers weren't allowed to tan more than a set number of days each week, yet some were trying to scam their way into doing more.

It provided an opportunity to see the curious side of human nature, but perhaps more significant were the lessons she learned about marketing. The tanning business was sophisticated in the way they collected and used purchasing data. They understood their market really well so they knew who bought what lotion. They knew who liked what, and who was going to be their client, and how they could get them to buy a bundle of things."

Olympia's career trajectory may have looked random, but what she didn't know at the time was that she was accumulating skills that would be the foundation of her future as a maggot farmer. One of those skills was in sales, and if managing a tanning salon was unexpected for someone who wanted to work on the land, working as a bank teller is even more unlikely. Unfortunately, this one did not have a happy ending.

One day a customer came into the bank to deposit a cheque. Handling this sort of request required the right combination of checks, signatures, marks, and circles drawn on the cheque for it to be approved. The finance officer went through all the steps, but she'd been on leave and came back the day after the process had been changed. It turned out she got it wrong. The cheque was a dud and the client lost money.

They were given what my uncle calls the DCM Award (Don't Come Monday) except there was no preamble, no discussion, and they didn't have until Monday. Her colleague was marched out the door, and Olympia was next. "They said, hand over your keys and take your personal items and leave."

"We both got fired." Olympia laughed again while telling her story, but says, "It was pretty stressful. You don't get fired from a bank and get another job."

War

Moving to the USA had given Olympia a break from her troubles in Australia, but her life was still unsettled. Then one night she went to a bar where she met Peter, a US Marine. "We just started talking and it felt really good," she remembers. "He offered some kind of friendship." Soon they were married and living in California when she got pregnant with her second child Clancy. If she'd been looking for a more stable life, it wouldn't last.

Early in the morning on the US West Coast on September 11, 2001, the first plane flew into the Twin Towers. Olympia had been working long hours and was asleep when her friend came and told her, "They're attacking America." Surely it was a joke, she thought, but they watched in horror as a plane flew into the second tower.

The Twin Towers attacks sparked a furious response from the US, which immediately launched military action. Within a day, Peter called to say he wouldn't be coming home. The boyfriend of Olympia's housemate who was also a marine was shipped to the Mediterranean with the US Navy. Olympia and Peter moved to Jacksonville, North Carolina where he was at the recruiting school. Clancy was born in March 2002. Then Peter was sent to the invasion of Iraq in 2003.

Now Olympia was a young mother while her new husband was off to war and she was facing the prospect that he might never return, or that he might return with injuries. "It was incredibly frightening because we had no experience. We couldn't expect the worst because we didn't know what the worst looks like. We knew it was going to be bad, but we had no benchmark to guide us."

Peter survived, but the relationship was in trouble. He'd provided friendship when she needed it, but it wasn't working and they parted.

Then in 2005, she met another US Marine, Eric Yarger. He'd also been sent to the Iraq invasion, and then the battle for Fallujah.

Ultimately he did six tours of service to the Middle East—four in Iraq and two in Afghanistan, including a stint with Marine Special Operations in western Afghanistan.

Olympia described what it was like to live in a military base during wartime. "As first lots of friends died, or people we knew died, or mothers of kids your son knew at school died, or people's husbands died—you start to realise it becomes a sort of a roulette conversation."

Over time the US military got better at preparing their troops for deployment. Soldiers wouldn't come home with an unexpected announcement. The transition of soldiers into a war zone became more orderly. The years 2005 to 2009 when the war was most intense were the worst. "It just didn't end," she says.

They were caught in one of two modes, and it was hard to say which was worse. While Eric was at war, Olympia would be waiting to see if he came home safely, but when he was home, they were stuck in a weird twilight zone. They spent their time trying to be happy, be okay, and enjoy life because soon Eric would be deployed again.

"You couldn't have arguments that might upset the apple cart. Everybody got magically good at walking on eggshells overnight."

"And then they would leave, and we would spend the rest of six or seven months waiting for them to come back. That was exhausting because you're waiting to see if you made it to the other end. You really don't have any control over whether you'll see them again or they'll come back wounded."

The war has taken a heavy burden on Eric. The accumulated damage of active service has left him with a skin condition, and repeated exposure to loud noises has damaged his hearing. He's only 32 and walks with a pronounced limp because of arthritis. He has a traumatic brain injury that was caused by repeated concussion from the detonation of IEDs (Improvised Explosive Devices). Then a 50-calibre round skimmed the top of his head.

An impact like that was obviously dangerous, but Eric did not go to the medic as he should have. That meant he didn't get the nine days downtime, and he just kept going. From that and the accumulated concussions, he now has memory loss. Olympia says, "When he gets stressed his short-term memory loss is really bad. But you know that's the price of being cool."

Olympia paused and said, "Yeah …" Then she laughed. But this laugh was not like her other laughs.

I come from an army family, so I sort of knew what she meant even if it's only remotely similar. My dad was shipped off to Korea, leaving Mum only a few months after they were married. As my war veteran friend used to say, "Old men send young men off to war." The thought of countless lives destroyed in a pointless fiasco was starting to upset me, so I changed the topic.

The Boudoir

Olympia had already told me that somewhere in her bizarre mix of careers she'd been a photographer. I'm a photographer myself, so we talked about that for a while and she showed me some of her work. It was really good, very professional. But how on earth had she jumped from being a wool classer, horse trainer, tanning salon manager, bank teller—and more—to photographer?

After losing her job at the bank, her options were limited, but she needed an income. Who would hire her if she'd been fired by a bank? But at the military base, she saw an opportunity where families were being constantly split by the war. She launched into photography "because it was the only thing I could do."

Jacksonville, North Carolina proved to be an ideal place to get started because it's a military community where everybody wants photos. The constant churn of people being sent overseas created a demand for photos for all the events—birthdays, Christmas, Thanksgiving, Halloween, Fourth of July, homecomings, farewells, and weddings. Olympia says there were more opportunities to photograph than any other community on the planet.

Again her marketing instincts showed. To begin with, she had no special skills in photography and she didn't even have a proper camera until her brother bought her one. The logical place was to start at the bottom by aiming for the low-value, high-volume market. She did as many jobs as she could, undercutting everybody by about $25—doing what she calls "shoot and burn stuff", like families on the beach. It was just enough to get by. To pay her bills each month she needed to make $2000, but after a while, she was making $2500.

It was enough to survive on, but she was running close to the bone. A simple mistake could mean losing two days income and then she'd have no money for petrol. Poverty focuses the mind and it was punishing if she missed a shoot or failed to follow up on an opportunity. She started looking for patterns such as clients who were likely to cancel. "Doing something when you have no other choice teaches you what it means to be agile. There's more than enough entrepreneur books on how to think in an agile way," she says.

Olympia needed to boost her photography skills, so she started reading everything she could find, which included picking the brains of people with skills. It's an approach that she still uses. When we met she'd told me she'd just been on the phone to someone who has written books on growing crickets. After she finished the call she told me, "He said, you probably already know all this, and I said 'no.'" That sounded like an Olympia sort of thing to say. Don't pretend you know something when you don't, just ask the right people and you'll keep learning. She says it's one of the things she does well, but sometimes it's not good because people see it as a weakness. "After a while, I started to realise that no one really knows, but you're the only one that is willing to admit it."

As her photography skills and her business improved, Olympia could progress from the low-cost bulk market toward the more discerning customer who was prepared to pay a little more. By this time, I shouldn't have been surprised by what she might do next, but then she told me about her next business. In many ways, it was a natural progression, and it happened by chance. One day a client asked if she'd be embarrassed taking photos with nudity? Sexually explicit poses? In her characteristic blunt way, Olympia replied, "'No, don't care.' I've worked in a sex shop. I didn't give a shit."

The client was asking if Olympia could do boudoir photography and Olympia says she didn't know what the client was talking about but agreed anyway. The client wanted photos of herself that were appealing and that she felt good about and would reconnect her with her husband overseas. She missed the intimacy and the feeling that she was wanted. Olympia's client told her that she was the first one she'd found who wasn't fussed about doing photography like this. Olympia says she didn't know where to start, so again she spent hours trawling the Internet to read everything she could find about boudoir photography.

The client was a young mother in her early twenties with two kids living in a typical military housing complex. Olympia says there was no childcare. "So we did it at her place. Her kids were everywhere, which was hilarious. We just sat them in front of the telly and when they knocked on the door, I told them to go and play. She wanted to wear his clothes and be on his bed."

"She wasn't nervous, she didn't care. She had two kids and was at her wits' end. It was the only time she had to herself, and she was going to have fun regardless. So we did—and it was great. We laughed and we looked at the photos. We went on the Internet to get ideas. It was a good first time, really."

"The photos came out better than we expected, and the client told her friends. And her friends were like, we want them too."

The boudoir photography business thrived and she went on to photograph other women who were divorcees or not in relationships. Often they were women at an age where the experience helped them feel empowered, or to capture the twilight of what they felt was their sexuality.

She says a sympathetic photoshoot is incredibly empowering. "To watch a woman not feeling great about herself naked, to then feeling really strong, seeing herself in those photos, and being astonished by the way she looks—that was very inspiring and fun. We had a good time. It was different."

By 2014, Eric had completed six tours to the Middle East, and it was starting to take its toll. Not just on him and Olympia, but on the people around them in the military community. There'd been many casualties and people were coming back wounded or psychologically damaged. There were divorces and often children were not doing well, developing depression or having trouble at school. Fathers were becoming suicidal; spouses were addicted to pain meds, alcohol, and other drugs.

It wasn't that the military system didn't try its best to ease the burden. They ran programs and counselling services to help soldiers and their families cope. I discovered this in a roundabout way in my first interview with Olympia when she rattled off a comprehensive, orderly account of her life.

"Wow," I said, "you've just given me a really neat, plotted story there."

"Well, I've had plenty of practice," she said. "That's what we did in all those counselling sessions."

Despite that, she says military life was becoming chronic. They needed to get away, and Olympia started to think about coming home to Australia. She says they shared doubts about America's incursions into foreign countries. "Both Eric and I believe that

America should never have gone into Iraq. There's a lot of regret for the actions of America." She stopped for a long pause, then gave an awkward laugh. "We've created a broken system. We refuse to change because we'll send them again tomorrow if we get a chance."

Eric and Olympia married and moved into a house with Clancy, their daughter Charlotte, and three dogs. Olympia loved having her place and even though it was small, it meant she could return to doing some small scale agriculture. It had a tiny backyard, not more than 25 square metres, but it was enough to grow some vegetables and raise chickens, rabbits, and even some fish.

But then the flies came, Olympia recalls. "That was making me really happy, and I was composting the dog poo. Then one summer I found all these maggots in there. It was just horrifying."

"I was trying to kill them and they wouldn't die, which is ironic because now that's my business. Eventually I thought, well fuck it, let's leave them there."

"So that was my first introduction to the black soldier fly, but I didn't know it then."

While Eric was getting out of the military, Olympia was writing business plans that would get them back onto the land. She thought about farming chickens and aquaculture, but there was the problem of how to feed the livestock. She wanted it to be environmentally sustainable and healthy for the animals. And of course, it had to be a viable business, but she kept running into the problem that the price of feed was constantly changing.

Animals such as cattle or sheep that range on paddocks mostly just eat the available grass, but those kept in feedlots have their food supplied by the farmer. Chickens and pigs, in particular, depend on feed that can be expensive and might be half or more of the farmer's total costs. But worse, much of their feed comes from grains such as corn, wheat, soy, and sorghum—which compete with human food. One year there might be an oversupply and feed is cheap, but the next year something happens to world markets and suddenly feed is expensive.

It's hard to start a business without knowing the costs. High costs could mean a large bank loan, which has to be paid, even if costs drop. Or if the loan is too small and costs suddenly go up, the business might run out of cash. Olympia says for the sort of sustainable farming she wanted, the cost of feed would be "absolutely crushing".

Maggots

It's official. I now love the black soldier fly, and that includes their maggots. Researching these little insects has helped me see they are actually a reasonably attractive creature and even their maggots don't look that bad. They're certainly not the repulsive things squirming in roadkill. The maggots—I think I'll call them larvae— look more like flattened, grey/tan-coloured grubs with slightly serrated edges. Unlike blowfly larvae, their skin is dry. The adults are easily mistaken for a small black wasp. In fact, I'd always thought they were a wasp, but it's a ruse. They mimic wasps so predators won't eat them.

Even better, the adult fly does not eat—they don't even have a mouth. That means they never hover around your barbeque, they don't buzz into your house and bat themselves against your windows and they don't carry disease.

That's a good start, but probably more importantly, the larvae can help convert mountains of food waste into animal feed. This is the same conclusion that Olympia had been drawn toward, although she didn't recognise it at the time.

In 2014, Olympia and her family moved to Canberra, and the problem of animal feed was still vexing. "I couldn't get a feed that would work," she says. She kept looking on the Internet until one day she did a search for nutrient analysis and came up with a website called *Feedipedia*. "Black soldier fly," it said.

Black Soldier Fly (photo by Rod Taylor).

It was maggots again. But even for a pragmatic person like Olympia, it was a step too far. "Being a sheep farmer, I couldn't just go there. So I looked at crickets." She wanted an insect that could be fed from food or agricultural waste. Crickets are produced for animal feed, but they're not as flexible with the types of waste as the black soldier fly, and later she'd learn they're not ideal for livestock feed. They'd looked promising, so she tried growing crickets in a compost bin in her backyard, feeding them wild corn.

The crickets grew okay, but the problem? Maggots! Always it was the maggots! If there's such a thing as fate, it was telling her that's what she should be doing. So she started laying traps and growing maggots in buckets. It had its funny side, too, because Olympia says her time in Texas had "involved killing a lot of maggots. I have never been so upset about the death of maggots in my life." She laughed and then said, "The irony of that statement is that I spent every part of my post-high school career killing every maggot I could find."

It was a double irony because while Olympia was having trouble with too many maggots, the world is slithering toward a food crisis. It's not clear how we are going to feed the world's population as it heads toward nine or ten billion people.

Clearly, something has to give, and feeding ourselves without destroying the planet's ecology is a daunting challenge. The Green Revolution mid last century provided a boost to agriculture, but since then gains have been incremental. The problem is huge, but in its own small way the humble fly will help. While the world population is growing, about a third of the food produced in the world for humans is wasted. That adds up to around 1.3 billion tonnes every year, but it's uneven because rich countries waste almost as much food as the entire food output of sub-Saharan Africa. This is happening while more than half the world's arable land is used to grow crops for animal feed.

The black soldier fly loves the edible stuff that we discard. It could turn mountains into food as part of a cradle-to-cradle economy where waste becomes a resource. However we do it, the industrial use-it-bin-it model can't continue.

The black soldier fly is a heroic little worker that can't resist the sweet smell of rotting compost. They lay their eggs and a few days later, the larvae emerge. The larva has to cram in as much food as it can because that's the last time it ever will eat. That gives them a ferocious appetite, and they chew through their own body weight in a matter of hours. When they're done, their bodies are packed with 45% crude protein. Each will eat half a gram of waste in a day, so one tonne of larvae can gobble down 2.5 tonnes of waste.

Once the larvae have had their fill, they pupate. A couple of weeks later, the adults emerge and their only mission is to mate. They enjoy a final fling before dying after about a week. The female lays up to 600 eggs and all up, they are 75-100 times more efficient at processing waste than earthworms. Then, of course, their eggs hatch, and round it goes in a wonderfully efficient waste processing cycle.

I watched a faintly disturbing time-lapse video of larvae chowing down a hamburger. A seething mass drags the contents back and forth across a tub and within eight hours it's pretty much demolished. It's not great viewing if you're squeamish, but it does show how effective the soldiers can be.

At around 10 days, the larvae harden, and a small kink shows in the bottom of their tail and they're ready for harvesting. Olympia says the fly is a wonderful thing commercially because the larvae harvest themselves. When it's ready to pupate, it walks out of the feed bin, up a ramp, and into a container. With a bit of processing, they become a healthy meal—42% crude protein and 34% lipids (fats)—that can be fed to pets, chickens, pigs, and fish. A bonus is they leave behind a bin of rich fertiliser.[8]

In all, it's a wonderful system that makes use of nature's inbuilt solutions for extracting every ounce from a resource. Humans can devise an artificial equivalent, but it's hard to compete with so many millions of years of fly evolution. The trick for Olympia is to tune it by using the right combination of temperature, the design of bins, and the type of waste they feed to the larvae. It needs a repeatable process that will give the same results every time for a predictable cost. You could say it's like taking a deep-fried chip from McDonald's. You always know what you're buying, whether it's a Maccas in Sydney, New York, or Tokyo because a chip is regulation size, cooked for three minutes.

Maggot farming brings fresh thinking to a stale resource (waste) and Olympia says Australian farmers are innovative and ready for a product like this. She decided to turn it into a business and in June 2016 she registered the company name "Goterra". She won

---

8   A tonne of larvae produces 180kg larvae meal and 250kg fertiliser.

a local government innovation grant to set up a pilot plant in the Canberra industrial suburb of Fyshwick. Goterra's first goal is to sell processed larvae to the animal feed market, but other possibilities might be compost or biofuel. They might even have potential for treating sewerage or pharmaceuticals. Olympia says her dogs like them too, making short work of any that drop onto the floor. They have a fishy smell a bit like fish food flakes, but not as strong.

Setting up and running the maggot business has been complicated, not least because there's a daunting checklist of things that have to work. Sometimes it's the big strategic thing, but sometimes it's the detail. When we met one day, Olympia was distracted by a minor issue with the air conditioning unit that keeps the plant operating at a constant 27°C, 75% humidity. If that fails it'll hurt production or worse, her crop of insects could die. Which is what happened in early 2017.

It was a minor disaster, but proved to be a painful lesson. Even though the Goterra plant is set up with all sorts of sophisticated monitoring, things can still go wrong. The air conditioning has an alarm system that fires an SMS alert if it detects an issue.

Another system is a daisy chain of sensors that monitor heat and humidity. Olympia had been at the plant in the morning and everything was fine, but when she returned six hours later, one of the sensors had gone down, taking the others with it. She was horrified to discover dead larvae on the surface of the bins. Digging her hands into the bins revealed more dead larvae. She'd lost all but 20 kilograms, and then nothing thrived for a couple of months after that.

It was a devastating blow, but now she seems unfazed. "It was a learning experience," she says. "We learned how it could fail, and that shouldn't happen again."

The pieces of the fly farming puzzle were coming together. Olympia had made good progress figuring out how to farm maggots, but it would be all for nothing unless she had a market and a way to distribute her products. To add another complication, she wanted a system that isn't just another monolithic, centralised factory. It makes sense to locate Goterra plants where the waste is generated to reduce the need to ship material over long distances. With a modular, distributed system it becomes not just a closed loop, but a closed *local* loop. It doesn't need a big capital investment to increase production.

Goterra will pack a self-contained production system into a shipping container, which can be operated anywhere. The owner of a shopping centre could engage Goterra to dispose of large amounts of food waste generated by their cafes and restaurants. It has financial advantages, too, because Goterra can ramp up by adding modules and training their people how to use them.

It's a brilliant solution that solves so many problems at once. While Goterra is getting itself established, it'll target the small producers such as people with a few chickens in their backyard and organic specialist farmers. Then they'll move up the chain to larger, higher volume consumers such as commercial farmers. That might be a challenging transition because it's one thing to sell to the small specialty market, but the larger consumer is more concerned about price and reliable supply. I can brew a reasonable beer in my garage, but that's a long way from selling to a supermarket. Start-ups often have a good idea, but getting them to scale is a big step.

If running a business is complicated, launching an innovative start-up is even more so, and it requires a diverse range of skills. Here I could see how Olympia's apparently random career has come together. It's marketing, finance, personal relations, science, and perhaps as much as anything, the willingness to take a calculated risk.

Around the time I was interviewing Olympia, I heard a radio program that talked about the many challenges that a business start-up has to face. I asked Olympia if she'd heard it and she took a deep breath. It was all a bit too much; yes, she'd seen a lot of this sort of stuff, but she already had a lot to think about. One step at a time; don't solve a problem until you need to. Running any business must be exhausting work, let alone one that's trying something new. Anybody with a bit of nous can open a coffee shop—it's been done millions of times. Not many people are growing maggots for a living.

If growing maggots is one side of the business, money is the other. She'd raised the starter capital from the ACT Government and to go beyond that she'd need to attract investors. I found an online video from November 2016 of Olympia doing an investor pitch to an audience of about a thousand people at an event sponsored by Rabobank. She's a good speaker, but in the video she looks nervous. And who wouldn't be? Most people rate public speaking at the top of their most-feared list and this was to a large, tough audience about a topic that's close to her heart. Still she ploughs on, giving a really good, clear explanation of why maggot farming is a great idea. She uses simple, effective slides to make the main points.

The pitch only lasts five minutes and then she has to face the evaluation from the moderator. Not quite reality TV, but frank and fearless advice. "Really convincing in your argument about sustainability," he says. "What was a bit disappointing was we didn't hear enough about how you'll go to market …"

It was tough feedback, but fair. In marketing, you learn that the most important lesson is the difference between "product focused" and "market focused". One says that what you're selling is inherently good and therefore people will buy. The other starts with what people actually want. An investor might care about the environment, but what they want more is whether they'll get a return on their money.

When I asked her about the experience, she looked pained and said, "Oh, I cringe when people tell me they watched that. I was terrified!"

"Well, it wasn't that bad," I added unhelpfully.

The experience was difficult, but she says it's the best thing she's done. Given the other life experiences she'd told me about, I could see why she might say that because she's not the sort of person to be put off by a hurdle. It was difficult, but now Goterra is attracting investors.

Then she had to do it all again. This time it was only a one-minute pitch to a much smaller audience. Even then, with the memory of the earlier event still fresh, it was an intimidating prospect. It was another chance, and she was acutely aware that the agriculture innovation sector comprises a limited number of people, and she'd only get a few goes before they tired of her. To help prepare, she wanted to simulate the feeling of being uncomfortable while delivering a talk. She paced back and forth in her hotel room, practising. Naked. She watched herself jumping in front of a mirror.

When the moment finally came she stood on the stage, briefly dazed. She'd lost a valuable four seconds before gathering herself to deliver a smooth pitch. It was good enough to win a $10,000 St George Kick Start innovation award. It's not a large sum, but it all helps, and Olympia is using it to build systems to automate production. She says that will make significant inroads to getting the prototype system running.

Girls in STEM

One afternoon, I met Olympia to record interviews at an outdoor coffee shop, and after about an hour she glanced at her watch, saying she had to be at the Institute of Technology at 4pm. "Of course," I said. "What will you be doing there?"

"I'll be talking to girls about STEM.[9] I'll be telling them that just because you have a vagina, it doesn't mean you can't do those things."

---

9   Science, Technology, Engineering, Maths.

"Right. That sounds good, but I won't quote you using the V-word," I replied.

"Well, that's up to you," she said, "if you want to give in to your unconscious bias."

Oh-kay. Thinking it over later, I had to laugh. Olympia knows I'm a sensitive soul and usually it's me provoking others during interviews. Time to eat my own dog food.

In spite of gains, the gender balance in so many fields seems an almost intractable problem. I was given a book for Christmas about the lives of 300 great thinkers in science, and it's not until page 112 that we encounter the first woman. The book is written by a woman.

Olympia would be a good role model. She's been inventive, doing something of value for the community—and she stands to make a lot of money if it works. In her home town of Canberra alone, there are 170,000 backyard chickens, but in the long run it's a seriously big market in Australia, with the combined market for feed valued at $800 million.

I went to visit Olympia at the Goterra pilot plant in Fyshwick. It's tucked away at the end of a narrow laneway in the back streets of the light industrial area. As I approached the large green tin warehouse, I started to notice the slightly acrid-sweet smell of compost. Not unpleasant, and it wasn't long before I forgot it was there. Olympia appeared, lugging a large bucket full of what looked like lettuce leaves. She picked up a handheld electric mincer, which I presumed she would use to chop up the lettuce for her insects.

She spends her mornings doing this kind of manual work. Feeding the larvae and driving around the various suppliers of food waste. In the afternoon she does the paperwork, emails, social media, etc. In the shed, she showed me the bins where they're growing the soldier fly larvae, crickets, and mealworms. Outside the protective mesh, there were a few escapees buzzing around harmlessly. Olympia dug her hands into the bins to show me the wriggling insects. I didn't find them unattractive and if I were a chicken my eyes would light up.

It all looks labour intensive with things patched together in a bit of a lash-up. But that's the nature of a start-up—everything is fluid. Over time it will evolve into a stable, routine production system and until then, everything is new, requiring fresh thinking to decide how to handle it.

I'm closing my eyes, rubbing my hands on my temples, imagining ten years into the future. Goterra has grown into a business with a couple of hundred workers. They've employed a CEO and a full-time finance manager, and are planning a transition to a publicly listed company. Olympia is Chief Technology Officer, but she still lugs around buckets of food waste, still digs her hands into bins of compost and wriggling insects.

By 2030, the erratic climate is making agriculture difficult and there's an additional one billion people to feed. Farmers are responding by finding ways to produce more food with less impact on the environment while companies such as Goterra keep innovating.

Mountains of waste that used to be buried are recycled into products such as animal feed. It's part of a changing attitude to waste that is revolutionising the entire economy. We've learned to see value in the things that used to go to landfill.

Olympia retains her passion for the black soldier fly, but she's still bouncing around with new ideas. Goterra runs a network of processing stations distributed across the country, establishing a business model that is being replicated around the world. They've tapped into a huge market and for the first time in her life, she's financially well-off.

The Accidental Activist
Charlie Prell

When the Millennium Drought hit eastern Australia, Charlie and Kris Prell found themselves struggling to keep their sheep farm as it spiralled into debt. After being on the land for four generations it would be a difficult decision. Not even selling a portion would solve the problem, because like any business they rely on reasonably predictable income.

Perhaps a sustainable answer could be found in the steady revenue from wind farms. And in a welcome twist, wind energy is an essential part of averting climate change—which itself is amplifying the frequency of ruinous droughts.

Wind farms held a promise, but the Prells didn't count on the toxic opposition they would encounter.

I didn't know much about Charlie Prell before we met, other than he's a grazier from near Crookwell and an activist for wind farms. For no good reason, I'd imagined a stereotypical farmer with craggy features, weather-beaten hands, and wearing a felt hat. I was right about the weather-beaten hands, but off the mark about everything else. Prell turned out to be medium build and wearing a trim suit. If I'd imagined a taciturn country character, I was also wrong because soon he was saying we should meet in the foyer at noon tomorrow.

We did meet for lunch, not for steak and chips, but sushi. The reserved farmer image soon fell away and almost immediately we were sharing details of our private lives. He told me about his struggle with anxiety and depression. I told him of my own battle with hearing loss. But this book is not about me and I felt obliged to make it clear: I'd assume anything he told me could be published unless he said otherwise. But no—everything is open, he said. Write what you think.

According to the conventional checklist, Prell should be a traditional Liberal Party conservative, which is how he describes his heritage of four generations on the land. In some ways he's broken with his tradition, but in other ways the seeds of his attitudes can be traced back through his family history.

In 1899, Prell's great-grandfather Charles acquired 2,000 square miles in Queensland's Gulf Country. The land was dry and the bank had been losing money on it. Their loss was his gain and he bought it for a good price. It was cheap, but it was also a gamble. Unless they could find a reliable source of water, the property would not be viable. The bank manager told him, "I wish you luck with it, Mr Prell, because it's been nothing but a sink to us." Charles Prell was witnessing the eternal connection between the land, water, and economics.

A hundred years later the same challenge would be pivotal in the life of his great-grandson Charlie.

For Charles and his young wife in 1900, the gulf country was uncomfortable. The rough slab house had calico walls and a corrugated iron roof. In the harsh climate, they were trying times and within a few months their first daughter died. Savannah Downs was a difficult 500 kilometres west of Townsville along a rough dirt road. Caroline and Charles Prell had to construct the coffin themselves to bury their daughter.

Finding bore water became an urgent problem, and without it

their enterprise would fail. After several failures, they eventually succeeded with one gushing "to a height of 10 feet, which was then a record for Queensland".

With their water supply secured, Savannah Downs developed into a thriving business, but it was not without its hazards. It was a large, unfenced area and the livestock ran wild. A 1951 biography describes how cattle had to be wrestled to the ground.

> The method used was to race after a beast on horseback, jump to the ground and throw it by giving a sharp tug to its tail while its hind legs were in the air. Then one hind leg was placed over the animal's horn and there it was left all day powerless to move.

Drought, too, could be devastating. During a dry period in 1902, a mob of sheep were being driven to Savannah Downs. Along the way, they fed on poison weed and hundreds died. Early farming practices in Australia were already being shaped by the variable climate. The Prells had prepared themselves by drilling bores and not overstocking the land.

Despite the difficulties, Savannah Downs thrived, and after only six years they sold it for a healthy profit. The Prells could now afford to buy land somewhere more to their liking. In 1904 they arrived in Crookwell where they found a sheep farm for sale. It was rough but looked promising.

> In places, the dead timber lay so thick that tracks had to be cut before the sheep could be driven through it. It was partly granite country consisting of poor light-grey soil from six to eight inches deep, lightly timbered with gum trees …

Gundowringa had 1,821 hectares and at its peak grew to 1,933 hectares. It's shrunk since then, but today it's still family owned. It sits on the attractive, lightly wooded hills of the Great Dividing Range.

The first white settlers arrived in the Crookwell region after the surveyor James Meehan and later, John Oxley had passed through in 1820. The name Crookwell is probably a corruption of Crookhall, the English family home of early settler William Stephenson.

Charles Prell named the farm "Gundowringa", the Aboriginal word for "watering hole". It seemed appropriate and probably also suited Prell's earlier time working with Aboriginal stockmen in the gulf country.

Before Europeans, the land had been occupied by the Gundungura people, whose tribal name means "west" and "east". The first Aborigines were here 40-50,000 years ago, but with the arrival of Europeans their numbers rapidly declined. They were devastated by an influenza epidemic and by 1848 it was estimated that only 25 were still in the Goulburn region.

Until his death in 1946, Prell was constantly experimenting. At first, he'd thought the way to increase production was just to lease adjoining land, but decided "there was not much in that". After moving onto Gundowringa, he visited England and France and saw how they approached farming. "I swallowed the pasture improvement germ," he wrote in 1940. It began with dividing the property into sections, which allowed him to treat each separately. It also meant he could test different techniques, comparing the results of one paddock against another.

They tried rotating crops of potatoes, wheat, and oats, followed by pasture. For several years they tried various combinations with limited success. Each time they managed a reasonable crop, but the grasses did not thrive as they'd hoped. They persevered until 1912 before abandoning the idea. Then Prell learned of experiments in Western Australia with subterranean clover, which looked promising. Adding superphosphate further improved the soil and crop yields. Techniques such as these were some of the many strands that led to the Green Revolution through the early-mid 1900s.

After years of experimenting, Gundowringa was able to carry more than double the number of sheep, rear 10% more lambs, and triple wool production. They were able to do this while improving soil quality and reducing erosion.

An episode that would lead to Prell being called "Crazy Charlie" by the locals was about his battle with rabbits. Their impact on the Australian environment and farming has been disastrous. At their worst, there were an estimated 600 million and until the myxoma virus was released in 1950 they were almost impossible to control. The story resonates with Charlie today as he tells what happened.

> He went out 150 kilometres west of [Gundowringa] and when he returned he started to build a rabbit proof fence. The locals asked, why would you do that when there are no rabbits? But it wasn't finished when the rabbits arrived and they came in like a plague.
>
> He finished the fences and then had teams of men getting rid of rabbits that had got in. That's the wisdom and the forward thinking of that man.

Another legacy Charlie describes is his sense of social justice. "I get really angry at the 'I know better than you because I went to private school' attitude. I've always had a strong sense of egalitarianism, which I think I got from my mother." He describes a similar attitude he sees in his great-grandfather.

> In the 1930s in the middle of the Depression, the government of Joseph Lyons accepted a proposal developed by Prell to try and get people off the road and give them a block of land

that would become a viable proposition for them. But that didn't go anywhere because the Second World War erupted and all of a sudden, everyone had a job.

That history is very strong in my blood.

Charlie is proud of this heritage, but sees it ebbing away in modern culture.

Kris

The 1951 biography of Charles Prell tells the story of a pioneering Australian. His innovative approach to productive farming helped shape the foundations of farming today. Clearly, he was a strong character, as is his great-grandson Charlie. But the book has a blind spot. It's written by men, about men, and the women are nearly invisible. They're only mentioned when there's a marriage or a birth. Social attitudes are changing, but surely strong men are almost always accompanied by strong women. "Partners" as we say today.

What then of Charlie's wife Kris? When we met, her response was straight. "I don't do interviews. Charlie does the upfront stuff." But wouldn't that leave the story unbalanced? What did she think of the women who were missing in the Prell family history? It was a provocative question that didn't need explaining. Well okay, she agreed, we'd record an interview, but only for *Fragile Planet*.

Kris's family moved from New Zealand when she was 14. Her mother worked with the Red Cross and her father ran an import business. Even now, at the age of 80, her mother goes into the Red Cross every week to help.

Nursing seemed a natural occupation for Kris. "I've always been very aware of social issues. I'm a very empathetic person and I can't bear injustice." She clearly remembers first meeting Charlie and can even recall the date, 22 November 1985. A friend had set them up on a blind date, but she was still feeling the effects of a recent breakup. "I thought, ooh he's so nice. He's too nice, too good-looking, something's got to be wrong." The relationship moved quickly and by April they were engaged. She was 27 and he was 29. Understandably, her mother had reservations. "Mum said, 'What are you thinking?' And I said, 'I don't know, Mum, but if I don't do it, I'll regret it.'"

Moving out of the city proved challenging. She knew Charlie, but in the early days she had few other social contacts. In her Greek culture, a new member would be drawn quickly into the family, but Australians are often more reserved. Breaking into a close rural social life wasn't easy and she didn't have a particular role in farming. "The women were not considered essential," she says. If the men were around to work, she'd be left alone, and unless Charlie was on his own there wasn't much to keep her occupied.

> For me, when I was home and Charlie was out working, I'd think, I'd like to go and visit someone. But they might be in town and they might be working with their husbands. There was no drop in or drop by. I had to make an arrangement if I wanted to go and see someone. It was very isolating.

Her fortune improved with a friend to help and soon her network started to grow. She also resumed her nursing career, mostly for the social contact. Initially, it was not particularly for the income, but with a crisis looming, that would change.

Charlie

The night before meeting Charlie, I stayed at one of Crookwell's three pubs. It's a country town with a population of about 2,500. It's small enough to retain its sense of history and there are no traffic lights. The Criterion Hotel had recently been renovated and painted a stylish dark grey. It was comfortable, but a little more expensive than I'd hoped. The bed was buried under a huge pile of cushions that had to move before I could get in. The next day I rode my motorbike 15 kilometres south to Gundowringa. It was a short way off the highway, along a dirt road with beautiful views looking east across the valley. Charlie had directed that I should take the right-turn to the new homestead, past the original colonial building where his father lives.

The driveway into the Savannah homestead. The original Gundowringa homestead is to the left (photo by Rod Taylor).

Well before you arrive at Crookwell, the wind farms are evident. They stretch west toward Boorowa and south toward Tarago and Lake George. They sit on the ridgelines that run north-south on the Great Dividing Range. Large parts of rural Australia are being transformed by wind power. Regions that once subsisted almost entirely on agriculture have a new source of income.

The driveway to the house they call Savannah is named after the property first owned by Charlie's great-grandfather. I rode slowly under the overhanging boughs of beautiful trees, taking in the scenery. At the house, I was greeted by a lanky red kelpie. It eyed me warily from a distance before trotting back around the side of the house.

Charlie waved me inside, but it was a dank day with misting rain rolling across the hills and my boots were muddy. I started to take them off, but Charlie told me, "No, this is a farm, leave your boots on."

Charlie's father Jeff, now aged 86, still occupies the older colonial-style house. Jeff's uncle Charles William died in World War I, and his father Harold served in World War II. The loss of his brother and his own war experience left scars from which he never recovered. He turned to alcohol, smoked heavily, and died young. His son Jeff was only 34 and was deeply affected by his father's trauma.

Charlie says his father is "strong, but emotionally detached", largely because he was affected by his father's war experience. Their relationship was also further strained when Charlie was sent to boarding school. It still hurts that he was forced to live apart from his parents during his formative years—first to Tudor House, not far away in Moss Vale, and then the King's School in Parramatta.

The prestigious King's School is Australia's oldest independent school, but Charlie's resentment shows, not least for the effect it had on his mother. "It tore her heart to pieces to see her kids go off to school," he says. His sisters had also been sent to boarding school.

The culture of King's at that time was a carry-over from the war years. "I think of myself as a soft-centred, emotional sort of person and Kings is a military school. It's about following orders, unquestioning obedience. If you do question authority or break the rules you are punished. It's something I've tried to forget."

The boys-only environment was damaging as well. "I left school at 18 as a social dinosaur. I didn't have any sort of cognisant relationship with women apart from looking at them as sexual beings. The boys-only environment meant that I had no experience with the fairer sex."

Charlie still remembers when his awareness of the environment first emerged. When he returned to the farm after a lengthy absence, he was struck by what he saw.

I remember coming home from school in the late 1970s into a really intense drought in 1979 through to 1983, and seeing this country so degraded and so barren after four years of drought.

It was very intense and I vowed to myself and the land that I would never ever let that happen again. Even through the millennium drought ten years ago, my first priority was to the land. That probably cost me financially, but I just did not want to see the land degraded to the point it had been in the 1970s.

For people living in cities, garbage disappears when a truck takes it away each week. But for people on the land, the connection is obvious.

On a farm in those days, you used to dump your rubbish into a gully because it was too expensive to take it into town. Then all of a sudden the gully would be full and when the rains came, the rubbish would be washed into the rivers.

This is partly because we are in a consumer society where rubbish is put in the bin and disappears out of sight.

The amount of fresh food that just gets thrown out ... I think to myself, when people are starving or living on two dollars a day, that seems a bit weird. Something like a third of all food produced gets wasted.

Looking across the landscape, it's impressive to think that the Gundungura Aboriginal people could live off this land. I imagined being stranded somewhere before white settlement. No roads, no electricity, no guns, no supermarkets, and definitely no restaurants. Without those, someone like me would soon starve. I'm completely dependent on the benefits of civilisation, but the Aboriginal people thrived here for 60,000 years. That number is so large I can't comprehend it. It dwarfs my life as well as recorded history by orders of magnitude.

Sixty thousand years is a long time, but it's only taken about 200 years of European settlement to utterly transform Australia and there's almost no corner that hasn't been touched. Living on Gundowringa, Charlie is conscious of this.

> The idea that Aboriginal people call themselves the custodians of the land, not the owners of the land, really appeals to me. I see myself as a custodian. The Aborigines don't even have a word for ownership.

I'm reminded of a line spoken by Paul Hogan in the movie *Crocodile Dundee*. "Arguing about who owns [the land] is like two fleas arguing over who owns the dog."

Falling off the Sheep's Back

Through the early 1900s, the sheep industry boomed in Australia. In 1936, Charles Prell wrote in *The Sun* newspaper: "It is plain that Australia's future depends largely on how much wool can be produced." Around that time, the phrase emerged that the nation "rode on the sheep's back", and for decades it was one of the nation's most important exports.

It was a profitable business, but farmers have always suffered the twin vagaries of the market and climate. They're punched from the left by drought and punched from the right when prices fall. Australia is more vulnerable than any other continent to variable weather, with floods one year followed by a run of droughts. Technology is also affecting the industry as the market shifts toward synthetics. Piled on top of fluctuating prices, the life of a farmer is uncertain.

In 1973, the Australian Wool Corporation was created, and with it came the Reserve Price Scheme. The idea was that the AWC would purchase wool for a guaranteed price, regardless of what the market was paying. When the price rose again, they'd sell the stockpile and recover their costs. It was supposed to be a buffer between the primary producers and the market. Had it worked it would have provided some certainty, but ultimately it was a disaster.

The plan was doomed before it started. Charles Massy describes the misplaced hubris: "The Australian Wool Corporation set about trying to convert itself into a giant Woolly DuPont: a transnational fibre marketer."

By 1990-91 the AWC had accumulated a vast wool stockpile with numbers almost beyond comprehension—4.8 million bales, nearly a billion kilograms of wool. They were burning $3 million per day—over $1 billion per year in costs of storage and interest. And worse, they were trapped. They had become such a large player in the market that selling the stock would have seen prices plummet. They would have been better off with a pile of used toothpicks, and in desperation, even considered radical plans such as burning the wool.

The AWB finally died with a spectacular crash in February 1991, with losses conservatively estimated at $12 billion. It was the largest-ever financial collapse in Australia. I dimly recall hearing about this in the news, but like most Australians, to me it was just another remote story. To Massy (himself a farmer), it was real. "The staggering sums do not include the incalculable opportunity, environmental, and social costs in Australia and overseas." Ten years later he wrote that the effects were still being felt. "Australia's once greatest export industry has been reduced to a third the size and value of what it was in 1990."

To sheep farmers such as the Prells, it was dire. The AWC crash triggered a crisis in the wool industry and farm incomes plummeted. Gundowringa spiralled into debt.

"The farm financial structure was totally broken … and we kept pushing the debt further out into the future," Charlie says. To stay afloat they had to drop luxuries such as family holidays, and Kris's nursing income became essential. They were forced to make some tough decisions such as selling 200 acres, but Charlie says, "It was not really a solution."

In 2015, he would tell *Farm Weekly*: "Family farming is a fantastic lifestyle, but at the moment it's a pretty crappy business. We're getting the same for lambs as we were 10 years ago, but the cost of fuel has doubled." It was a mild assessment that doesn't capture the depths of their experience because after the wool crisis of the '90s, they were hit by the Millennium Drought. Definitions of when it occurred vary, but the dry began in late 1996 and didn't let up until 2010/11. It plunged southern Australia into a decade of hot-dry weather, which became the worst drought ever recorded.

Scientists are conservative by nature and they're reluctant to pin a particular weather event on global warming, but evidence suggests the Millennium Drought was more severe because of it. In 2017, the news became even more serious, with research suggesting that extreme El Niños will be twice as common[10] as the world warms by 1.5°C. That's conservative because on our current trajectory warming will go well beyond that. Already we're locked into 1.1°C and with conservative obstruction, staying under 2°C seems unlikely.

---

10   "Expert Reaction: Extreme El Niños twice as common in a 1.5C warmer world", *scimex*, 25 July 2017, www.scimex.org/newsfeed/extreme-el-ninos-twice-as-common-with-1.5c-rise-in-global-temperature.

Now there's a growing realisation that humans are causing a new geological epoch in the Earth's history. It's an extraordinary step and the word *Anthropocene*[11] has ominous connotations. Never before has a single species transformed the planet on this scale. We're meddling with every part of our world, from biology, water, climate, and even the geology of the planet. It marks the end of an unusually stable period of climate called the Holocene, which has allowed human civilisation to flourish.

At its simplest, global warming is a rise of average temperature, but the real impact is more complicated because entire weather patterns are being affected. Greenhouse gasses emitted by humans are trapping heat. That is beginning to disrupt the climate, with droughts and storms becoming more frequent and more severe. In 2017, the Gulf of Mexico and south-east parts of the USA experienced unusually intense hurricanes.[12]

Global warming often seems to be an abstract problem, but farmers can see what's happening. Charlie says they've witnessed the changes on their property. "The extremes of weather are going from very wet seasons to very dry seasons and also huge variations in temperature within a very short time."

Charlie says when a drought hits, the first thing that happens is farmers put their hand up for help from the government. Commodity prices dip, and with it goes farm income. Farmers have to act quickly. "Unfortunately, most farmers do not plan. They're not prepared with some sort of insurance like a couple of paddocks

---

11   On a lighter note, a surprising attribute of the Anthropocene is … chickens. If ever a future palaeontologist digs up the layer we're now creating, they'll find an abundance of chicken fossils. The current population is about 23 billion!

12   According to Wikipedia, "The 2017 Atlantic hurricane season was the costliest tropical cyclone season on record, with a damage total of at least $294.92 billion (USD)", https://en.wikipedia.org/wiki/2017_Atlantic_hurricane_season.

ready in case. But I understand that because it's a consequence of the really tenuous economics of farming."

In a drought, farmers find themselves wedged between falling income and land under stress. They need to reduce stock while feeding the animals they keep. Soil needs care to hold back erosion when the rain returns. Their costs are high, but their income is under pressure. "The land gets degraded and the soil is degraded. Often trees will die after an extended drought. It's not good environmentally and it's not good economically."

I remember the Millennium Drought, but living in the city I took no notice of what was happening on farms. To most shoppers, food comes from supermarkets wrapped in plastic. What we did see were severe water restrictions, and cities such as Goulburn faced a crisis when reservoirs fell below 10%. Occasional dust storms blew in to remind us of the intimate connection of farms to the soil. During the earlier drought in 1983, a huge dust storm smothered Melbourne. Denuded land was stripped by strong wind, carrying Australia's food production system as it went.

Civilisation has provided us with abundant food, but it's also disconnected us from our origins on the land. It's a risky proposition when we take food for granted. It's said there are only seven meals between civilisation and anarchy.

Charlie has grave concerns about how humans have got to this point. The contrast with his conservative family background is stark. "Despite my parents' political beliefs, me and my sisters are progressives. We are all concerned about climate change. We're all worried about the culture that rampant capitalism has created."

Anxiety

I met Kris and Charlie at a pleasant rural bakery, overlooking a vineyard. The clatter of coffee cups and the hissing espresso machine were not good for recording audio or my poor hearing, so we took our drinks and moved outside. Well, it seemed like a good idea at the time.

Charlie Prell at Gundowringa (photo by Rod Taylor).

I wanted to hear their shared perspectives on how they survived the difficult years through the wool crisis and the Millennium Drought. Charlie recalls that it even got to the point where they faced having to walk away from four generations on the land.

> I had two young kids. I was about to turn 40 and I couldn't see any opportunity for me to live out the rest of my life on this farm. Kris and I were starting to think there has to be something more to life than this. We were considering selling up, which wouldn't have been easy because of the family tradition.

Both Charlie and Kris found themselves struggling with anxiety and depression. As we spoke, Kris seemed positive as she feels things have improved, but I could see Charlie was reliving those days. He frowned and rubbed his hand across his forehead.

It was a difficult conversation, but it quickly became very odd. BANG. I was trying to figure out what was going on, and then again: BANG. Air guns. The vineyard uses them to keep birds off the ripening grapes. It was like a Tarantino scene where death meets the banal. My recording of the session is punctuated by those noises, but soon it became even stranger.

There are two houses on Gundowringa. Charlie told me about his mother Jess, who lived in the original colonial-style building while Charlie and Kris occupy the newer house not far up the hill.

> Mum was from a broken marriage. She was very attractive and was a good catch, but she wasn't from the right side of the railway tracks according to my father's family. She kept the family together for 50-odd years.
>
> She could see the torment that I was going through in my mid-forties as I started to question the whole sustainability, liveability, and financial circumstances we were in.

In 2007, Charlie remembers he was writing an email when Kris took a call from his father. Jess was not feeling well and she was vomiting. He wanted to know if it would be all right to give her some Mylanta. Kris described what happened next.

> I was the nurse, so I was the go-to person for anything medical. I said," Yes that's fine. Has she eaten something?" He said, "No, I don't think so. She came back from her walk not feeling well."
>
> He told me the Mylanta was 10 years old, so I said if she's really crook don't give her that because it will only make her feel worse. Then it popped into my head that maybe something else was going on and I asked, "Is she sweating?"
>
> Yes, she was sweating profusely.

The story they were sharing was painful and deeply personal, but our vineyard setting was becoming surreal. We'd persisted in spite of the air guns, but then a farm dog trotted over with a lump of wood in its mouth. It dropped it at Charlie's feet and looked at him expectantly. It had decided we were going to play catch. It stood there staring at us and the message was obvious. Dog. Stick. Human. Hello? We did our best to ignore it, but "No" was not an option, and nothing would make it go away. Kris ploughed on.

> So Charlie and I went down there and our niece Dimity was standing in the driveway looking shocked and waving frantically waving. "Quick, quick."

It was a harrowing account, but the dog and the air guns would not be deterred. BANG. WOOF. We tried everything to get rid of the dog, but nothing worked and for the rest of our conversation we had to talk over them. It reminded me of other pivotal moments in life. The profound and the ridiculous, side by side. Kris continued.

> We went into the bedroom and basically she had passed away. She wasn't breathing and I couldn't feel a pulse … so Charlie started CPR doing compressions, and I was doing mouth-to-mouth and I managed to get out to Jeff, "Have you rung the ambulance?"

They kept it up for 20 to 25 minutes until the ambulance arrived, but it was too late.

A post-mortem revealed that a third of her heart had died and there were signs of an earlier heart attack, but she'd never complained. "She was not interested in feeling unwell. She was more concerned about looking after Jeff and she gave very little thought to her own aches and pains," Kris says.

For the Prells, the incident would have long-term consequences. To Charlie, the immediate aftermath seemed unreal. They still had the mundane chores like going to the supermarket and moving sheep around the farm. But at the same time, they were arranging the funeral. "You feel like the train has stopped, but the train is still going," he says. Piled on top of the long-term problems on the farm, it was a trigger for anxiety and depression.

Their daughter Alexandra was very close to her grandmother. "She was waiting in our house for two hours on her own, not knowing what was going on." She had to attend trauma counselling. Kris struggled with depression and also needed counselling, but it took her some time to understand the extent of her problem. Eventually, she came to appreciate her sense of shame—for being a trained nurse yet unable to save her own mother-in-law. The lingering sense of failure has been hard to shake.

Wind

In March 2017, a headline in the *Canberra Times* caught my eye: "Wind farm stirs big outcry". A Spanish-Australian venture was proposing to build the Jupiter Wind Farm at Tarago, near Canberra. It had already been knocked back by planning authorities and now they were hoping for a smaller project with 88 turbines across 23 rural properties.

I had to read the article a second time because ... why would wind energy advocates be opposing a wind farm? The article read in part: "Among the objecting organisations ... the Australian Wind Alliance, in an unprecedented move formally objecting to a wind farm."

In 2014, the Australian Wind Alliance approached Charlie Prell after hearing about the outspoken Crookwell farmer. The Australian Wind Alliance describes itself as a community-based advocacy group sharing a common vision of harnessing Australia's world-class wind resources. It was a natural fit for Charlie and since then he's been heavily involved.

I met Charlie soon after the Jupiter news broke and his frustration was evident. He's been here before. "I have some sympathy for the farmers. We talked to them 18 months ago and said, 'This is bullshit.'"

He vividly remembers a day in the 1990s when someone asked him if he knew about wind farms. "I didn't have any idea about them, or what the benefits were, but I had a sense that it was a game-changer. Now the generational change renewable energy is offering to rural Australia is just huge." At that time they were just going into the Millennium Drought and things were bad financially.

Farming will always be an uncertain business, but wind turbines provide a reliable income. It's a buffer through drought, storms, and market gyrations. Reducing uncertainty is not just a psychological boost. Fluctuating incomes make it hard to invest in remedial work on creeks, trees, and fences, and it's a temptation to boost cash flow by overstocking. To Charlie, it made perfect sense that they should have some turbines on their property too.

Australia's first turbines were connected to the grid in 1998 near Crookwell, but by April 2017 there still weren't any on Gundowringa. The promise was there, but making it happen proved more complicated. There was an endless array of obstacles, locally and nationally. Just as they were negotiating a contract for the wind farm for 2004 to 2008, the anti-wind farm movement started to reach a peak. The election of Kevin Rudd gave him some hope, but Charlie says, "He turned out to be more hot air than action."

More immediate was resistance from the local council. There were stories about turbines killing birds, affecting people's health, and causing land devaluation.

Charlie sounds exasperated. "I was thinking, well we are running a grazing operation, and the turbines are probably only going to take up 100 square metres at the base. What's wrong with having a few turbines on your farm?"

Charlie feels the council lacked courage, caving in to the "viciousness of the anti-wind farm brigade". The debate had become so toxic that even those in favour stayed silent. He found himself becoming a spokesman for the wind farm companies. "I used to get really sick of people walking down the street and saying to me, just quietly, 'Good on you, Charlie. Go for it.' And I would say, 'Can you say that a bit louder?'"

Debate in the shire council became nasty, and to make it worse it coincided with his mother's fatal heart attack. As he told me his story, he laughed, but it remains a painful memory. In one session he was accused of being "as corrupt as Eddie Obeid",[13] that he was in the pockets of the wind farm industry. Charlie says he doesn't mind a bit of robust discussion, but "that really got my goat and that's when I decided, bugger these guys, I'm going to fight back."

He was criticised for missing a council inspection of a local wind farm so he told the council, "I couldn't be there because I was burying my mother."

Recalling the incident is difficult for Charlie, and as he spoke, he paused, sighed, and then continued. "I was really angry." At a subsequent council meeting, he made a statement defending himself. His words had an impact, and now Charlie reflects: "The councillor involved was severely chastened and has since become quite a good friend."

Charlie may have been seen as a spokesman for the wind farm companies, but they were part of the problem. He is scathing about how some of them approached landowners. "Some of the companies were often bullying, arrogant, and sometimes breaking the law." They were asking farmers to cede the rights to their land and "we'll

---

13   NSW politician found guilty of corruption.

let you do stuff we think is appropriate". If landowners accepted, they'd turn farms into subsidiary operations for the turbines. He tried to get the council to support local farmers who were tempted to sign up but weren't well educated in the legal issues involved.

Riding through the beautiful Crookwell landscape, I found myself with mixed feelings about how turbines look. They're prolific, and if your preference is for unspoilt nature they can be intrusive. The first one I ever saw was in Albany, Western Australia, and then it was a novelty, but now they are common. A former Australian treasurer famously called them "utterly offensive", but that has a flavour of politics more than aesthetics. Beauty or otherwise, they are nothing compared to the ugliness of global warming.

The gently swooshing blades generate a low rumble that mimics the opposition from some anti-wind farm groups who say the infrasound is related to "wind turbine syndrome".[14] Charlie remembers that one of their neighbours thought turbines would electrify the ground because they were generating electricity and that "I was a selfish bastard because I just wanted the money and didn't give a shit about my neighbours. It was going to destroy the land." They would say "anything that sort of stuck".

By October 2016, some of the rhetoric hadn't progressed, with Rowan Dean on the Bolt Report[15] sounding like he was commenting on concentration camps.

---

14   This is just one episode in the curious history of concerns about the effects of new technology. It's important that we do this as long as it's grounded in science. Trains, for example, were a trigger for huge technological and social change that were not always welcomed. "Women's bodies were not designed to go at 50 miles an hour", and people worried that "[female passengers'] uteruses would fly out of [their] bodies as they were accelerated to that speed". "Early Trains Were Thought to Make Women's Uteruses Fly Out", *Mental Floss*, 26 August 2015, http://mentalfloss.com/article/67806/early-trains-were-thought-make-womens-uteruses-fly-out.

15   "Lunar right go crazy over 'genocidal' wind turbines and solar power", *Renew Economy*, 2 May 2017, www.reneweconomy.com.au/lunar-right-go-crazy-over-genocidal-wind-turbines-and-solar-power-89735/.

Let me remind you that every year in Australia, at least 2,000 birds are killed by windmills. In Germany, Andrew, it's 6 million birds every year killed by renewables, by windmills. In America, it's a couple of million every year. So if anybody has blood on their hands, Andrew, it's the Greens, it's people like Adam Bandt, who have forced these genocidal bird holocaust machines across our landscape.

And yet, they sit there gleefully putting more and more of them and telling us they're doing it for the good, when … it makes no difference to global temperatures, and they are massacring birds and they are destroying jobs for no difference to global temperatures.

Progress around Crookwell wasn't helped by the attitude of companies. Charlie says, "It really annoys me that the actions of the wind farm companies were often less than honest and less than ethical. That fed into the hyper-partisanship debate in relation to wind farms, which has fed into the political heat over renewable energy, which fed into the empowering of Tony Abbott and his right-wing group, and led to stagnation."

Charlie says he finds the opposition strange because to him wind energy is a pragmatic choice. "The Australian Wind Alliance is not simply a support mechanism for the companies regardless of what they are offering. The Alliance aims to get the best possible outcome for landholders, neighbours, and small regional communities as well as for the companies. The companies respect us, but they're also wary of us because potentially we're like union organisers for landholders."

Prell's neighbours had been frightened by the anti-wind farm brigade, but that has mostly changed and by 2017 many had signed up for turbines. Charlie's paid a high price for his advocacy, but now he can see the results. He takes some pride in knowing that he and other farmers have a reliable income to buffer them through flood, drought, and unpredictable markets. Numbers vary, but a typical 50-megawatt wind farm will pay landowners $250,000.

Even better, Charlie says, the farms are now producing food *and* energy.

The Accidental Activist

When I visited Gundowringa in March 2017, Charlie was expecting to see the turbines going up in a few months' time. It would be cool, I thought, to visit and watch some of the action. First it was going to be November, then it was March, but it was not until July 2018 that I learned it was finally going ahead. The delay? Drought. Again it was drought! Charlie told me this one was potentially worse than the Millennium Drought. Importantly for the wind farm construction, it meant they had no water for construction and for keeping the dust down on roads. And then he said he couldn't be certain of exactly when the workers would be on site. "It's ironic," he told me, "but they can't put up the turbines while the wind is blowing."

It was a crisp winter's day travelling north from Goulburn, and for while I was immersed in pea-soup fog. As I crested the hill it suddenly cleared, and I was greeted by a beautiful blue sky. There they were, on the far side of the valley—Charlie's wind turbines. Well, technically they're not his, but I felt a surge of excitement. I've seen plenty of them before, but in a tiny way, I felt part of this project. For Charlie, though, it's the climax of a long struggle. How did he feel? "Excited, elated, relieved." But there was a tinge of nervousness. Would it all go well? It'd still be weeks before the turbines could be connected to the grid.

The nearest turbine is 500 metres from Charlie and Kris's house. From the back door, it's clearly visible through the trees. Running underground from each is a power line to a local substation and from there to the grid. Each unit can generate 3.4 megawatts. According to the common "per house" metric,[16] that's about enough to supply 1,500 average homes. I still can't quite imagine that, so I did a conversion that reveals that a single turbine is the same capacity as 20,400 of the solar array we just installed at home (6 kilowatts).

Charlie had invited some other friends to enjoy the spectacle. The turbines towered over us, pristine white against the blue sky. We shared a sense of optimism to see what could be achieved with persistence. Above us, the huge blades gently turned, making a slight whirring sound. Not loud, we thought, but noticeable. Then we realised something seemed strange ... terribly wrong ...

"Run," we yelled. "Infrasound!" We had to get away or be struck down by Wind Turbine Syndrome!

It was a silly joke, of course—there almost certainly is no such thing. It's hard to imagine how a sound below the threshold of hearing might inflict a range of maladies that includes cancer, congenital abnormalities, and death. Even the slightly more benign list runs to symptoms such as sleep loss, fatigue, nausea, headaches, tinnitus, disturbances, and more. If it really were true, you'd want to stay away from cities and beaches. One study[17] measured infrasound levels in the Adelaide CBD at 76 decibels.[18] At a beach, 25 metres from the high-water line, they measured 75 decibels. Meanwhile, the loudest wind farm they recorded from 85 metres[19] was 72 decibels.

---

16 I'm always slightly bemused by this method of measurement; it reminds me of the "width of a human hair" scale, but I guess we need to relate it to something we can understand.

17 "Measurement and level of infrasound from wind farms and other sources", *Acoustics Australia*, Vol 40, No 1, April 2012, www.acoustics.asn.au/journal/2012/2012_40_1_Turnbull.pdf.

18 Technically, it was dB(G), which indicates the sound pressure levels that's weighted for this type of measurement.

19 Sound pressure level halves each time you double the distance, so at 170 metres, that 72 dB is reduced to about the volume of a TV set.

Numbers like these don't deter those who inhabit websites such as the provocatively named StopTheseThings. It's a strange island universe where the only way in is virulent opposition to wind energy and the only evidence allowed is negative. The stories posted feature spectacular images of turbines that have caught fire.[20] One such story delivers this damning assessment of a wind farm not far from Gundowringa.

> The Gullen Range wind farm has been a disaster from the get-go—with hundreds of homes lined up as sonic torture traps ...

Charlie knows about the website. "It's a depressing place," he says. The problem with anti- activists such as these is that their loopy approach clouds the genuine issues that can occur. Charlie's seen poor behaviour from wind energy companies, but the unbalanced opposition obscures sensible debate, and where companies behave badly, they should be held to account.

Even with the best intentions, companies sometimes go astray. Communities can be a fickle thing, as Dr Rebecca Colvin learned when she investigated a wind farm project on King Island. There, the company did all the so-called "best practice" community engagement things, but they had to withdraw when the local people became deeply divided. Wind farm companies are mindful of those pitfalls and are spending time and money to win people over. Community Energy Funds channel money into the local areas

---

20   As one website puts it amusingly:" Wind turbines are essentially small buckets of lubricating oil on top of a large metal stick, with rotating wings attached. Add a strike of lightning, a short circuit or a mechanical fault and they occasionally set alight. "They say that between 1995 and 2012, there were 200 involving fire. "How often do wind turbines catch fire? And does it matter?" Global Wind Energy Council, www.gwec.net/how-often-wind-turbines-catch-fire-and-matter/.

where it pays for a range of activities in education, health, and the environment. They need to do this because a wind turbine is a large, obvious structure on the skyline and sometimes they sit within one farmer's property, only a few metres from the neighbours. When neighbours are unhappy, the company has a problem.

Now with a more secure income, Charlie and Kris can ride through the tough times on Gundowringa. And there are, he says, many others who could benefit from the same thing. There are huge amounts of wind power yet to be exploited that will help other rural communities.

Meanwhile, climate change continues to bite, and Charlie has picked his next target. He represents the group called Farmers for Climate Action. Their job is to advocate for people on the land who have been abandoned by politicians. Even the National Party, once called the "Country Party", is now promoting the giant Adani coal mine in Queensland that seeks to pump not just water from limited aquifers but dollars from the Australian purse. When we met, Charlie had just been meeting senior politicians to lobby for action on climate change.

It's not a course he ever planned. More, it's the unlikely path where life has taken him. "I am," he says, "an accidental activist."

The Thoughtful Salesman
Leonard Cohen

Here was somebody I had to meet. Who could convince a struggling car company and a government to spend a million dollars planting trees?

Leonard Cohen—yes, he's (part) Jewish and yes, he plays guitar, but this Leonard is still very much alive. He's also part Māori, a former teacher, and founder of the carbon farming organisation, Canopy.

Standing on the edge of the city of Auckland, New Zealand is an enormous tree. As a boy, Leonard Cohen would sit here, dwarfed in both size and age of the towering structure. He was already contemplating life and nature. Sixty years later, his memory of those days is still strong. He looked wistful as he described it to me, saying, "I formed an affection for this tree. My family would joke that Leonard's gone to talk to Tane, the God of the forest."

What he didn't know then, was how this tree would shape his thinking and signal his future. "We had this funny little boy intellectually curious who was programmed culturally to relate strongly to the environment, living in the intersection of the affluent middle-class and the indigenous world in suburbia on the edge of rainforests. All these forces swirled around in my developing psyche," he told me.

Many years later he would return to the kauri of his childhood. For 45 years he's visited it almost every year, but now he experienced one of those rare insights. The old farm had been recently sold and subdivided and the new owner, Wade Cornell, was sensitive to the significance of the tree. Leonard is grateful and says Wade is now "custodian" of the tree. When Wade took Leonard to see it and Leonard looked up, "I thought, shit, it hasn't grown, but the canopy section was much thicker. We were all looking, saying, what lovely trees."

Leonard describes what happened next.

> The bush there is dark and dense, the big trees cutting down the light—sparse undergrowth for a rainforest. I was a little disconcerted at being escorted. It was like being introduced to someone you know well. I can't complain because he's looking after it well.
>
> We passed through the gate and I didn't look for the tree. I knew where it stood so I kept my eyes on the ground until I was at its base—I don't know why. Then I put my hand on it and looked up, and tears rolled down my face. I had no warning and didn't understand quite why. I spent a while walking around it. I picked a tiny piece of gum from the bark to experience that camphor smell—so evocative.
>
> Wade asked me if I'd like a little longer with the tree. It felt like leaving a child at a bus stop or your mum in a retirement village.
>
> Suddenly it hit me that the most significant thing in my life was not a Western artefact. It was a living thing.

Now aged 72, Leonard was contemplating his journey as a boy living near the kauri to his adult life as a teacher and the work he would do planting trees. "I never understood where the sense of shame came from until two months ago. I was sitting at the foot of a tree and I thought 'You bastard. If you had been doing in 1971 what you're doing now, think of how much good you could have done. What a shame. *What a shame.*'"

Leonard at his home in the Adelaide Hills. He was excited to spot a koala in the tree above (photo by Rod Taylor).

The kauri tree is an amazing thing, not just because they can be extremely tall (they can grow to over 50 metres), but because they look odd. Leonard describes the one from his childhood in his particular style. "They look like a big tube with no branches and a bubble on top. It was one of the largest trees around Auckland, it was kind of an anomaly. It was the biggest tree for fucking miles."

It didn't take long for me to learn that Leonard is a curious blend of intellectual and salesman. It's an unusual combination because often people can be intellectual, but not practical—or practical, but not a deep thinker. At one moment he'd be telling me, "The universe is conscious—the post on my veranda doesn't have a lot to say, but it's part of the whole," and the next he'd be describing how he'd convinced a car manufacturer to spend money planting trees, or how he managed to wrangle his way into the state premier's office.

Leonard has the blended heritage of an ex-British soldier father and a mother of Māori descent. His namesake Leonard Cohen, who had died not long before we met, was famous for being Jewish and playing guitar. I'm told this Leonard also plays guitar although I've yet to hear him play. The Jewish comes from his father's side, but he doesn't identify himself as such.

More influential, perhaps, has been his mother's indigenous background that gave her a particular view of the natural world. Māori culture is governed by various deities, and his mother would say, "Ikatere has been good to us because we have fish." It's an animist religion where things have souls, such as Punga, the god of deformed, ugly things and the ancestor of sharks, lizards, and rays. Tane[21] is the god of the forests. Leonard's family were guardians of lizards and orca. His mother Sam would drop fern leaves for them at the foot of a large tree.

A kauri can be 14 metres around the girth, which I find hard to imagine, so I got out a tape measure. By the time I paced out 14 metres, it was almost the length of my house and the word "big" doesn't seem adequate. Their age, too, is remarkable. The largest tree named *TaneMahuta* is about 1,200 years old. It's thought they can live as long as 2,000 years, maybe more. Some kauri have been found buried in swamps where they've been preserved for over 45,000 years, which is an astounding length of time if you consider that is roughly ten times older than civilisation.

---

21   Pronounced Ta-nay.

The great kauri towers not just over a human, but over the whole of humanity. The first kauri appeared between 190 and 135 million years ago during the Jurassic period when the world was warmer and wetter, and the great dinosaurs were still around. The dinosaurs[22] disappeared when an asteroid crashed into the Gulf of Mexico 65 million years ago, but the kauri lived on. Homo sapiens have only been around about 200,000 years, which means that kauri have been on the planet for more than 300 times longer than us. Kauri survived the cataclysmic encounter with a 15-kilometre lump of rock. And then they met humans.

Deforestation began when the Māori arrived nearly 1,000 years ago, but real progress had to wait until the arrival of Europeans and mechanisation. From their settlement in the early 1800s, it only took until 1900 to remove 90% of the original kauri. The one-time profit continued and, by the 1950s, only 1,400 square kilometres remained in 47 forests depleted of their best kauri. Today only about 4% of the original forest remains in isolated pockets.

When I asked Leonard how he felt about this, he said, "I don't have anything to say about the loss of these great trees that isn't trite."

Even though Leonard's mother was Māori, she had an eye on Western culture and the industrial system. She gave Leonard a book by Brooks Stevens who popularised the term "planned obsolescence". It's a brilliant insight into how we allow ourselves to be manipulated by marketing. The key was "instilling in the buyer the desire to own something a little newer, a little better, a little sooner than is necessary".

She gave him the 1960 book *The Waste Makers* by Vance Packard, which categorised marketing as a "systematic attempt by business to make us wasteful, debt-ridden, and permanently discontented". The practice remains blatant today, with endless

---

22   Almost—birds are descended from dinosaurs.

updates to devices such as smartphones that become either technically or socially obsolete almost as soon as you buy them. They come with specialised screw heads[23] and glued-in batteries so they can't be repaired. The average smartphone has a lifespan of about 21 months before it becomes as valuable as a half-eaten hamburger—often not because they break, but because we get bored with them. Or the manufacturers introduce some software "upgrades" that won't install.

Leonard says the idea hit him "like a ton of bricks. I thought," hit, everything is like this. It means more and more burdens are being imposed on the natural world."" Then he went on to read Rachel Carson's *Silent Spring* and works by Ralph Nader about the impact of DDT pesticides and the nature of the consumer society.

Leonard's father, Keith, had returned from World War II emotionally and physically damaged. Leonard says his father spent most of the war "walking backward", starting in Greece as the Allies retreated to Cyprus, and then North Africa and Libya. In North Africa, they encountered the Afrika Korps led by Field Marshal Erwin Rommel in a highly mobile war across the desert.

During the fierce desert battle for El Alamein, Keith was shot in the arm. He managed to find his way to the field hospital before being repatriated to New Zealand. He'd arrived home, but even that wasn't safe as the Japanese swept across the Pacific. There was a real fear that invasion was imminent, so the local authorities began preparing defences. There were blackout curtains, fire buckets full of sand, and a Home Guard. Large trapezoid-shaped concrete tank traps were installed on roads around Auckland. These were designed to slow tanks, but they were also a traffic hazard. One night Keith was in an Austin Seven car driving along the Great North Road

---

23   I once met someone who'd been a smartphone repairer and he described to me the bizarre screws used in the Apple iPhones that are designed to prevent them being repaired. "I'd never buy an iPhone," he said.

when it hit one. Leonard's sister Lianne says with a hint of irony, "his fine straight nose was mushed".

Keith Cohen had gone to the war as a good-looking man, but when it was over he couldn't use his arm or wrist properly and his face was scarred. His scarring wasn't a gross disfigurement, but Leonard says it made his father self-conscious and like most men of the period, he didn't talk about it. The bullet had gone through his left arm and he could no longer play his violin.

The war left Keith with a sense of failure and Leonard says, "He was a sad case. He'd been traumatised and from 1946 to 1956 he was screaming in his sleep. He was a successful businessman, but the way he dealt with his family was affected by his experience." He was a bit of an authoritarian who came from an affluent middle-class family.

War for many people is a terrible experience, but World War II was even riskier for someone of Jewish heritage. As Leonard's sister Lianne dryly notes, "A person with the name of Cohen should not have volunteered, knowing the consequences of capture."

It took Leonard a while after leaving school to decide what he wanted to do with his life. But first, he wanted to explore the adult world. "I studied snooker and advanced girls, which saw me married at age 20. That was a badly designed course," he says.

Then he went into law, but hated it and turned to teaching secondary school English instead. "I discovered I was good at that," he says. His love of teaching has stayed with him and now that's how he views his life. Whether it was carbon farming or energy efficiency, the goal was always the same. "The trees were incidental to climate change. What really mattered to me was to show a way to deal with climate change. I am a teacher."

Some say teaching is an undervalued profession, but it's hard to overestimate the impact of a great teacher. Changing a person's thinking generates ever-expanding ripples that can have an effect far beyond what we imagine. Leonard told me about the letters he still receives. There's a familiar pattern, he says. They read something like: "Dear Mr Cohen, you may not remember me, but you were my teacher a long time ago. I still remember that you taught me …"

The Kauri at Forrest Hill.[24]

After he quit teaching in 2000, his own thinking was changed when he met author and environmentalist Gael Rudwick. She told him, "Everything spreads, and nothing disappears. Things still exist even when we put them in the bin—and we've been using the sky for a free rubbish dump. I don't have to pay to dump the rubbish from my car because it goes into the sky."

---

24   Sir George Grey Special Collections, Auckland Libraries, 4-1535, www.aucklandcity.govt.nz.

Humans are causing a great dispersal not just of rubbish, but of plants and animals, and it seems every day we discover another introduced pest. Leonard read about sustainability and the so-called "triple bottom line", which values the environment and people as well as profit. He read about the idea of the "externality", which describes costs that are ignored by profit and loss statements. If a company strips a hillside but doesn't pay the cost, that's an externality. If I dump my car's engine oil by the roadside, that's an externality because someone else pays.

It was a revelation, he says. "I completely remember the feeling—where was I, down on the beach?—I thought this was astounding. I realised I was part of a gigantic experiment being conducted on the planet." He read about climate change. "It was exhausting, I couldn't stop, I was overwhelmed. It was a bit like the first time I read Marx, I became a communist for at least six weeks. I was a Marxist and all for the revolution." His interest in Marxism didn't last, but he remained committed to doing something about climate change.

Telling his story, Leonard seemed quite cheerful and unconcerned by the dire challenge of global warming. By chance, I'd also been talking to Clive Hamilton who'd said how the experience had left him deeply depressed. Unlike Clive, Leonard was unfussed. "I was never daunted by climate change, I'm still not. Before we get depressed, how about we just know? I'm excited about that. First you need to know what the impact is, and then you decide what to do about it. I'm a warrior. I like a bit of a stoush. It's good."

Gael Rudwick had planted an idea, but now Leonard needed to find a way to do something about it. Being retired meant he had time, but the question was, where to start? Rudwick suggested he should investigate the Green Fleet who can boast they've helped to offset carbon pollution by planting 8.9 million native trees across 475 biodiverse forests. Given his deep connection to the kauri, sequestering carbon by planting trees was the logical thing. But this is Leonard and he wasn't going to do it by half. This was the chutzpah I'd been wondering about. Leonard decided he was going to enlist a senior state politician and a car manufacturer. He'd start at the top and work his way down.

That's a good theory, but getting the attention of these people wouldn't be easy. Their days are full of people calling, emailing, or sending letters, all wanting something. He needed an approach that would stand out, something that would offer a thing they wanted.

Then he hit on an idea. He walked into the office of the Minister for Environment with a seedling and a note attached saying, "This is for the minister. You can get more like me in order that I and my friends can grow in South Australia."

Almost immediately he got a call from the minister asking, "Who are you?"

I'd been told that Leonard can be persuasive, and if he could pull off that sort of manoeuvre, he must be. At this point, he had no money, no organisation, and nobody to actually plant any trees. All he had was an idea and nibble of interest from the state government.

The first thing they asked was how his plan was going to work. He suggested that if the government built a small levy into the next vehicle registration cost increase, nobody would notice. "Find something that people are already paying and tack on to that," he thought. The carbon offset wouldn't necessarily match emissions, but as a matter of principle it was worthwhile.

The minister liked the idea, but his government had been elected on a platform of no increases in taxes or charges, so it would have to wait for their next term. Leonard wasn't particularly concerned because part of his plan was to get them thinking about climate change, and he'd already achieved that.

To get to this point, he'd started at the top. He'd used a bit of humour and now he needed to be adaptable, so he came up with a new plan that involved one of South Australia's car manufacturers.

They'd been struggling since Australia dropped import tariffs under the ironically named 1984 Motor Industry Development Plan. One of those companies was Mitsubishi Motors who, like the others, had stayed in business with the assistance of huge government subsidies.[25] They weren't likely to have much spare cash to plant trees, so Leonard needed a way to make sure it wouldn't cost them anything.

He formulated a plan: The state government had money and a desire to be seen to be doing public good. Mitsubishi Motors was in a tough business, they obviously wanted to sell cars, and the publicity might help them too. The South Australian government was even more concerned about the future of Mitsubishi, whose manufacturing plants were major employers and a significant part of the state's economy. Leonard's idea was to build a small increase into the cost of the 800 cars the state government was buying each year. It was a classic win-win because it would boost Mitsubishi's green credentials, helping them sell more cars, while the government would help a major local industry.

The small premium paid by the state fleets would buy carbon credits to offset emissions for up to 60,000 kilometres on each car. Leonard would do the calculations to work out how many trees, how much land, and how long the carbon would be sequestered if landholders were paid to plant trees.

Playing on the notion that the politicians and the car company both wanted publicity, he suggested a photo opportunity. He'd get the state premier and the CEO of Mitsubishi on the front page of the *Adelaide Advertiser*. With his characteristic wry humour, it appealed to Leonard, who says, "Not everyone necessarily understands, but everyone loves trees."

---

25   And since then, the car makers have left anyway.

Physics and Metaphysics

Clearly, Leonard knows a few tricks, but I had a lot to learn about how someone could come from nowhere to do something like this. Leonard had been suggested as a possible story for *Fragile Planet*, so I phoned him. He was friendly, and within minutes we were talking physics, metaphysics, renewable energy, and trees. "The fact that we humans are here to observe it means that the universe is self-aware." We rambled on in this vein for an hour, mulling over life, the universe … Luckily, we didn't get onto Schopenhauer philosophy because the only thing I know about that is the intimidating name.

At some point, Leonard got on to describing himself. A narcissist, he said. It seemed a self-deprecating, un-narcissistic thing to say, so I didn't take it seriously but made a note to ask him more about this later. It reminded me that people are a tangle of contradictions. When I met him the first time, he told me, "A patient man coming to talk to you about yourself is every narcissist's dream. If you are an egotistical arrogant and conceited narcissist like me, you made my fucking my day by turning up."

Wow, I thought, he didn't hold back, but did he really want to portray himself this way? Apparently so. "That's what insight does. With that knowledge, you rejoice. It gives you an infinite capacity for self-mockery," he says.

Now the contradictions were really showing, but I couldn't help feeling that it was an insight into self-awareness. He says the first step is to understand your inner nature, accept it, then work with it. As he says, "A friend taught me about reflection and about humility. From her, I learned to accept that I am a narcissist, but I'm like a non-drinking alcoholic. If you're a humble narcissist you will learn who you are."

Leonard was telling me this story and then in his characteristic way he laughed again. "The great narcissist joke is: anyway, that's enough about me—tell me about what you think about me."

This was the clue I'd been looking for. Understanding himself helps Leonard to better understand others. He says he's more successful working with other people because he can see their motivations, but doesn't assume they are the same. "It's a mistake to try to make people do what you want," he says. This was the heart of how he'd win the cooperation of influential people.

What he described was revealing about how to sell. "It's probably going to work well if I know more about them than they know about me. And as long as I have a moral compass everyone wins." He was raising the topic of ethics, so I decided to quiz him about it later.

A Big Green Umbrella

In my front yard, there's a mannifera eucalyptus tree that was planted not long after our house was built 35 years ago. They are the most beautiful things, with smooth white bark and patches of deep green. When I'm feeling playful and climb it, it leaves white dusty marks over my clothing, which gets me into trouble when I go back inside. As they get older, they develop enchanting twisted limbs with wrinkles that look like the folds around a fat man's legs.

Our mannifera stands 9 metres tall and 1.5 metres around the girth. Before the tree was planted, the soil around it was flat, but now it's bulging where the roots have grown. The stuff that makes up the trunk, leaves, branches, and roots had to come from somewhere. Some obviously originate from the soil, which includes a large amount of moisture, but it's a small percentage of the whole tree. The rest was drawn from the air. Our tree is a carbon capture and storage system. Even better, creating it didn't need any engineering work. It needed no plumbing, no construction, and no wiring. It's also free.

An online calculator tells me that our mannifera has pulled about 2.2 tonnes of CO_2 from the air since it was planted, but it's a tiddler alongside Leonard's kauri. With a girth of 14 metres, the same calculator estimates a kauri would account for 428 tonnes of CO2.[26]

Our mannifera. This angle makes it look bigger than it really is (photo by Rod Taylor).

Travelling to meet Leonard and the others in South Australia meant driving 3,240 kilometres. I could feel smug writing a book about the environment, but according to another online calculator, my trip sent a quarter of a tonne of CO2 into the sky. It's not much, but it adds up, and in 2015 we passed the grim milestone of 400

26   In the atmosphere, the mass of CO2 is greater because it is bonded with oxygen. In my mannifera, that equates to 0.6 tonnes of carbon. The kauri stores 116 tonnes of carbon, which would be 428 tonnes as CO2.

parts per million atmospheric CO2. It's hard to comprehend how much carbon that is, but one researcher[27] likened it to "burning enough coal to form a square tower 22 metres wide that reaches from Earth to the moon."

I could claim the tree as an offset, but it didn't grow that much while I was away. As an average Australian, I'm among the worst polluting people on the planet and this year I'll be responsible for about 16 tonnes of CO2. At that rate, I'll need to grow nearly eight of our manniferas every year to soak up my CO2. I can't grow trees that quickly, but I could invest in an organisation such as Canopy.[28] Leonard founded it for that very purpose.

With his usual wit, he originally named it "Big Green Umbrella". With that, the pieces were starting to come together. He had the state government and Mitsubishi, but he still needed people to actually plant trees and somewhere to plant them. But first, he had a more pressing problem, because some companies had acquired a shaky reputation for what became known as "greenwashing".

"Leonard can be persuasive," I was reminded. Apparently so, because here was someone who'd been selling to car salesmen. Car salesmen, really? The old jibe is that you can quieten a noisy car by stuffing a nylon shirt into the gearbox. This was my cue to prod him with a question about ethics. The business of capturing carbon by planting trees is complicated, which sounds like a lot of effort. Would it, I suggested, be tempting to fudge it?

"Fudge? Like what?" he asked.

"You know, perhaps take a few shortcuts. Just plant the trees, but skip the carbon calculations. Or maybe save a few dollars on the watering."

---

27 Eelco Rohling, "We need to get rid of carbon in the atmosphere, not just reduce emissions", *The Conversation*, 20 April 2017.

28 Canopy has since been sold to Greening Australia.

Nice try, but I'd have to work harder. His answer said as much about sales as it did ethics. If they played games with, say, their carbon calculations, sooner or later they'd be caught out and the whole enterprise would be for nothing. Or as Leonard says, "If you're going to be successful and you haven't got integrity then you'll eventually unravel. A sustainable business is about trust."

To make his point, he told me about what happened to the car company Saab (then owned by GM). In 2008 Australia's consumer watchdog (ACCC) mounted a case[29] against the car manufacturer. Saab's "Grrrrrreen" campaign told people that "every Saab is green, with carbon emissions neutral across the entire Saab range." The ads promised that their CO2 emissions would be neutral over the life of the vehicle, when in fact they were only planting 17 native trees, enough to offset a single year.

To maintain people's confidence, Canopy had to avoid those sorts of incidents. Planting trees will help only as long as they actually grow, and the timber is retained in some form. If it burns or rots, most of the carbon will return to the atmosphere. To do what it says on the label, it has to be done properly and carbon should stay put for at least a hundred years.

With Canopy, Leonard set up a process that could be tracked and was backed up by models that scientists had produced to calculate how much carbon would be stored for a given planting. The model is fairly complicated because the way trees grow depends on things such as where they are, rainfall, soil, and the type of trees. When Leonard plugged the numbers into the model, it showed that their site near the Coorong would hold 10-20,000 tCO2e at maturity. I

---

29   "Saab 'Grrrrrreen' claims declared misleading by Federal Court", ACCC, 18 September 2008, www.accc.gov.au/media-release/saab-grrrrrreen-claims-declared-misleading-by-federal-court; "ACCC tackles growing trend of false green claims", 22 January 2010, *Sydney Morning Herald*, www.smh.com.au/world/accc-tackles-growing-trend-of-false-green-claims-20100121-mp2p.html.

can't comprehend how much that is, but if I imagine my mannifera growing across 300 hectares (3 kilometres square), it seems like a lot of carbon.

The topic was starting to get technical, but then Leonard launched into another story about selling cars and ethics. Leonard's friend said he couldn't be a used car salesman because he felt you can't do that without being a liar. "But you're wrong," Leonard replied. "If you sold used cars you'd be the biggest dealer in South Australia because you can't tell a lie."

Leonard described a family business that is one of the biggest Toyota dealers in South Australia. "The old boy set it up two generations back," he said. "On everybody's desk is a sheet of paper that reads, 'You're known by your good deeds. You must tell the truth.' If you were a car salesman with that dealership and they caught you lying, they'd sack you. This guy has been many years in the used car business. He diversified the business and now turns over a billion dollars a year."

"You can tell the truth and still make money. The head of sales in Mitsubishi told me to find out what people's needs were first and told them how he could make them go away. You don't sell—you enable people to buy."

Planting

The pieces of his plan were starting to fall into place. Leonard had the state government, Mitsubishi Motors, CMI Toyota, the Commonwealth Bank, and a scientifically rigorous way to calculate the carbon captured by trees. Now he needed the people and the places to plant them, so he got in contact with a range of environmental groups. "I stuck them in a room and I said, 'Listen, guys, if we had $1 million, what would you do? Who can plant the trees?" he said.

"And they all said pick me!" Leonard was relishing the story with a bemused grin. "As soon as you say I have $1 million everyone becomes highly motivated," he added.

Greening Australia came up with the best proposition, so he chose them. In the end, they didn't quite get the million dollars because of taxes, but it was still enough to plant a lot of trees. Where exactly was to be decided. Again, with an eye to the publicity potential, he suggested to Mitsubishi it would be more visible if they planted on Aboriginal land. They agreed and he went to the Ngarrindjeri community where the Murray runs into the sea.

The land is managed by the Aboriginal Lands Trust. Leonard asked them if they'd like to plant trees there, and it wouldn't cost them anything. He told them the trees would need them to stay there for a hundred years at least. "They understand those timescales," he says.

The idea of planting trees on Aboriginal land had a special appeal to Leonard, given his Māori heritage. The words of his mother were still with him: "I have to do something to help those poor Aborigines, they don't have a treaty." When he approached the communities, he made sure they knew about his Māori background. "They called me their brown brother from across the sea," he said. He remembers it was a special moment when they gave him a welcome to country.

It's not that long ago that Aborigines were described as "primitive"[30] and to the first white settlers, they were. When the First Fleet arrived in Sydney Cove, they found people living in bark shelters without books or guns, and wearing few clothes. They had no obvious farms or system of government that the newcomers recognised. Their people didn't have "jobs". They'd rub their bodies with fish oil to keep mosquitoes away, which meant they smelled, well, like fish. These were superficial impressions, but what we are slowly learning today is the extraordinary sophistication needed

---

30   I am disappointed to read that my hero Charles Darwin thought there was a progression of races from "savage" to "civilised". For one thing, there is no scientific definition of "race". Mind you, Darwin was also a product of his time.

to live in a land such as Australia. They'd survived here for tens of thousands of years, while our more advanced society relies on stripping resources that cannot be replaced.

The locals may have been "primitive", but the First Fleet settlers came close to starving when their resupply ships were slow to arrive. As they became desperate and Governor Phillip was forced to impose severe rationing, theft was common. The Aborigines were quite comfortable living off the land, while the new arrivals couldn't survive without importing food.

Leonard and his colleague Ted Byrt secured a government grant of $250,000 to travel to communities around Australia to tell them about climate change and help them plant trees. They had the funding, but getting people to meetings wasn't easy because, as Leonard says, "Aboriginal communities are the most over consulted people on the planet. They would turn up to 200 meetings a year with various government organisations," so they paid each person "a hundred dollars and a slap-up lunch to show up".

One place that sits in his memory is the South Australian Umuwa community near the Northern Territory border. It was hard to get to, he says, "a terrible place". Then he sighed and added, "Awful pain and sorrow." He didn't elaborate, but I could imagine the scenes of damaged communities.

Travelling to the communities gave Leonard insights into the ways we are degrading our environment. Cane toads are perhaps Australia's most hated pest, not least because they're ugly—and spread like cane toads. They were deliberately introduced from Hawaii in 1935.[31] Less well known is the product of another bright idea that went horribly wrong: buffel grass.

---

31   There's a surprising number of other countries where cane toads have been introduced: Martinique, Barbados, parts of the United States, Islands of Japan, most Caribbean islands, Jamaica, Dominica, the Bahamas, the Philippines, Puerto Rico, Fiji, and New Guinea.

In the early 1960s, buffel grass seeds were spread by cattlemen across the centre of Australia because it grows ... like buffel grass. In dry lands, it spreads prolifically, which is good for stock. There was even a strain introduced by the CSIRO in the 1970s called "American". They planted it around the Alice Springs airport to keep down dust.

Spreading across the Umuwa land was a huge amount of buffel grass, and Leonard laments, "The native grasses burn much slower. But these things just stay there and come back again." After rain, it soon produces green shoots, which looks vibrant, making it popular amongst some graziers although its food value is poor. But a weed is forever and once they arrive, they're friends for life—the type that park their backsides in your lounge room, drink your beer, and leave chip packets all over the floor.

Buffel grass is a scourge, but with the resources of Canopy, Leonard wanted to provide employment and improve native lands through carefully managed tree plantings. With Greening Australia, Leonard travelled to communities looking for more places where they might plant trees. One of the early sites was on the Murray River with the Peramangk people. They had a problem because there were burial sites on top of the dunes that have been cleared for farming. The exposed soil was blowing away and uncovering the remains of their ancestors. They hoped to solve the problem by planting trees, but Leonard found they didn't have the strength as a community to make it happen, so he had to abandon the idea. Instead, he went to the Ngarrindjeri people at the mouth of the Murray. Greening Australia found funding to employ them to gather seeds and plant trees. This was repeated on the lands of the Narrungar people.

The Cohen Method

Tree planting was just one of many projects that Leonard threw himself into. Canopy was one of the first organisations to devise life-cycle analysis for biodiesel in Australia and then to provide a carbon offset program. To do this, they worked with chemists to calculate how much carbon would be saved. Then he moved onto the idea of offsetting the carbon emissions in the embodied energy of a skyscraper and electricity in the building. That, too, meant finding a way to credible carbon calculations.

By now I could see a recurring pattern, which I'll call the Cohen Method. Leonard will like that. It's also not a simple 1-2-3 step program because it's subtle—more a set of principles where adaptability is essential. He'd hatch an idea such as linking carbon capture to car sales. Then find an organisation with motivation and money who might be willing to fund a project. Then he'd find people who could deliver the project while demonstrating credible results.

For his skyscraper-carbon project, he found someone who was selling floor space and, to make purchases more attractive to the government, the price would include offsets to plant trees. Instead of wasting time trying to navigate his way up through the lower tiers of an organisation, he'd go to the top because, he says, "Coming from the bottom, everyone gets in your way." He'd use stunts such as sending a seedling to the minister with a note attached.

On one occasion, he set up a meeting in the Mitsubishi boardroom with all the executives. Leonard clearly enjoyed telling his story. "So think about this," he said. "What would be going through your head if you're an executive with a 9 o'clock meeting? What are they feeling?"

He was applying some simple psychology, which he told with a chuckle, "They're thinking—*I'm running late, skip breakfast!*"

"So I took in a big tray of muffins and they fell on them with glad cries and ate the lot!"

He had, it seems, charmed his way into the upper echelons and he knew exactly what he was doing. "By this time, I now know both the head of marketing and the head of fleet sales. So they think I'm a nice guy. I wanted to spend time with powerful people in Mitsubishi and twist them around a bit." It didn't really matter that he couldn't hold the attention of everyone in the room. "One Japanese executive went to sleep while I was talking, but he wasn't too good with English."

Dead Trees

Leonard likes to tell stories of how he danced around obstacles to achieve all these things, but it seemed too easy. Surely, I wondered, there must have been some difficult patches, times when things were going pear-shaped? What were his failures? I asked. When had his cunning not worked? At first, he didn't tell me any, so I asked again, gently prodding. That might've annoyed someone else, but he wasn't the least fazed, saying, "Oh sure, I fail all the time. I fail all the time! There have been errors of judgement, making mistakes about people."

Could he be more specific? Was there a particular time or place he could describe? "My greatest single failure is what my family calls *Leonard and the bright shiny things*." He went on to describe a series of projects where he'd start, then lose interest before launching into another.

Canopy was the first in Australia to devise life-cycle analysis for biodiesel and then to provide a carbon offset program. They worked extensively with chemists to calculate how much carbon would be offset. The biodiesel project was going well and Leonard says he could have extended it to every manufacturer across the country, but he "got bored with it".

He tried a similar approach to offset the embodied energy in a skyscraper. He found someone who could do the carbon calculations and a real estate agent who was selling the floor space. That was also going well, but eventually he grew bored with that too.

Well, I suggested, this could be seen as a failure, but it looked to me like someone playing to their strengths. Leonard is an innovator with the ability to take a fresh idea and make it work. He'd combine it with his natural salesmanship and a commitment to rigour. He'd take the idea, get it running and then find other people to keep it going.

The world needs both innovators and managers. Surely it's a good thing to let someone like Leonard loose on innovation, as long it has ongoing merit and someone else is there to pick it up when they get bored.

What I'd really been asking was whether his journey had been more difficult than it seemed. What adversities had he faced? Instead, he was cheerfully cataloguing his character flaws. Then he launched into another story about the day he was driving in the country and he got a call from the ABC. They wanted to interview him about a project that had become a highly visible, expensive failure around South Australia's Lower Lakes and Coorong district.

Leonard, who was by then with Greening Australia, says, "The premier was driving around and he noticed there were no trees. So he spoke to his people, and said, 'Let there be trees.' But he didn't say let there be trees in the right spot. There were *never* trees in that spot."

The *Australian* newspaper picked up the story, saying, "Former premier Mike Rann allocated $5.7 million to the scheme in a bid to woo the Greens before the 2007 South Australian election … Thousands of trees died in the initial planting zone between Morgan and Renmark because of drought, locusts, bad soils, a ban on watering, and poor site choice …"

Leonard says the lesson was that having money and a good idea is not enough. "You actually have to do the science. If you spend cash and the trees all die, it will have no impact and it will damage your credibility."

It was a painful experience, not just because it hurt their reputation, but because it was bait for people with another agenda. Leonard says, "… and then all the people came out of the woodwork like those who deny climate change." These people infuriate him, but he's also disappointed with people who accept climate change and yet do nothing. "I find it incomprehensible because how could any adult know about climate change and not do anything about that?"

The Kauri Leprosy

Today, small pockets of kauri have survived European loggers and burning by Māori, but a new threat has emerged. Kauri collar rot has been spreading through forests, carried on people's shoes and animals such as feral pigs.

The disease is a type of Phytophthora derived from the Greek for "plant destroyer". It gets into the soil and the roots, causing the leaves to wilt and turn yellow. The canopy thins and branches start to die. A girdle of lesions forms near the base of the trunk, which then bleeds resin until the tree is ring-barked. If trees could get leprosy, it might look a bit like this. There is no known treatment beyond prevention, and eventually the tree succumbs.

It's remarkable when you think about it, that a tiny microscopic organism can cause the death of something as large as a kauri. Phytophthora—or any lethal disease—attacks critical parts of its host, but usually it's not that simple.

A tree is more than a collection of roots, leaves, branches, and bark. They are elaborately connected, and something special happens when they work to form a whole, in the same way that a violin is more than a set of strings. Or a house isn't just a roof and a few walls. The parts come together to form a system where every part affects every other. Damaging one part can lead to cascading failures in other parts until the system flips into chaos and then collapses. Phytophthora infects the roots, which triggers a series of knock-on effects that ultimately kills the tree.

Our planet, too, is a system. Like the kauri, it dwarfs the organisms that live on it, and like the kauri, those things are capable of killing their host. You'd think that killing off your host is a poor survival strategy and yet that's what collar rot does. If it made sense to imagine a disease has intelligence, you'd say it's a stupid thing to do.

That may be a disturbing thought, but every system has checks and balances. They're the opposite of the so-called positive feedbacks that change a system then loop back around to amplify themselves. People like Leonard Cohen are a type of negative feedback, helping to moderate the dangerous oscillations that occur when a system—our planet—is disrupted. Like each of us, Leonard is part of a deeply connected set of interacting parts: the trees, the land, and the people.

By the time I'd met Leonard, he was moving on to a new phase of his life. He'd handed everything he'd learned to Greening Australia, plus the assets of Canopy. They now have 15 carbon sinks in South Australia and many more around Australia, all controlled by systems he helped create.

We walked around the beautiful, extensive garden where he lives in the Adelaide Hills. Not surprisingly, it was a quirky, rambling affair with large deciduous trees dropping yellow leaves on the lawn. "Isn't that terrible?" he quipped.

Not likely, I thought. Leonard could enjoy some quiet years here, but it's not his nature. Already he's working on his next project. Something darker, not bright and shiny—juvenile offenders in the criminal justice system. I'm not sure if even he knows how he's going to do that, but it's a good bet it won't be conventional.

The Politician
Susan Jeanes

Interview former Liberal MP Susan Jeanes, they said. Okay, interesting proposition. Given the recent reputation of the Liberal Party on climate change, how would that qualify her for a spot in my book?

Still, this was a trusted source, and it turns out that Susan Jeanes has been a champion of Australia's transition to renewable energy. That would be worthwhile. Plus meeting her would give me a peek into the weird machinations of politics and, in particular, the conservative side.

We don't have a problem with science. We have a problem with politics, so I decided I would talk to Susan.

It didn't take long for Susan Jeanes to break the politician mould. She has a self-deprecating charm and she'd sprinkle her stories with wry amusement, such as the time she was chased down a person's driveway, or was harangued by a duck hunter. It probably wasn't fun at the time, but now she sees the humour and punctuates her stories with laughter.

On many issues, she has progressive views, such as what it means to eat meat. At university, she'd read Peter Singer's *Animal Liberation*. The controversial 1975 book contains many provocative quotes such as, "People may hope that the meat they buy came from an animal who died without pain, but they do not really want to know about it."

"That was an awakening moment," Susan says, which prompted her to become a vegan. "I was struck by the idea that there was no rationale for defining whose flesh it was ethically okay to eat, across all societies."

"I was more struck by the non-defined way societies choose what to eat. Better to be a cow in India rather than Australia, and terrible to be a cow being shipped live to a country that does not respect civilised laws around killing animals. Better to be a dog in Australia than in China. Better to be a human in a country where cannibalism is no longer practised. Flesh is flesh."

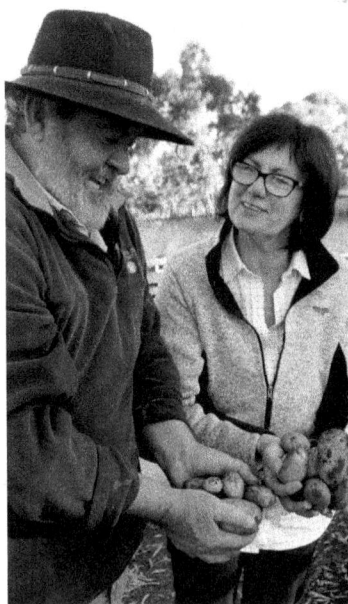

Susan and her husband Kim (photo by Rod Taylor).

It's not just the welfare of animals that concerns her. It's also the amount of resources needed to farm meat, and what they do to the environment. As Singer writes, "We are, quite literally, gambling with the future of our planet—for the sake of hamburgers."

These thoughts played out some years later when, as a Member of Parliament, she was visited by two bearded men from Animal Liberation. They sat in her office and described how hunters were going into the wetlands to shoot ducks. Susan wanted to know, are the shooters breaking the law? No, they were out during the duck season, but what they're doing to the poor animals is cruel and unnecessary.

Her visitors calmly asked what she might do about it. "Well, I thought, this is very contentious, but I'll go along. There was a lot of speculation so I decided to see for myself," she says. Then late one night Susan and her then-husband set out from home and arrived at the wetlands around sunrise the next morning when the shooters were starting their hunt. They weren't going there to protest or make a fuss. The plan was to watch, keep a low profile, and rescue injured ducks.

When they arrived at the wetlands, the morning sun was rising and great flocks of birds were overhead. They squawked loudly as they flew against the coloured sky. The scene made a big impression on Susan, who says, "I've never seen anything like that before. There was this most spectacular light. It was one of the most amazing things I've seen. The water birds took off and we heard this great roar of wings as their necks craned."

On any other day, it would be a moment to enjoy, but instead they encountered people wearing camouflage outfits, vests, and waders. Resting on their shoulders and cradled in their arms were shotguns. Susan's story reminded me of a sign I once saw on the back of a truck in a county town.

If it moves, shoot it,
If it stands up, chop it down,
If it's green, piss on it.

Susan walked out into the wetlands with her companions, but they were concerned that she might be recognised. It was a touchy time with the gun lobby because the Howard government had recently introduced restrictions on gun ownership and they would not have welcomed a visit from a vegan Liberal MP. Susan laughed as she told me, "It was a bit of a worry because these people all had guns, and they might know what I did for a living."

"I remember what struck me was that they were laughing because we were expressing concern. They thought it was funny when we went to rescue a duck, but what really, really, really upset me was when a pair of ducks flew over the top of the reeds. The shooters had hit one, and it was madly trying to keep up with the other one. They were laughing, and I just thought that was awful."

Across the water, another duck was desperately flapping after being hit, so Susan waded out to rescue it. She put it in a sack and carried it back to triage on the shore where they found it was carrying injuries from an earlier encounter with the shooters. The crows had been harassing it and its wing was broken. It had been living like that for some time.

The experience prompted Susan to write an article for the *Adelaide Advertiser,* which a witty subeditor titled "Day of a Dead Duck". The story so irked the shooting lobby that they published an item on their website claiming that Susan Jeanes knew nothing about ecology and nothing about how ducks die naturally in the wild. Shooting ducks, they said, was "good for the environment". Then a pair visited her electoral office.

"They tried to humiliate me," she says. "So I chased them out. Or more like, I invited them to leave. Immediately."

The incident was a turning point for Susan, where she says she "tried to get into the headspace of people who would kill an animal for sport".

Early Life

I arrived at Susan's house, which has views across the valley toward Lake Alexandrina on the mouth of the Murray River. A medium-sized dog trotted out to inspect me, barking to make sure everybody knew I'd arrived. Inside I met Susan's father Bill. He was nestling a small, soft-furred dog on his lap. It barked. Bill had just returned from the hospital after having some tests. Nothing serious, but he was feeling the effects of advancing years and still mourning his wife, Susan's mother.

Outside, Susan's husband Kim had been driving a small ride-on tractor, reducing the fuel load by piling up wood to make a bonfire. Two years ago a fire had swept down the hill through the neighbour's property until suddenly the wind changed. It raced up the hill with such ferocity, they thought their house was lost. It wasn't safe to stay so they retreated to another neighbour's house. The fire burned the entire property, including the fences and destroyed the garage that contained their daughter's belongings. The flames were hot enough to disintegrate the gold in a few pieces of family heirloom jewellery. The rusting hulks of a burnt-out Kombi van and a Beetle car are still parked around the side. Miraculously the house survived, but many of the old trees were destroyed.

We walked down the hill to inspect the dam and pick up golf balls. It's a practice range, Susan told me. Later we watched the sun go down as the stars came up and Kim's bonfire lit up the night. We drank red wine from the vineyard on the property and discussed the state of the nation.

Susan says she "hit the jackpot" with her parents, who provided for their needs but set a high benchmark. Her mother taught her there "wasn't anything I couldn't do because I was a girl". Susan says her mother was very capable, but in those days you were either a secretary or a teacher, and even then "you gave that up when you got married".

Kim: hazard reduction burning (photo by Rod Taylor).

For many years, her father Bill was a draughtsman on the Snowy Mountains Scheme, and for a time they'd lived in the mountain villages of Jindabyne and Khancoban. The Snowy has been quiet for many years since then, but now it's back in the news since Malcolm Turnbull announced plans for "Snowy Hydro 2.0". It was an attempt to win back the initiative after South Australia launched its own plan to fix the recurring failures in their electricity supply. For a few weeks, the state and the federal governments were jockeying to show the public who could fix the problem.

Susan became aware of politics when she was only nine. She remembers going to (Old) Parliament House in Canberra in 1967. "There was something about it that really took me. I was fascinated by the building and there was something about the green interior. It seemed like the centre of the universe."

For a primary school project, her class was told to choose the best site for a new dam, which was to be either at Dartmouth at the head of the Murray River or another location further down at Chowilla. In retelling the story she used a curious turn of phrase, saying she "aligned" herself with Steele Hall rather than Don Dunstan because his arguments were better. It sounded like she was already destined for politics.

First Blood

Some years later, Susan's first political blood was drawn during party preselection in 1986, but in this case, the blood was her own. Before the vote, party members were jockeying for support to get themselves or their preferred candidate voted in. There were quiet, back-room conversations with other party members and a few friends had promised to support Susan's bid, but when the vote came, people who said they'd vote for her didn't. She'd been stabbed in the back.

Why would they do that? It hurt that confidences were betrayed, but it turned out she was just a small fish swimming among political sharks. They'd encouraged her to nominate so that she would draw votes away from a candidate whom they didn't want. It wasn't until later that she understood she was a pawn in a larger game.

Clearly, it was unpleasant, but now Susan is stoic. "I learned lessons then. It was a really blooding lesson about politics. People often don't have the courage to tell the truth. I wasn't used to that. It was a hard lesson to learn. These people were friends I thought I could trust, but you have to be stabbed in the back to understand how nasty it can be. Once you know that, you're well-armed."

It was a hard lesson and as Amanda Vanstone once told her (quoting Harry Truman), "If you want friends, don't look for them in politics, get a dog instead." Susan had witnessed a minor example of political brutality, but she did make friends and she remains close friends with another former MP, Chris Gallus.

The incident helped to crystallise Susan's political views. "I learned that I really wanted to align myself with the moderates. Not just because of what happened, but because their values are much closer to mine." There were Liberal members such as Robert Hill and Peter Baume who advocated "a kinder liberalism". Many of her views were more progressive, but she wasn't attracted to the Labor Party because they were too close to the unions.

Susan missed preselection in 1986, but another opportunity came around in the 1996 federal election. This time she won, and on this occasion it helped to be a woman because the party had decided they needed better representation from women. She made the point with her typical sense of irony in her preselection speech, saying, "I'm the best man for the job."

In 1902, Australia became one of the first countries to give women both the right to vote and the right to stand for parliament, but the first woman wasn't elected until 1943. In 2017, gender balance seems a long way off with only 43 women out of 150 in the lower house, and in the Senate only 31 out of 76 are women. Susan had been discouraged by a teacher, who'd told her, "Politics is no game for a girl," but that was balanced by her mother who "never let me think I couldn't do anything I wanted".

Winning preselection was satisfying, but it was just permission to enter the race. If she was going to win the seat of Kingston in South Australia, the real work was about to begin. Campaigning for the seat meant relentless hours attending community events, handing out leaflets, and door-knocking. Usually, the reaction was non-committal, but sometimes it was hostile. On one occasion, she was chased down a driveway. Susan laughed as she remembers: "It was a toothless woman with a hose, shouting, 'Get off my property!'"

On another occasion one of her campaign workers was approached by some men who'd been out fishing. She was putting up posters and "they threw a fish at her. It hit her in the face. It was terrible."

The prime minister at the time was Paul Keating, who had ousted Bob Hawke in a Labor Party internal struggle. It was good timing for a new Liberal candidate since the Labor Party had been losing the support of its traditional base. The "Howard battlers" shifted and the Liberal-National Coalition swept into power with a 29-seat swing.

In Kingston, Susan's opponent was the sitting member, Gordon Bilney. Susan says, "We could see he'd run out of steam. When you're in government, you're so busy getting on with business that you tend to lose track of changes that are coming." Making it harder for Bilney was that he was Minister for Pacific Island Affairs, which left him little time to look after the people in his electorate.

They could feel there was a mood for change and the polls were showing the coalition was likely to win. Bilney was a curious character, described by journalist Alan Ramsey as a "free and roly-poly spirit with considerable style and acerbic wit". After Bilney left parliament he quipped, "One of the great pleasures of private life is that I need no longer be polite to nincompoops, bigots, curmudgeons, and twerps."

Back in 1996, less than 1% of Australia's population had an internet connection and there was no such thing as a smartphone. Technology has changed since then, and on election night in 1996, Susan and her party members watched live coverage on the television from the tally room in Canberra. As the numbers rolled in, they were posted on a huge board showing the progress in each electorate. By the end of the night, the results were clear. Susan Jeanes would now be the Liberal Party member for Kingston.

Her family travelled to watch her first day in parliament. It was an exciting moment, but tempered by the death of her grandmother three months earlier. Her knees shook as she delivered her maiden speech to the imposing chamber. She felt that being recorded in Hansard meant that she was now a part of Australia's history. Still, that didn't mean holding back on her characteristic sense of humour.

> On the night of the election, I do not think I really realised that I had won. When my opponent rang at about 9 o'clock to concede defeat, all I could think of was to say, "Are you sure?" This did not seem to please him much. He sent me a warning on national television that he would leave a message for me in my office. And what a message he left!
>
> As my staff and I entered the office for the first time, no one took much notice of a report that was left in the front bookcase about the viral diseases in rodents and ruminants. Nor did anyone bother to look at the chapters about the effect of these diseases on humans.
>
> It was not until we went into the kitchen that the meaning of the message began to be understood. There were indeed many little messages left in the kitchen drawers and the cupboards. The small, brown creatures that left the messages had my staff and I were squealing with delight— not terror of course—as we stood on our desk tops and desperately dialled the department for the pest controller.

Guns

Susan's first day in parliament was tempered by another event, reminding her again of the potential of guns. Normally the first sitting of the new government would be a time of excitement, but after recent events at Port Arthur in Tasmania, the mood was sombre. Often politicians are portrayed in the media as heartless individuals, but like most Australians, they were horrified. It seemed wrong to celebrate on such an occasion, so they decided to cancel the ceremonial opening of parliament.

Susan's story reminded me of my own frightening glimpse of what guns can do, although it didn't involve any crime. On one level we can read about the cold technical details of the weaponry used in the Port Arthur massacre, but it does give a vague sense of the horror. The Colt AR-15 is a semi-automatic version of the lightweight military weapon similar to the one used by a gunman in Orlando, Florida to shoot and kill 49 people while wounding 53 others. The SLR semi-automatic military rifle can fire 7.62 mm rounds at 823 metres per second velocity from a 20-round magazine and a skilled shooter can get off three aimed shots per second.

Our instructors in the Army Reserve would tell us that being hit on any part of the body by one of these weapons would remove the entire limb. Firing gives a hefty kick and we'd end a day at the range with bruised shoulders. We were sore, but at least the force was spread across the butt of the rifle rather than the sharp tip of a bullet.

Martin Bryant was known to be mentally unbalanced. With an IQ of 66, he was borderline mentally disabled, and a psychologist recorded that he'd been torturing animals. He was suspended from New Town Primary School in 1977 because of his disruptive and sometimes violent behaviour. In April 1996, Bryant had both Colt AR-15 and SLR semi-automatic weapons that he used to kill 35 people and injure 23 others at Port Arthur.

Australians were dismayed by what happened in Port Arthur, but they were also alarmed to discover that a person such as Bryant was able to obtain military-grade weapons. Prime Minister John Howard was as shocked as his colleagues and committed himself to improving gun control, but it was deeply unpopular with sporting shooters and his counterparts in the National Party. Behind the scenes, MPs were checking with their electorates to gauge community reaction. In her electorate, Susan found that the police wanted better gun controls, but the shooters were angry. They tried to address some of the sporting shooter's concerns by designing protocols to allow their access to their guns and ammunition.

In spite of their vocal opposition, one of the first acts of the new parliament was to tighten gun laws, and Susan says, "Most of us [MPs] were very proud to be a part of Howard's decisive response."

The Right to Die

These were the laws that infuriated the duck hunters, but there was another issue that generated even more hate mail: euthanasia. In Australia, the debate has been highly contentious. For a brief period in 1995, the Northern Territory had the "*Rights of the Terminally Ill Act*" until it was nullified a year later by federal parliament. Susan notes dryly that the "right to life" movement doesn't believe that people have the right to their own life.

Without legal means to end their lives, people have been forced to make tragic choices. In 2008, a couple faced manslaughter charges for providing Nembutal to Graeme Wylie. They were found guilty even though they'd provided evidence that Wylie wanted to die "with dignity". In 2011, a 66-year-old man received a two-year suspended sentence for assisting the death of his long-term 78-year-old partner who'd been suffering severe pain from a spinal condition.

Hearing Susan Jeanes talking about her involvement with the euthanasia issue was particularly poignant because only a day earlier Monica Oliphant had told me about how her mother was riddled with cancer and longing for death. Without anybody who was able to help, her mother was driven to multiple failed suicide attempts. There are parallels with Susan's own story where she'd witnessed an aunt who was dying from bowel cancer. "She wanted to choose her time of departure and not struggle on through the pain and the agony of watching her family watching her die."

Of all the issues Susan dealt with, this one drew the most

vehement reaction and a stream of hostile letters flooded into her office. Those from far-right on the Christian spectrum were particularly nasty, she says. "They damned my soul to hell. They were very unchristian like."

The experience drove her conviction that "with the right protections, people with verified and imminently fatal conditions should be able to choose the way they die. If death is inevitable, dignity and freedom from pain should be a person's own choice."

Media

Backbenchers are mostly ignored by the media, who are more interested in high-profile ministers, but one way to get noticed is by making a silly mistake. Parliamentarians have to deal with a huge range of issues and at any moment they can be caught unprepared. Susan has some sympathy for "that poor [politician] in the western suburbs of Sydney who couldn't answer a fairly basic question about policy". On that occasion, a backbencher was caught on camera by a reporter asking about taxation. Sometimes though, they get noticed by putting out a provocative media release. That's what Susan did with a release saying that Pauline Hanson should be black-banned.

In an opinion piece for the *Adelaide Advertiser*, Susan peers mischievously at us in an accompanying photo. Her words were blunt: "The One Nation message is one that the Australian people do not need to hear. It offers nothing that has any positive value ..." She was prodding the nest, knowing it would bring out the wasps. And stir it did, because she soon got a call from Stan Zemanek asking if she'd agree to an interview. Zemanek was a radio broadcaster who had earned the title "shock jock" with lines such as "feminists are women who need to change the batteries in their vibrators".

Susan didn't know Zemanek so she asked a New South Wales colleague for advice. What was he like and how should she handle him? It was a clever move, because now she was forewarned about Zemanek's acerbic style. When he didn't like a caller, he'd cut them off, saying, "Because you're an idiot." Zemanek knew he was an entertainer and wasn't much interested in reasoned debate. He didn't care whether listeners loved him or loathed him, as long as they boosted his ratings. Besides, he and much of his audience had sympathy for the hard views of the One Nation leader, Pauline Hanson.

Her colleague's advice was good: "Just talk and don't let him get a word in because he can't handle it," they told her. When Zemanek got her on-air, he said, "Who the hell do you think you are, telling us we should black-ban Pauline Hanson?"

That was the cue for Susan to launch into her tirade. When she finally stopped, he said, "You Labor people can talk underwater." Now he looked silly because he hadn't done his homework and she told him, "I'm actually not Labor. I'm Liberal." Then she said, "You choose every day who makes the news. She is your problem." Susan says Zemanek didn't like that.

Susan didn't enjoy that sort of confrontation, but sometimes that's what politicians have to do to get into the media. She says modestly, "It wasn't my area of expertise," but more experienced performers have come undone at the hands of people like Zemanek. The trick was to know he wouldn't follow the normal rules of debate and there was little point trying to win with careful arguments because his method was about emotion, not logic. Susan was describing a type of media where insulting people is entertainment and important issues submerge into trivia.

Some politicians skilfully exploit this and Susan is infuriated by the prominence given to Tony Abbott's chief of staff, Peta Credlin. Susan says she's attractive to the media because she's "influential and vindictive", the sort of person who generates sound bites. Credlin and Abbott were calling the carbon pricing scheme introduced by the Gillard government "A Big New Tax". Credlin said publicly that they knew it was untrue, but they did it anyway because it got attention.[32]

"Where is the credibility and honour in journalism when they continue to give people that public profile? "Susan asks.

Susan's views on hunting, euthanasia, Pauline Hanson, and renewable energy placed her on the progressive side of the Liberal Party. She held similar views on gay and Aboriginal rights, earning the title of "maverick" from columnist Alan Ramsey for her willingness to risk censure from her colleagues. Another columnist, Tony Wright, said after she lost her seat there'd be "few tears from the hard noses in the party", and she'd become known as "the Independent Member for Kingston" for her fearless criticism of Prime Minister John Howard and Treasurer Peter Costello.

Kyoto

Negotiating international agreements is always complicated and the Kyoto Protocol was no exception. Prime Minister John Howard was saying, "If we adhered to the protocol … that would disadvantage the resource industries of Australia." Environment Minister Robert Hill was sent to the 1997 climate conference to negotiate what would become known as "the Australia clause". They gained a major concession that allowed Australia to include carbon emissions due to land clearing.

It was controversial because Australia could claim against a peak in land clearing in 1990, which then sharply declined. This meant that under the protocol, Australia could increase its CO2 emissions by 8% on top of an already high base. Even then Howard refused to sign the agreement—that would have to wait until Labor Prime

---

32   Judith Brett, "He will never stop", *The Monthly*, August 2017, www. themonthly.com.au/issue/2017/august/1501509600/judith-brett/he-will-never-stop.

Minister Kevin Rudd signed it in 2007. Susan takes the pragmatic view, saying that Australia has a carbon-intensive economy and the Kyoto agreement was about what she calls "equal pain", and she's "happy for the Howard Government to be criticised for not ratifying the protocol".

The Kyoto target meant that in 2015, Environment Minister Greg Hunt could claim that Australia was "one of the few countries in the world to have met and beaten our first round of Kyoto targets", leading Clive Hamilton to suggest that "Australia hit its Kyoto target, but it was more a three-inch putt than a hole in one." Susan says that's an unreasonable criticism, but she's even more unsympathetic to the renewable energy opponents who say renewable energy will put up energy bills so that some people can't afford them. The alternative will be far worse if we ignore carbon emissions and she asks, "Do they wonder what uncontrolled climate change would ultimately do to global communities?"

The initiatives they introduced helped nurture the birth of renewable energy in Australia, and 20 years later costs are falling rapidly. Renewable energy was once a champagne solution, but now it's common beer, undercutting the fossil fuel alternatives.

After Kyoto, Robert Hill with help from Susan Jeanes wanted to push bills through parliament that would spur the transition to renewable energy. The Mandatory Renewable Energy Target (MRET) legislation would give it a real boost.

The Renewable Energy Target

Getting a bill passed is a long, arduous process that is largely invisible to the public. It must be passed by both houses, the House of Representatives and the Senate. A bill can start in either chamber, but it must then be reviewed and passed by the other. Often there are amendments, which can be requested in either chamber but have to be approved by both. In between there are various administrative processes, paperwork drafted and signed, with public servants and legal specialists checking that everything is done properly. In all, a bill goes through a complicated dance bouncing back and forth between the chambers and a small squad of public servants.

In the final hours of the final sitting of parliament in 1999, the RET Bill was almost ready. Robert Hill and Susan Jeanes knew they had the numbers to push it through, but as always there were amendments. Time was running short and if it failed in this sitting, it would be forced to wait for the next, with no guarantee of success. So to get it through Susan needed to sprint.

There were a whole lot of deadlines we were not going to meet, so at 11 o'clock at night I grabbed the paperwork and took it to the leader of government in the Senate and I chucked it in front of his face for him to sign. Then I walked the bill between both Houses of Parliament in the middle of the night and sat in the Senate Chambers.

In the early hours of the next morning, the bill finally got through.

That was definitely a big high. At 4:30am we went to Robert Hill's office and in the fridge we found a bottle of champagne and smoked salmon. I was vegetarian so I didn't have any of that. Then I had to get on a plane for a 6 o'clock flight to get home to Adelaide, go to bed, and have a sleep.

Susan spared a thought for the two public servants she'd been working with. "I got to go home to have a sleep, but they had to have a shower and then go back to work."

Kingston had been a marginal seat that Susan held by a slim

2%. When Howard called an early election in October 1998, the Coalition's majority was cut from 40 to 12. On election day, again they watched results televised from the tally room in Canberra. In Kingston, the count could go either way. It was a tense evening, but when the results were finally settled, Susan had lost by the wafer-thin margin of 0.47% to Labor candidate David Cox.

It was, she says, a painful experience—life in politics is a tenuous thing—but overall it was a positive experience. Aside from her work on renewable energy, Susan feels she had a strong sense of caring for the people in her electorate. It could show even in a hostile situation such as a public meeting when the mood turned ugly. One of the people yelling at her was a 17-year-old man.

I imagined what it would be like to face people in that kind of situation. It could go in many ways—return the anger, or maybe retreat. Instead, she drew on her sympathy for the man, which undercuts the common view of the self-serving politician. A cynical view might be that she'd do that only for show, but having got to know Susan a little that seems unlikely and I believe her concern was genuine.

"I felt a bit sorry for him," she recalls and invited him to visit her in her office the next day. His partner was pregnant and they were living in a caravan. She arranged counselling and access to community health for his girlfriend. "It was good when you could make a difference," she says.

Power Struggles

In March 2017, Australians witnessed an extraordinary impromptu TV press conference.

Federal Energy Minister Josh Frydenberg is sitting next to South Australian Premier Jay Weatherill. Weatherill has his arms folded across his lap and his head cocked slightly to one side. On the surface he's listening, but his body language says he's winding up for a premeditated attack. It looks like a calculated move[33] when Frydenberg asks, "Is this a bit awkward?"

"It's about to be," Weatherill whispers.

Then the pair are seen standing as the press conference starts. Frydenberg looks uncomfortable and is rocking slightly, trying to contain his composure as Weatherill takes him down. It looks like a primary teacher delivering discipline to a naughty pupil. Frydenberg can be seen pushing his tongue into his left cheek, displaying what psychologists call "displacement behaviour". The cameras are rolling and he has little choice other than to wait for Weatherill's humiliating tirade to end.

There's a delicious, guilty pleasure we all enjoy in watching another person's downfall and it's no coincidence that much humour relies on slapstick, slipping into puddles and walking into doors. It's all the better when the target is a politician, but was this schadenfreude justified? Susan thinks not. She says he's "very smart", but he's wedged among forces he can't control.

Frydenberg had already been humiliated after saying that an emissions intensity scheme would be the "best" policy, only to be shut down by his own prime minister, who promptly dismissed the idea.

Flip-flopping government policy has undermined the confidence in energy investors. Clancy Yeates summarises the knock-on effect of this uncertainty:

In the past decade, we've had John Howard propose an emissions trading scheme; Kevin Rudd propose then abandon such a scheme; and Julia Gillard introduce one, only to have it torn down by Tony Abbott in favour of "direct

---

33   Nick Harmsen, "Jay Weatherill's tirade on Josh Frydenberg a calculated move by SA Government", *ABC News*, 17 March 2017, www.abc.net.au/news/2017-03-16/jay-weatherill-tirade-josh-frydenberg-calculated/8360354

action". The upshot of this back and forth is investors doing the equivalent of sitting on their hands.

From outside politics, it's often hard to know who contributes what, or what a politician really thinks. Party discipline can force politicians to defend the party line even when they don't agree. In other words—sometimes they must lie and if they can do that convincingly, they get caught. It happens often enough that people don't trust them.

Susan has sympathy for Frydenberg, saying that he really wants to do the right thing, but "Josh has to balance what he can get past his party room". She feels he was caught between the hard climate denialist conservatives in his own party and the state premier who "held a gun" to his head. The clash of ideologies, where each end of the debate sees it as a winner-takes-all situation, hasn't helped. It'd be much better for Australia to invest in clever R&D and make a smooth transition to renewable energy, without the blackouts and escalating prices.

The best is the enemy of the good

Recent times have not been good for Liberal Party moderates such as Susan Jeanes. She sounded frustrated as we talked about how the hard-line conservatives have undermined Australia's energy policy and the response to climate change. Around the time we met, events were playing out in South Australia that illustrated how they've frustrated the drive toward renewable energy.

An abiding memory of my father is of him saying how it is amazing that hot water comes out of a tap. What a complete loon, I thought. To my unsophisticated teenage mind, it was obvious: there's a tap, there's a heater—simple. Now with advancing years, I see what he meant. The modern electricity and water supply systems are a triumph of civilisation. It's extremely sophisticated and if you add the chain of services that deliver the pipes, taps, and electrics to our houses, it's mind-bogglingly complicated. That's just the technical bits, the plumbing and the wiring. They don't get into your house without an army of salespeople, accounts managers, and workers who make it happen. We can plug a kettle into a power point, and somehow we get boiling water. If I think about the amount of whirring and clunking it takes to get it there, it makes my head spin. Amazing.

The swan, as they say, glides gracefully across the pond while its feet paddle furiously through mud. We don't notice until something goes wrong, which is what happened when South Australians found themselves without power in 2016 and 2017. Ironically the outages were triggered by storms and heatwaves that are becoming more prevalent as global warming bites.

The power loss story quickly submerged into political sludge with simplistic notions that the problem was caused by renewable energy when really it was more complicated. Mostly it was the result of a national failure to plan. It'd become a high-profile issue that didn't need new science or technology. It wasn't the science or the technology that needed fixing, it was the politics.

Australia's Chief Scientist Dr Alan Finkel was given the job of writing a review that could fix the complicated technical problems, but still have a chance of getting through the political mire. In particular, he would have to weather attacks from the hard-right led by Australia's most destructive politician, Tony Abbott. It was a problem for Malcolm Turnbull because before becoming prime minister (now deposed), he had said that humans are conducting the largest-ever experiment on the planet and reducing greenhouse emissions is urgent.

Susan Jeanes has some sympathy for Turnbull, saying, "Malcolm has to represent the noisiest, nastiest rump of the party and I find it really frustrating. The politician who stands up and is true to him or herself finds there's a big price to pay." She laments the rigid two-party system, but it's also the media who feed on conflict. A lot of the bad rap that politicians get is from the journalists who swoop in on a difference to make a story. She says reasonable debate becomes tangled with an obsessive focus on personalities. "There are some really bad journalists who thrive on finding conflict and that's not a good thing for the public."

These forces were played out when the Finkel review was launched. Within a day it was being undermined as conservative forces claimed it was biased against fossil fuels when Australia should be building more coal-fired power stations. Alan Finkel always had to live up to impossible expectations. On one hand, there were groups such as the Climate Council saying the recommendations were far too weak and would fail to meet the looming global warming crisis. On the other, it was a cue to the renewable sceptics saying only coal and gas can provide reliable power.

Perhaps the most important lesson Susan Jeanes learned was from her former boss and mentor Robert Hill is that politics is the delicate art of compromise. "If you go into a room, it's not just about winning or being clever. It's about people leaving the room with honour." The critical two-letter word in negotiation is not "no". It's "if", signifying flexibility to accept another view, but holding onto what's essential.

Finkel had produced a report that needed to be stronger on climate change, but one that might still make its way through the broken system of politics. Still fresh in political memory is the failure of the first carbon pricing scheme that was rejected when the Greens said it wasn't strong enough. Then the second pricing scheme passed by Julia Gillard's government was overturned as soon as Abbot got into government. Susan sees Finkel's approach as something that is possible, even if it isn't perfect. "The best is the enemy of the good," as my Dad would've said.

After Politics

Nearly 20 years after her term as an MP, Susan has settled into a new life devoting much of her time promoting renewable energy. She did a stint as Chief Executive of the Australian Geothermal Energy Association and is now on the board of the Australian Renewable Energy Agency. It's the same goal as the RET legislation back in 1999, pushing the transition to renewable energy.

ARENA funds innovations such as the Karratha Solar Farm. Susan clearly loved talking about what they were achieving in projects such as these. A problem for grid operators is the sudden dips and spikes in power as clouds move across solar panels. Balancing the grid is a complication that will become serious as variable generators become more prominent, forcing solar farm owners to spend money on batteries and other equipment to smooth output. A clever solution is cloud tracking technology that predicts changes in sunlight so that the solar farm can feed their electricity into the grid more gently. With assistance from ARENA, the project has saved more than 20% in battery storage.

The Karratha project is one of many that Susan enthuses about as she describes the work of ARENA. With this and other investments, she can show how renewable energy will deliver cheaper, reliable energy.

Another strand of her work is the consulting company she founded with Dave Holland, helping start-up companies move from the lab into business. It's a difficult transition for an innovative start-up to grow into a stable business, and many fail. The early phases of a start-up are driven by innovation, which is always challenging because they're doing something that hasn't been done before. There's a fluid period before a business can settle into a more stable operation that has to adapt to the demands of finance, profits, labour, construction, and government regulation. Australia has a proud history of invention, but a poor record of bringing them to market.

Jeanes Holland Consulting helps start-ups by using their networks to raise money. The consulting service is like a bridging service that helps them navigate the complex maze of government and financial regulation. Sometimes technical people don't appreciate that it can be the softer skills that make the difference, and Susan says they can be dogmatic, "wanting to tell you how it's going to work". She coaches them on skills such as body language and the value of good relationships. One of the problems she sees is start-up companies going to the government thinking they'll change the world, but often they're talking to people who've heard it all before. Jeanes Holland advises on how to develop a pitch and establish credibility.

Seventeen years after the long night passing the RET, Susan can see how the renewable energy world has shifted from the fringe to the mainstream. In 2016, Bloomberg estimated that Australian investment in clean energy totalled more than $4.29 billion, with 3,150 megawatts of new generating capacity. Along with technology improvements and plunging costs, the RET has been a major force behind kick-starting the revolution.

The Kyoto agreement drew criticism, but as is often the way in political life, the positive side often stays hidden and Susan is pleased with what they were able to achieve. Part of the Kyoto package was establishing the Australian Greenhouse Office, which was the first agency anywhere in the world dedicated to overseeing a reduction of greenhouse gases.

This, and measures such as the RET, have been one piece of the puzzle contributing to the transformation of Australia's renewable energy now underway. The economics have changed to the point where the coal-fired power stations are closing and it's unlikely that any new ones will be built.

As we wound up our interview, I asked Susan what she felt was her greatest achievement. I thought she might say getting into parliament, or helping get the RET legislation passed, or winning a position with ARENA, but she didn't hesitate. Instead, she said, "The thing I'm most proud of is my husband Kim, and bringing up my children to be educated and caring adults. That's the greatest thing you can do for anybody. My children are my greatest achievement."

The Climate Game Changer
Inez Harker-Schuch

The stories of some of the people I've met in this book have been, well, chaotic. One of those is Inez Harker-Schuch, whose story begins as Darwin is flattened by a cyclone. From there, her journey to the present has continued the theme, with unexpected turns from life in a dysfunctional family, to being a cinema candy girl, a fashion model, and a teacher. Then, in one of those rare epiphanies, she saw a way that kids could learn about climate change—while having fun.

On Christmas Eve in 1974, Inez Harker-Schuch was three years old, huddled with her family inside their flimsy Darwin house. Outside, Cyclone Tracy was demolishing the city in what was perhaps Australia's worst-ever natural disaster. Peak winds on the day can only be estimated because the wind-gauge was destroyed, but it's believed to have reached over 240 kilometres per hour. Inez still remembers the terror of seeing sheets of corrugated iron flying across the street. One wrapped itself around a tree, which contorted, then snapped to become more flying debris. "It was as if the world had gone mad," she recalls. "It was the shriek of the wind, the violence, and the destruction. It seemed as if Hell had opened up and spilled its guts into the atmosphere."

Earlier, on 20 December, Cyclone Tracy had been forming

over the Arafura Sea about 370 kilometres north-east of Darwin. From there it tracked south-west, away from the town, and wasn't considered a threat. Then on the morning of 24 December, it veered to the east, straight into Darwin.

By late afternoon it was raining heavily and the wind was becoming gusty. Many people had ignored the warnings, believing the cyclone would pass them by like the one a few weeks earlier. Families were preparing for Christmas, but by evening it was clear the cyclone was about to strike when it was too late to leave. Inez's parents drove to the supermarket to stock up on food with Inez and her brother on the back seat.

Inez described what happened next: "I think I had my first real panic when my mother left the car. It was very gusty, very frightening. There was stuff already flying around the street." Her mother had left the car and disappeared into the supermarket, and Inez started to panic. "My father was clearly nervous and he reached back and smacked me across the face. I think he was at his emotional limit. In the early '70s, those kinds of behaviours in Darwin were not uncommon."

Inez's family went back to shelter in their house. It was very old and built on concrete stilts. They closed the shutters, though Inez says in the face of the storm it was futile, but they did it anyway as a kind of gut reaction. There was a feeling of disbelief that something like this could happen, especially on Christmas day.

We've all seen images on TV of violent storms, but what they don't convey are the terrifying sounds. Inez looked distressed as she grappled to describe how it felt. "You can't even say 'wind', because the shrieking was no longer just gusts—it got into a crescendo of such impossible ... I don't know how to say it."

As the intensity of the cyclone increased, the house started to collapse around them. The windows imploded, showering them with glass, and they had to flee. Her father took her sister first, down the stairs to their Volkswagen Beetle parked under the house. Then he came back to get Inez and wrapped her in a blanket. "I remember us going down the stairs, and him putting me in the car, then going back to walk my mother down."

Her memories from such a young age are detailed, but for Inez it was such an intense experience that it is still vivid.

We were hit with everything. Even small leaves became missiles, and there were tin cans smashing against the house. At some points, you could see everything in the strobe lightning. It was flashing everywhere. It was like being in the most insane disco.

When they talk about hell—*I imagine hell looks like that.* Then inside the car, the glass shattered and fell over us. We reached a point where we just had to wait for the outcome. Either we were going to die or survive.

My sister was sitting on the back seat; I remember exactly what the leather felt like. Then we saw the neighbour's house. I could hear this suddenly through the storm ... this really weird groan like somebody with a bad stomach ache.

Suddenly my father was looking out the window and we could see the roof of our neighbour's house lift off and disintegrate and disappear into the night ... and then our neighbour ran through the cyclone to get into our car.

As they entered the eye of the storm, the wind abruptly stopped. There was an eerie silence and Inez could hear water dripping. It was the "absence of everything else," she says.

Tracy was one of the most compact cyclones ever recorded, so the eye was small. It was quiet, but it wasn't peaceful because once the eye had passed they would enter the other side. There was a feeling of doom as they waited.

Then the storm started again, and now the debris was being blown in the opposite direction. During the first half, they'd been sheltering in their little car and even with five people in it, it had been pushed down the driveway and onto the street. When the wind returned, it pushed them back up the driveway again.

By the next day, Tracy had killed 65 in a city of 47,000, caused $837 million in damage, and left 41,000 people homeless. Inez's family home was one of the 80% that were destroyed. Once the wind had torn down the wall and roof, the contents of their house were then blown away. Inez's toys, her bed—almost everything was gone. Among the few things they retrieved were a doll and a single wedding photo.

Photos from the time show entire suburbs flattened in scenes that look like something from Hiroshima. When the storm subsided, the people of Darwin began to realise the extent of the destruction, but nobody else in Australia knew until someone managed to get a radio signal from Tennant Creek.

The events are now over 40 years old, but Inez now was becoming distressed as she relived it. She began to cry as she described what happened next. It was from the trauma, but also the generosity of Australians who stepped in to help in a time of crisis.

> I have heard stories—crazy stories—of one woman who arrived at Brisbane airport, and this guy was sitting there in a car and he says, "You've been in the cyclone, can I help?" She said, "Look, could you possibly take me to the bus station?" He actually drove for the next five hours to take her to her family.

It now became urgent to evacuate people as quickly as possible and Inez, her sister, and her mother were sent on the most packed plane that had ever flown in Australia.

We arrived at Sydney airport. I had blood up to my thighs from all the glass and stuff we'd walked through. When my uncle David picked us up from the airport, he said he's never seen anything that's broken his heart so much as watching his sister and her two children arrive.

The idea that people can unite behind something is one of the best things about humanity, and also one of the things that I keep reminding myself of when we are facing these problems.

Ultimately over 30,000 people were evacuated, but Inez's father was a policeman and had to stay behind for the clean-up. His family had survived, but there was more trauma to follow. Inez thinks he had a predisposition to mental illness, which started to show from around this time.

Many years later he told her some of the things he saw, including a body virtually decapitated from flying corrugated iron. The hardest thing was finding the body of a 12-year-old boy. He took him to the centre where they were collecting the bodies. "I was so distraught to find this boy that I forgot to tag his body," he told Inez.

"I wrestled with this for decades afterward because I just did not know if that family ever found their boy, or how long it took for them to find their boy after that error."

He said he was so horrified by the impact of the loss of this kid that he just couldn't function properly. Inez thinks he never recovered from that.

Inez remembers the cyclone with a surprising amount of detail for someone of such a young age. It was a brutal demonstration that when climate systems bite, humans become spectators. For all the hubris and imagined power of civilisation, we cannot control climate, and if we continue to provoke it, ultimately we will lose. In 1974 it wasn't obvious, but now greenhouse gasses are warming the planet and as the oceans bleed off more heat, storms such as Tracy are becoming increasingly common.

The cyclone on Christmas Day 1974 was a spur that changed the course of Inez's life and sparked a life-long fascination with climate science. Now that ambition has translated into helping people understand how our planet is being affected by climate change.

Post Cyclone

Inez stayed in Sydney with her mother and sister for a few months until they could return to Darwin when essential services had been restored. Where their house had once stood, they found only a concrete slab, and for the next four years they lived in a caravan. It was a sparse existence, she says. "We didn't have anything. We really had no toys."

They had a basic lifestyle, but the emotional trauma was worse. Inez's father was becoming unstable. He suffered PTSD, but also was bipolar. The Australian Black Dog Institute describes how people who are bipolar experience periods of low mood, feelings of hopelessness, extreme sadness, and lack pleasure in things. They have manic episodes with extremes of agitation, racing thoughts, and little need for sleep. Later in life, he developed psychosis, believing he could hear the voice of Badger from *The Wind in the Willows*, and that he was the son of God.

They were troubling times, but now Inez can see the humour in it. "The son of God?" she quipped. "I wish he could be more original."

Life at home was made even more complicated by her mother's condition. With her attractive green eyes, Inez's mother Janine was talented and well educated, but she'd been spoilt as a child, and a car accident when she was 20 had left a scar across her face. More serious, however, was being diagnosed with multiple sclerosis when she was pregnant with Inez. The symptoms such as fatigue, dizziness, vertigo, and weakness were challenging, but with them came anxiety and mood swings, which Inez feels affected their relationship. "Somehow she associated that with me."

Inez's story illuminates something I've often wondered about. How does a person lift themselves out of a dysfunctional upbringing, but then go on to achieve remarkable things? Why do many fail, but a few succeed? This is something that each of the *Fragile Planet* characters have in common—they do not see themselves as powerless. Why did Inez do that instead of falling into despair?

We talked it over for a long while and she thinks perhaps it began in her early childhood when she began to take responsibility for her siblings. Inez is the second of six children with three sisters and two brothers. Her father's unpredictable behaviour made life at home challenging and her mother wasn't coping. Inez says they had no toys and even at Christmas time they wouldn't be given presents. She'd escape into the backyard, playing with things she found in the garden and at night she'd hide under her bedsheets, reading. She was inspired by the autobiography *I Can Jump Puddles* by Alan Marshall, which tells the story of his childhood in rural Victoria while suffering from polio. Something in his makeup gave him the strength to achieve despite the hurdles. For Inez, looking after her family was important. It was something she could actually do.

Then, when she was only 12, she was diagnosed with depression, and as she describes it: "I went to the doctor and I knew something was wrong. I was in this place that had no life, had no meaning. I had nothing. Nothing came through, nothing made me cry."

The night after Inez told me that story, I read that to test mice for depression, researchers dangle them by their tail. Most will wriggle, but the ones that are thought to be depressed hang passively.

And then her mother became pregnant again, with what was to be her brother. But instead of the joy of a new sibling, she was resentful. "I thought, *what's wrong with you people*? Why would you do this to another innocent person? I *hated* him before he was born. I hated the fact that they were going to do that to us," she told me.

Telling her story, Inez was becoming visibly upset and I was struck by the way she said *hated*. She resented him, not just because he was being brought into an unhappy world, but because she knew she'd be forced to look after him. "It was going to come to me ... he would fall under my care because they didn't give a shit."

Inez paused and then her emphasis abruptly changed. "But then he was born, and I *loved* him. In that moment when I should have despised him ... I should have despised him because he was the long-awaited boy."

Now, she said *love* with equal intensity, but with the opposite effect. "He gave me meaning and his birth took me out of the hole I was in. He made everything mean something again. I did everything I possibly could to let his life be not like ours. He was my self-esteem. He was where I knew that I could make a difference."

By the age of 14, her parents had separated and she was living with her brothers and sisters at their mother's house in Armidale. While she was studying for school she was helping her younger siblings and caring for her mother. By now her mother was crippled with multiple sclerosis and could only move her shoulder, and she could neither feed nor wash herself.

While Inez was studying for her end of year exams, her mother was becoming increasingly demanding. One day she came home from school and told her mother told her, "I've been thinking, you can't manage going to school as well as looking after me. You're going to have to leave school at the end of the year so you can care for me full-time."

It left Inez with an impossible choice, but life at home had become intolerable. It wasn't a palatable option, but she felt she had no choice other than to escape to her father's house where he was living with his mother.

Moving to Sydney allowed Inez to solve one problem, but now she was with her unpredictable father. She went to high school and worked nights in a cinema as what she describes as "a little candy bar girl wearing a dress with purple trimmings". One day she was studying for her Year 11 exams and her father walked in and asked, "Where's my tea?" She looked up with surprise and said, "You didn't ask for any."

He said, "I shouldn't have to ask," and he hit her.

The next day she went to work with a black eye and the manager of the cinema asked, "What happened to you?" When she replied, "I walked into a door," he said, "No, you didn't. You're not going back there again. You can come and live with us."

She was nearly 16 when she moved in with Adam and Tony, and later Cameron. They were, she says, "my first heroes". Today Inez says she hasn't seen Adam for many years, but they keep in touch. Telling her story now, Inez's voice shows a glow of the gratitude she still feels when she says, "He knows I'd do anything for him."

The Life of a Model

When I met Inez in 2017, I learned that she was in the middle of a Kickstarter campaign, trying to raise money to build a computer game to teach climate science. It was, I thought, an interesting venture and perhaps I could help. So we made a time to record an interview and take some portrait photos for a newspaper article. I suggested she wear dark clothes, and I bought a cheap globe of the Earth to use as a prop. We did the photoshoot and I was impressed by how natural she was with the camera. Usually, I have to fuss around with a subject to get them to pose because most people don't understand, but she knew immediately what we were doing.

Looking at the results later, I felt a disconnect between Inez in the photos and Inez the person. She cuts a striking image, looking more like someone who'd be on the cover of a fashion magazine, which didn't seem to line up with the intense personality I was getting to know. Then I learned that the reason she seemed like a model was because she was a model. Or at least, she became a model at almost 17, which she continued for about seven years. It began by accident when she was on a beach with some friends, and a man approached her. He gave her his business card and said, "You should be a model. Call me."

Inez Harker-Schuch (photo by Rod Taylor).

Her initial reaction was to dismiss him. By now she was an attractive teenager getting a lot of attention from boys, and this one didn't look much different. But when she showed the card to her friends, they said he was from a major modelling agency, and she should take it seriously. So she did, and not long after she went to her first photoshoot.

The move into modelling proved a boon, and she was almost immediately successful. For the first time in her life, she had financial independence. Her first assignment was a lingerie shoot for a major magazine. On another occasion there was a big shoot on Bondi Beach for evening wear where she remembers, "I had my hair up and looking all glam." That was a more up-market occasion, but mostly she modelled swimwear.

The work started to roll in and she was given jobs in Europe, taking her to places like Vienna, Amsterdam, and London. It was lucrative, but like most "dream" jobs it wasn't all glamorous. There were practical things like waking up at 4 am so somebody could pluck her eyebrows. It became clear she'd become a product to be sold to the consumer. That meant having her personal space invaded. "I hated that they would come up and adjust my underwear. There's a very fine line—somebody grabbing my crotch and adjusting my underwear."

Even though modelling paid well and was an opportunity for international travel, Inez had reservations. One friend was horrified, calling it "jumped up prostitution". She laughed, then said, "I agree with him now. I'd stop working for a while because I was wrestling with my conscience. I got jobs as a secretary or a waitress or a barmaid, which gave me skills I needed later on."

In the years since then, she's been conscious of how a woman's appearance can affect the way others perceive them. She says, "If you look good and you're in a serious business, you're in trouble and that affects the way I dress. I dress in a non-threatening way."

Curiously though, she says it's not always the men. "In a professional environment, I found that men are often much more conscious of their role than are women. Sometimes it's they who are predators."

During this time Inez started getting involved with charities. There was one in Vienna that helped foreign women who got pregnant. She felt the need to do something, but by now her religious conviction had faded. It wouldn't have mattered, but she had to leave because she felt the strong Christian element interfered with the way the charity was offered. "I couldn't stand it, it was the wrong thing to do. I don't believe in religion with a bowl of rice."

She left, but the notion of getting what she calls a "real job" was simmering away. The hours observing nature in her backyard and her time with her uncle loomed in her background. Then there was the vivid memory of Cyclone Tracy. Science is sometimes thought of as a cold, impersonal way to digest facts, but it was science that helped fuel her curiosity and somehow make sense of the events that shaped her life.

At around the time she was thinking about these things, evidence for global warming was beginning to emerge from the background of noisy data. Climate data naturally wobbles about from year to year and it takes time to spot the trends. Scientists had long known it was likely, but around the year 2000, it was becoming clear that the planet was warming. It's like a child walking uphill with a yo-yo. Like temperature, the yo-yo goes up and down, but the trend is upward.

University

With these thoughts, in 2001 Inez enrolled in a science degree at the Open University. It was a bold move because she was now 30 and had two small children. It'd been 15 years since she'd last studied and she was convinced it would be too difficult. "I didn't tell anybody because I was so sure I'd fail. I made it this big golden secret," she says.

"I didn't think there was any possibility of finishing, no chance. But when I got my marks, I had this incredible experience. I discovered I'm good at it and I loved it." Her success encouraged her to continue on to an honours and then a masters at the University of Vienna and the University of Copenhagen, studying agriculture and environmental science. "I could not believe that I was doing this," she says. "I was going to have a degree in science." She'd started late, but she had the inspiration of her grandmother, who'd earned a degree in literature when she was 86.

After graduating, Inez became what she calls "a happy worker bee", supporting online students in Copenhagen. Then on a trip to

Jamaica, she saw something that again would change the direction of her life. The people there, she says, are just as smart as her, but they are hindered by their lack of education. "Why are we depriving them of this? Why do I have access to this, but they don't?" she asked. Education would improve their quality of life and help them understand what's happening to the planet.

It's easy to think of environmental problems and especially global warming as a first-world problem, but climate change has no respect for borders. Developed nations are responsible for more atmospheric pollution, but it's the poorer people of the world who will feel the effects more. Pacific Island nations are already finding their land under threat as sea levels rise. Helping to improve education in less developed parts of the world gives them more opportunities as well as better equipping them to hold the big polluters to account.

A Climate Adventure

From university, it was a natural transition to teaching in schools, focusing on environmental issues and, in particular, climate change. She soon found teaching a room full of kids was exhausting, but it was also rewarding. Sometimes the class would get the point, and other times they seemed clueless. One day Inez could see that something was missing. Her epiphany came when she realised her class of 12-year-olds weren't connecting with the lesson on climate change. The subject was too difficult; it was too abstract and the kids didn't get it.

Making it more difficult was that teachers had made assumptions about what the children already knew. Maybe, Inez thought, there's a better way to engage the kids' curiosity. The kids should be challenged without being stretched too far. She wanted to set them onto the road to understanding climate change without terrifying them.

Could she perhaps create a computer game? One that is targeted toward children aged around 12. That would be ideal, because at that age their worldview is open to change. They can take in new information in a way that their older selves might not. They could play a game in the classroom with a teacher to help, and then continue at home.

Importantly, a computer game should be fun. The players would learn new things in a way that is tangible, exciting, relevant, and visual. If learning brings pleasure, the kids would be drawn in without coercion. She imagined a strategy game where players fly through the solar system exploring, going on missions, and solving puzzles. By tracking the progress of a player, the difficulty of each step would be tuned to match their skill.

It was a wild idea, but where to begin? Inez had only a vague notion of what it would mean to create a computer game. She didn't even have experience in software, but it was worth a try.

It'd be a long search to find the money, the organisation, and the technical resources. The answer turned out to be a PhD scholarship at the Australian National University in Canberra where her research would allow her to begin work on a climate game. CO2peration was born.

Now she had a concept for the game and some funding, but computer software—and especially games—is not trivial. And to make it more complicated, Inez says she had "zero programming skills". What could go wrong?

The first challenge was to find people who could build such a game. Inez knew she'd have to solve technical problems, but there was one she didn't expect to have to solve: theft.

A promising start would be the ANU Tech Launcher program that introduces computing students to researchers. Feeling optimistic, she went to her first meeting to find a few that were willing to join her. The game was now looking like a real prospect until, on the way, her wallet was stolen. Inside was a down-payment of over $4,000, and with it went her hopes. The loss was a crushing blow and yet another delay. After more applications and pleading, she managed to raise the money again. Now she could try again to recruit her programmers.

That's the theory, but to actually get them interested meant delivering a pitch. She says, "I went in there with my heart beating. I had a few minutes to say, 'Listen, guys, come onto my project.'" It worked and she got her first group of student programmers, but it was challenging because while some students were high achievers, others were only interested in doing the minimum possible to get a degree. Not all the programmers were particularly skilled or motivated, but she pressed on and by early 2017 they'd completed the first prototype.

Building the game meant overcoming a lot of problems because the technology didn't work reliably inside schools. It was one of the many hurdles they had to overcome, but eventually they got the first version of the game working. It was rough, but it was good enough to try on the first classrooms. She found schools who were happy to give it a go, and now they had 800 students to play. It'd taken many hours of planning and construction to get this far, and for Inez it was a tense period. Would the game work?

The classes were abuzz with the usual noise and clutter in school. Inez wandered around the room, peering intently over the kids' shoulders to see how they were reacting to the game. Then a teacher walked toward her saying, "I want to give you some feedback on the game." Inez remembers thinking, "Uh oh, here it comes …"

Then she said, "I have a student here who suffers from ADHD. I have never seen her concentrate on something for longer than a few minutes. She's been playing your game for ten minutes and she hasn't looked up once." It was the spark she needed. "To have that [feedback about]somebody who has learning difficulties was a big moment for me," she says.

Now that she was confident the game would succeed, Inez needed a source of funding to finish development. When I met Inez in 2017, she was a few weeks into a Kickstarter campaign where she hoped to raise $38,970. We did a session on the radio and some newspaper stories, and other supporters appeared from unexpected places to help push it along. She even got a request from Yale University to record an interview.

It was exciting to see the first pledge roll in, which came from a person she didn't even know. He even suggested a few marketing ideas. "It was," she says, "terrifying and exciting at the same time. To have that validation from someone, to have a complete stranger give you some money for your game—it's humbling."

Even better, seeing people offer their own money was validation of an idea that some people had said wouldn't work. Why build a computer game when there are good textbooks? "We never thought we would get this far," she says, "and yet here we are. It was a dream of ten years. It took a lot of willpower because some people just couldn't see the sense of it."

The Kickstarter was an all-or-nothing campaign and as the end date approached, it became clear she wouldn't make the target. "But that's okay," she told me. "I have backup options."

That didn't surprise me; I felt sure she'd have a few more options up her sleeve. As it turned out, I was right—she had a Plan B, Plan C, and I suspect Plans D and E too. In the end, the Kickstarter fell short with $12,066 in pledges, so she moved onto Plan B—another Kickstarter with a smaller target of $6,284.

She took the failure with good humour and sent a message to sponsors, which read (in part):

And yet, in spite of those bewitching titles and seductive fantasies, you chose CO2peration.

You validated a project that's been close to my heart for

more than 10 years—a project I have been working toward with all the determination and single-mindedness of a despot (we can only say visionary, apparently, when we succeed).

Inez has now seen enough of students' reactions to the game to feel confident that the full version of CO2peration will be a success. It starts by motivating players to reach a goal, and that makes learning fun.

CO2peration is a climate adventure where players can fly through the solar system on missions, collecting information to help them answer questions such as why there's so much water on Earth. The kids learn an abstract science without the fear and emotional noise that often goes with climate science. They're not asked to confront the dire consequences of climate change or figure out how to avoid it. Inez says research shows that younger students are less alarmed when learning about climate change than adolescents.

At its core, the climate system is extremely simple. Heat from the sun pushes the Earth's water and atmosphere around the planet. Inez uses a lava lamp to demonstrate convection currents. Warm blobs of oil rise toward the surface until they cool, then sink again, and around it goes.

If the basic principle is simple, the details soon make it wickedly complicated. The devil is the feedback loops because there are many moving parts in the climate system, each interacting with the other. As the ocean warms, it sends more moisture into the air, which generates clouds. The clouds create shade, but water vapour is a greenhouse gas. Greenhouse gasses increase warming, making it a positive feedback loop, but it's partially mitigated by the cloud cover, which is a negative feedback. Already it's getting messy, and there are a few other feedbacks besides. Their combined effect is one thing that makes climate science difficult.

The frightening thing about climate change is that we're meddling with a system that is vastly bigger than any human, and when we prod it hard enough it will bite. Just how and when it's impossible to know for sure, because when the positive feedbacks kick in, the system will flip. To make it harder, it's operating in timescales that humans are extremely poor at managing. If we reach a tipping point, it's too late because the climate operates on a scale decades beyond the political cycle.

Inez describes a few more of these positive loops that players learn about in the game, one of which is already showing disturbing signs—of having been disturbed. The Arctic ice sheet is a vast reflector at the top of the globe, bouncing heat back out into space. The linear rate of sea ice decline for November is 55,000 square kilometres. From 1979 to 2017, sea ice has declined by 5.14% every decade.[34] White ice is being replaced by dark sea that traps heat.

These might sound like dull statistics to some national leaders, but imagine the reaction if world share prices dropped by that amount in a year. There'd be instant panic and we wouldn't see denialists campaigns funded by fossil fuel companies.

A few weeks after the first Kickstarter failed, Inez sent a news update about the second attempt. Now she could celebrate reaching her goal, and CO2peration would live after all. It was a lot smaller than the first attempt but, she hinted with a wink, that wouldn't be a problem. And with her characteristic wit, the announcement read:

---

34   "Charctic Interactive Sea Ice Graph", National Snow and Ice Data Center, nsidc.org/arcticseaicenews/charctic-interactive-sea-ice-graph/

**38 backers pledged AU$6,284 to help bring
this project to life**

Mercurians are getting ready to host a welcome party in our honour.

It's going to be a pyjama party (and a chilly one at that)—so do remember to pack your woolliest, cosiest PJs as nights on Mercury drop to -173°C—and it will be a long night as it lasts for just under 59 Earth days.

This is a good thing, as we will have to leave before dawn on the morning of the 58th day as the diurnal temperature is 427°C.

In view of this, I think it's probably just best that we plan to party all night—what do you say?

In one sense, building CO2peration is in for the long haul because it'll take years before those players become influential adults. Unfortunately, those are years we don't have because we've spent the past 25 years saying we have 10 years to fix this problem. We've frittered away our free time, converting a difficult problem into an almost impossible one.

Still, the way influence works is more subtle and each of us affects the thinking of others to some extent. Even with the younger target audience of CO2peration, we probably won't have to wait to see some results. My brother and sister-in-law changed their votes in the last election because of their opposition to the vast Adani coal mine. They're inclined toward more conservative politics and weren't particularly environmentally conscious. Or at least they weren't until their children inspired them to change their thinking.

Multiply that over thousands of kids playing climate games and that could be a big change.

The Advocate
Professor Kate Auty

An independent commissioner has to be ... independent. So what would you do if the man who's your political boss suggests you should change your report to suit his agenda?

That's what Kate Auty faced when the Liberal Victorian State environment minister read her climate report. And what should she do when the public service was instructed to say that "climate change" was now "climate variability"?

It was probably inevitable that Kate Auty's childhood home would be raided by ASIO. During the 1950s and 1960s, her father would load his Gestetner[35] onto his motorbike and ride off to Communist Party meetings.[36]

Kate Auty was never a communist, but it's not surprising that she'd evolve into an advocate for social justice given her heritage. Her mother Jean had grown up in a working-class background in Brisbane where Kate's grandfather was in the building trade. They'd tell stories of how the first thing they did when rebuilding houses was

---

35   The Gestetner was a forerunner of the photocopier.

36   Australia's focus on communism didn't get to the level of McCarthyism in the US, but getting attention from ASIO wasn't necessarily benign, and Robert Manne suggests that the employment of 358 people was "adversely affected" between 1951 and 1957.

pull down the staircases, and the last they did was put them back up.

"At home, we'd have lively discussions," she says. I could imagine that. The Auty family sounds like my own (though we had no communists)—robust debates, always probing, always challenging, testing ideas against each other. It's a skill that would serve her well in her future legal career, which relies on the ability to articulate a strong case.

In the early 1960s, her days were spent in a tiny school in the remote far north-west of Australia. There was a single room with a single teacher who'd been sent from Perth. Sitting up the back of the room were the Aboriginal kids from Ivanhoe station across the Ord River, while Kate and her brother Peter would sit toward the front with the other white kids.

The Kimberley region is about as far as you can get from the populated south-east corner of Australia and still be on the continent. Kate remembers it as "a very strange, faraway place". The family had bought a 1959 Citroen Goddess, and bounced their way across the Nullarbor gravel roads to Perth, then up to the Kimberley where her father John could complete a master's degree in veterinary science. Kate, her mother Jean, and her brother Peter spent the next three years at the Kimberley Research Station.

In many ways, the school was just like any other, where the kids would learn how to hold a pen, how to write, and memorise multiplication tables. Their artwork would be pinned on the walls and before they could go to lunch they had to answer a spelling question. It was a regular school, but in other ways it was different, and one particular day stands out. Sitting at the back of the class was a small Aboriginal girl, wanting to go to the toilet. She crossed her legs with ever greater urgency, but she was frightened of the teacher. Inevitably, she lost control and wet herself. When the teacher saw the urine trickling onto the floor, he shouted and rubbed her nose in it.

Kate was only seven at the time, but she and her brother were horrified. Nobody should be subjected to that kind of treatment, and the fact that the girl was Aboriginal should be irrelevant. To Kate and Peter, all the kids were just like them. To play, have fun, learn, to just do what kids do. When they got home, they told their mother, who then told their father. He was outraged. He and a colleague drove out to see the teacher and loaded him on the next plane from Wyndham airport. "I'm sure it was an uncomfortable trip with this school teacher," Kate muses. "Off they went in the Citroen in a cloud of dust. It was 60 miles away on dirt roads."

Now without their teacher, the school dissolved for three weeks. Kate and her brother had a wonderful time, but schooling continued while their mother taught them. "A for apple, B for bat." She's not sure what kids from Ivanhoe Station did, but probably they had three weeks off, enjoying the Ord River riverbank with their families.

Kate has other, happier memories of those days. Her mother would take photos with an old-fashioned camera in the fields of wildflowers. "I remember the great paddocks of yellow. It was a childhood where we could get dirty, wag, behave badly, and play naughty," she says. It was "a very free childhood", helped by a mother who didn't coddle anyone, and an adventurous father. "They didn't restrict us, which provided a sense of independence."

Those early years triggered an emerging sense of living in the environment. They watched the crocodiles beside the river, and they'd scratch their legs walking through the spinifex. They'd watch Hollywood westerns at the open-air cinema while the occasional flying foxes would fly through the light. One day they found a wedge-tailed eagle beside the road with a broken wing. They took it home so their father could tape it up.

All this was blended with their experience of Aboriginal culture. They went to school and played with the other kids without much thought that they were different. They'd go for long walks and find wonderful rock paintings. Kate's best friend was an Aboriginal girl named Carol.

Kate observes that Aboriginal people see themselves as living *in* the environment. They—and it—are deeply entwined. "Look after the environment and it will look after us," they say. Meanwhile, we have debates about the environment versus the economy as if they are separate things, as if we could have one without the other.

The incident at school was a defining moment, a stark awakening of her sense of social justice. "It was an occasion that I've never forgotten," she says. "It showed me it's important to take action, and it's important to be considerate of what role you could play as a person in a position of authority." If it hadn't been for a bunch of scientists at the Kimberly Research Station, that incident would have gone unchecked. Looking back now, she reflects on the question of how power affects our relationships, who can do what and when, whether it's okay to rub a girl's nose in her own urine, and how two small kids can make a difference.

In a single-teacher school, their teacher was all-powerful and could do more or less whatever he wanted. "My brother and I knew we had created a palace coup even though that wasn't what we intended. We didn't go home to get our teacher fired."

"And this was really only shortly after the time that Aboriginal people were chained up in 'justice' settings and contemporaneous with them being arbitrarily moved around the country, taken away in the stolen generation."

On another occasion during school holidays, her friend Carol came to stay for a few days. They had fun, but the adult Kate still thinks about it. "I don't know whether Carol's parents thought it was okay, or whether they felt they had no choice because it was a power relationship."

Although the events of the Kimberley school remain strong in her memory, Kate keeps it in perspective because there were many good parts too. "We were very close to the Aboriginal kids. It was an environment of play." And importantly, their culture remained strong. "No one stopped them from speaking their own language." Her encounter with the world's oldest culture seeped into her psyche and continues to affect her thinking about community and our place in the environment.

The Law

By now I could see that Kate is the sort of person who might be talking to a state premier one moment, and a person in need the next. She seems interested in character more than status, and what she said next made me think of my own unconscious bias of a different sort. My rare encounters with the legal profession have left me with the impression of a strange ethereal world remote from ordinary people, of expensive and complicated processes where Capital Letters embody Special Significance. Maybe there's some truth in that, so I was a little surprised when she said that after high school she studied law at Melbourne University. Why would anybody who cares about ordinary people go into law?

More likely it reflects my lack of understanding, because she then explained that law is about politics, and politics is about social justice. Law has given her access to people in power, and with that she can advance the cause of social justice. "I didn't know exactly what I wanted to do, but I always thought it would be about remedying inequity," she says. "I've found that I could achieve more by being outside politics."

"I vividly remember going into a tutorial, and there was this person who was a real silver-tail, and she talked about all the things she was going to do. I said to her, 'Don't you think you have a social responsibility because you're here getting an education, and you could be improving other people's lives?' She looked at me and said 'No.'"

As her story unfolded it made me wonder about my own position as a white professional middle-class male. I've never been arrested, never done drugs other than a few puffs (I did inhale, but not much), and none of my family are on welfare. It hardly leaves me in a position to know what it means for so many Aboriginal people who are far more likely to come in contact with the law.

Law was a canny choice because now it's clear that the path gave her influence in the legal system that affects the lives of so many Aboriginal people. It would pave her way into prominent public office where she can affect government policy and behaviour. With that, she has access to places inaccessible to people outside the system.

Toward the end of her bachelor's degree, Kate needed to find a topic for her honours thesis, something that would interest her and be worthy of study, one that would bring together themes that would shape her future—history, Aboriginal heritage, and the law.

Kate's father told her about a royal commission into a massacre not far from her childhood home on the Kimberley Research Station. That, with her connection to the local people, made it a compelling topic. The 1927[37] Royal Commission report makes sober reading. The title puts it succinctly: *An Inquiry into Alleged Killing and Burning of Bodies of Aborigines in East Kimberley and into Police Methods when Effecting Arrests.*

---

37   1927 almost seems like ancient history, but it's not when I remind myself that my grandparents arrived in Canberra in 1927.

The report describes a 1926 massacre of Aborigines that occurred around the Forrest River Mission in the East Kimberley. The mission's object was "to Christianise the natives, instruct them in various useful occupations, assist them, and furnish them with the means of subsistence in return for work done".

The commissioner, GT Wood, Esq describes the mood at the time. "I was impressed with the evident ill-feeling entertained toward what may be termed the bush blacks, as distinguished from the domesticated blacks, on account of the killing of cattle. There is no doubt in my mind that the white settlers have a real grievance against the blacks on this score."

There was ill-will on both sides, and accounts recorded by interpreters refer to the testimony of the Aboriginal man named Lumbia.

A witness to the royal commission describes what happened in a confrontation between Lumbia and pastoralist Fred Hay. "Hay assaulted [Lumbia] over the head with the butt of the handle of his stockwhip and also over the back with the lash. Lumbia still has the scar on his forehead. He fell down; then jumping up he ran for his spear when Hay fired his revolver at him. Then the native speared him in the stomach."

A 1926 photo of Lumbia shows a youngish man in about his mid-twenties with his head shaved, wearing a loose-fitting shirt and baggy pants. His unbuttoned shirt reveals rows of horizontal scars across his chest and stomach, presumably from his initiation ceremony. He wears heavy chains wrapped around his waist, joining him to another member of his tribe, and next to them are a pair of Aboriginal trackers. Lumbia and his companion stand, heads down and shoulders slumped, looking forlorn.

After Hay was killed, police patrols went in search of Lumbia and subsequently several sites were found where mass killings of women and men had occurred. The inspector of the Western Australian Aborigines Department, EC Mitchell, visited two massacre sites where he found human teeth and skull fragments in campfire ashes. He sent a telegram[38] saying, "Shocking revelations, saw place Forrest River, rocky higher bed where natives chained small tree killed there then bodies burnt improvised oven."

The report concluded that 16 Aborigines were killed,[39] but the actual number is uncertain and Kate believes it was closer to 30. Even then, after all the hearings, the court found there was insufficient evidence, and acquitted the two policemen.

It appears to be a dark episode in Australia's history, but at least, I asked Kate, given the royal commission, wasn't there an attempt at justice? She wasn't particularly impressed, saying, "I question why they only charged the two young coppers. They could have charged at least one of the special constables who was on board for at least two of the fires." She referred to another incident in the Coniston area involving returned soldiers (light horsemen): "… and they've been valorised. We've been celebrating what they did." These men were war heroes, which meant they were almost above the law. They even had their legal costs paid.

On one hand it was returning war heroes—and on the other it was Kimberly Aborigines. "You can't let a black fellow win," Kate says.

In Melbourne in 1841–42, two Tasmanian Aborigines from a group known as *Palawa* were executed in what one observer[40] describes as "racially motivated deformed justice". It was a story that Kate thought should be told, and with Professor Lynette Russell wrote *Hunt Them, Hang Them.*

---

38   Neville Green, "The Evidence for the Forrest River Massacre", *Quadrant*, Vol 47, No 7-8 , July-August 2003.

39   Lumbia survived the affair, and was imprisoned on Rottnest Island. He later contracted leprosy and died at Forrest River in 1950.

40   Richard Frankland, review of Kate Auty and Lynette Russell, *Hunt Them, Hang Them,* Justice Press, www.justice-press.com/publications/434-hunt-them-hang-them.

According to the blurb, "Three women—Truganini, Planobeena, and Pyterruner—were returned to their country, grieving and brutalised." The name Truganini is well known as the last surviving Tasmanian Aborigine from a group exiled to King Island.[41] The blurb continues:

> ... the conduct of an erratic and incompetent trial judge (Willis) who had failed in other jurisdictions and who was now 'in charge' of a fledgling colonial justice system, and of a Protector, G.A. Robinson, complicit in a great injustice.

> ... Readers will be shocked by the treatment of the Palawa in this tragedy—not Shakespearean times, but Victoria in the 1840s.

On a day we met, Kate had been reading Neil Black's journal about another incident in the western districts of Victoria. She read about how Black's shepherds would routinely take Aboriginal women and sleep with them, and if they didn't like them, in the morning they would shoot them.

Usually, Kate presents a calm image, but now her voice had an edge. "That wasn't everyone, but you only need enough people to be a complete brute to telegraph a message to people, *shut your mouth and sit down*. You are told 'don't cause trouble'."

"We overlook the brutality that occurred in this country. I frankly think there was a lot of stuff at that level of brutality that we simply don't know about."

It's not a view shared by revisionist historians. The 1927 Kimberley incident is the target of Rod Moran's book, *Massacre Myth*, which claims the royal commission did not present credible

---

41   She died in 1876; according to Wikipedia, not the "last" since people in the Census still identify as such.

evidence. It was a myth, he says, promoted by a disturbed missionary. Then Keith Windschuttle wrote in *The Fabrication of Aboriginal History*, challenging what he called the "orthodox school" view of violence between Indigenous Australians and settlers. Politicians such as Prime Minister John Howard played on the notion, saying there was too much "black armband" in Australian history.

By now it was clear that Kate has strong views on the topic, so I could predict the reaction I'd get when I asked her about the history wars. She didn't hesitate and I think it's the only time I've heard her use an expletive, even if it was mild.

"Oh, it's bullshit."

Kate was suggesting that the black armband label reveals more about ideology than it does about history. "You can cherry-pick this stuff as much as you like. It wasn't some demented missionary who just made it up. I don't know what motivates them. Maybe notoriety or maybe being right when others are wrong."

Learning about these disturbing episodes left me feeling concerned—not that we should hide from these, but that we might paint an unrealistically gloomy stereotype. Clearly, there are difficult parts of our history but, I wondered, might we cause more harm by being too negative?

Perhaps, she says, the answer is to tell the stories in a straightforward way. Allow the facts to speak for themselves without being emotive. "We don't want to be shocking people about that massacre in 1926. It shocked me, but you need to engage people. In any case, there are many positive stories we also can tell." We should look at the inherent strength of Aboriginal people whom she says have been "enormously adaptable and generous".

It was a sentiment Kate would repeat many times during our conversations. She'd say this Aboriginal person was "impressive", or another was "inspiring", and then she'd talk about the many good things that were happening.

For a year after graduating, Kate worked for a small criminal law firm in Footscray. It was the standard path to follow after a law degree. "It's just what you do," she says. It wasn't something she saw as a long-term career, but it did give her insights into how people who are less well-off interact with the justice system. Back then, Footscray wasn't the gentrified place it is now. Many were migrants and people working in factories who had limited language skills and education.

It wasn't about excusing criminal behaviour, but it did involve understanding social disadvantage. We tend to think that what people do is simply a matter of personal choice. Choice is critical, but we overlook the effect of our environment. We only need to look at the famous Stanford Prison experiment to see how easily supposedly average people can veer into antisocial behaviour. When they hit the courts, a lack of knowledge and resources can make things worse. Improving access to the justice system is essential if we are to build a more equitable society.

In 1980, Kate quit the law firm. She didn't have a clear plan of what she'd do next, but walking down Gertrude Street in Fitzroy she had a chance encounter with an acquaintance. There was a job going at the Aboriginal Legal Service; perhaps she might apply. She did, sending her on a new path.

In her new job, Kate represented Indigenous children, men, and women, mainly for criminal law matters. They could be charged with offences when they were caught tampering with a car door— not because they wanted to take the car, but because they were looking for money. When that happened, parents might be told their child was not being looked after, and be served with a care and protection order.

There were so many unfortunate stories. Kate became animated as she described one incident where a boy was facing a court charge. He was living with his grandmother, who probably had some reading and writing skills from living on a mission. His grandmother was raising him because his mother was dead, and his father had shot through. Kate described what happened next.

> The offence was to do with dishonesty; I think it was shoplifting. He didn't come to court because people's lives were a mess. Rochelle Patten and I went out to pick him up and take him to court. We went into the house where his grandmother was.
>
> In the house, there was no carpet. It was a housing commission house—and this was in Shepparton, which has pretty brutal winters. When we walked in, what immediately was apparent was a glass furniture cabinet. It was the most significant bit of furniture in a house. It was full of sports trophies.
>
> I said to this little kid, "So whose trophies are these?"
>
> When he started to talk about his achievements and his trophies his face lit up. He was full of pride. He was wanting to tell his story. He'd gone from being a shy and retiring kid to being assertive, to being a child who had a story to tell.

All the sporting trophies were for football and running. Not squash or cricket, or anything that required uniforms or expensive equipment. "You can run in your bare feet and you can play football in a Jersey," she says. "Every one of the cases had that sort of specialness."

Years later she was in Shepparton as the senior magistrate setting up an Aboriginal sentencing Koori[42] court, and those stories came

---

42 The Koori Court provides an informal atmosphere and allows greater participation by the Aboriginal (Koori) community in the court process. Koori Elders or Respected Persons, the Koori Court Officer, Koori defendants and their families can contribute during the court hearing. Source: magistratescourt.vic.gov.au

rushing back. They had senior people with the magistrates, helping them understand people's situations. The Koori court was a way to make what would otherwise be an inscrutable system accessible. When a person appeared in court, often they lacked the most basic knowledge of how the legal system worked.

In telling me her story, Kate made a surprising admission. "As a non-Indigenous lawyer being exported into these communities, I was always aware of how little I knew." Given her years of close contact with Aboriginal people and her senior position, it reflects a degree of humility. We've all encountered the puffed up petty official, but it takes a certain strength to say "I don't know". I wondered how much better it'd be if we'd pause from certainty or feigned confidence to ask a good question.

"It's not all about doom and gloom. I came away from that job thinking that Aboriginal people had *real* strengths. Just last week I heard Rowan Foley (the General Manager of the Aboriginal Carbon fund) talking about how their people were taking control of land, and its capacity to be turned into carbon sinks."

"He was absolutely inspirational. I think we need to remember that Aboriginal people have their destiny in their own hands."

Around the time I was interviewing Kate for *Fragile Planet*, the contentious issue of Australia Day was hotly debated in the media. 26 January marks the day in 1788 when the British ships arrived at Port Jackson carrying the first white settlers. That event permanently changed the future of Aborigines in a land that the Europeans called *Terra Nullius*. Some refer to it as "invasion day", insisting that the nation should celebrate an alternative date.

Prime Minister Kevin Rudd issued an apology in February 2008, acknowledging "the suffering caused by decades of mistreatment of Indigenous Australians". It was a great moment, but the issue remains vexed and we don't seem much closer to an answer. And as the History Wars have shown, political attitudes intrude. I wondered how this might affect Kate, so I prodded her with a slightly pointy question. Did she think she might be seen as a white middle-class do-gooder professional?

She rolled her eyes, but wasn't fazed. "Probably," she replied, "but I have a bit of a broad Australian accent and I was probably pretty realistic, so when the police pushed me around, I pushed back. I was probably reasonably assertive."

She launched into a story about a case in Heidelberg where an Aboriginal person was charged with driving while disqualified. The policeman had watched him reverse down his driveway and then drive back in. They came along and charged him. These coppers were looking for a charge, she said. "Many police would have said, 'Mate, don't do that again. If you do, we will book you.'"

But they did book him and the hearing was set down for 26 January—*Australia Day*. Kate and the man charged sat up the back of the court. "We're happy to sit here all day. I'm not in a hurry," she told the clerk of the court.

When eventually the matter did arise, Kate addressed the magistrate. "How ironic," she said, "that I should be standing here on 26 January representing an Aboriginal man who has driven five yards and been charged with this offence. I would like you to take this into account and put him on probation."

Given his history, he could have been given a prison sentence, but the magistrate said, "I have been sitting here thinking exactly the same thing." And he gave him probation.

As Kate and the Aboriginal man walked out of the court, the two young coppers approached them, saying, "We'll be appealing that decision."

"Feel free," she replied. It was bravado of course; she knew they wouldn't.

Kate's story gives another insight into the legal process. She says she knew the magistrate and that he would be receptive to the message. "None of these are straightforward," she says. "It's never straightforward, it's never objective."

After about three years with the Aboriginal Legal Service, Kate left to set up a private practice in inner Melbourne with Jelena Popovic, specialising in welfare law representing women's refuge clients and Aboriginal people.

Deaths in Custody

Lloyd Boney[43] was born on 23 December 1959 in Walgett, New South Wales, and by the time he finished school he'd already received his first conviction for breaking, entering, and stealing. In subsequent years he was convicted of a range of similar offences including driving under the influence of alcohol, minor theft, and assault, and on 6 August 1987 he was arrested again for breach of bail. An hour and a half later, police found him dead in his cell. He was hung by the neck with a football sock.

Subsequent legal enquiries found that the police did not have a case to answer for homicide, but people were not convinced, and after the funeral at Brewarrina[44] cemetery on 15 August, Aboriginal residents clashed violently with police.

The incident gained national attention, and a few days later a newspaper report described the house where Lloyd Boney had lived.

---

43   Tim Rowse, "Boney, Lloyd James (1959–1987)", *Australian Dictionary of Biography*, Vol 17, (MUP), 2007, www.adb.anu.edu.au/biography/boney-lloyd-james-12229.

44   Perhaps it's an irony that what might be the oldest human construction ever found are the fish traps at Brewarrina. These are known by the Ngemba people as Baiame's Ngunnhu (pronounced By-ah-mee's noon-oo). They date back at least 40,000 years, making them 10 times older than Stonehenge. Chris Graham, "Outback Tour: Australia Has One Of The Oldest Human-Made Structures On Earth. Meh?" *New Matilda*, 5 February 2019, www.newmatilda.com/2019/02/05/australia-one-oldest-human-made-structures- earth-meh-nmfhpotae.

Most Australians would not regard the Aboriginal houses at Barwon Four in Brewarrina as fit for a garden shed or a garage for the car. The flimsy tin-and-fibro constructions, with tyres and bricks lying on roofs to secure them in a big wind, have housed a community of about 150 Aboriginals for the past 30 years. Pregnant dogs walk among dumped cars and rubbish. For one house, running water comes from the nearby Barwon River to a single outside tap. With no proper sewerage, the smell of human excrement is rancid.

The report went on to announce that the Federal Minister for Aboriginal Affairs, Jerry Hand, was "seeking urgent talks with state ministers on how to deal with the problem of deaths in custody". Soon after, Prime Minister Bob Hawke announced that a royal commission would investigate Aboriginal deaths in state and territory prisons. Initially, one commissioner was appointed to investigate 44 deaths, but when they discovered there were in fact 99 deaths, additional five commissioners were appointed. It also became apparent to the commissioners that they should broaden their scope to include why Australia's Aboriginal population has *20 times* the risk of dying in police custody and *10 times* the risk of dying in prison.

One of those commissioners was Pat Dodson. Photos of Dodson show an unmistakable character with a thick, bushy white beard growing down to his chest. He wears a black, wide-brimmed hat with a yellow-red-black sash matching the colours of the Aboriginal flag. Dodson was not legally trained, but he was well respected in both the Indigenous and white communities.[45] Assembling the royal commission report was a substantial task that demanded a strong set of skills. Dodson needed support from someone with legal expertise and especially someone sympathetic

---

45   And since 2 May 2016, he has held a Western Australian seat in the Senate.

to the Aboriginal cause while being impartial. Kate Auty was an ideal choice, and she joined his team as a senior solicitor.

It was difficult work, involving travelling across Western Australia from the far north down to the southwest. They heard the harrowing stories not just of the deaths, but of the circumstances and the effect on people around them. A third of the 99 deaths investigated had occurred in Western Australia.

Kate says that all the cases they investigated were pretty horrible, but one stands out. Nita Blankett was a 41-year-old mother of five, serving a sentence of six months at the Bandyup Training Centre for drink-driving offences.

The report's description of the final hours of her life reads like a dark comedy of errors. It was well known to the custodial officers and nursing staff that Nita was a chronic asthmatic, but when, on the night of 14 January 1982, she suffered an asthma attack, they seemed almost incapable of responding.

Those who've suffered an asthma attack say it can be a terrifying experience. They begin to wheeze and it feels as if someone is sitting on their chest. "It's like you're drowning in air," as one puts it. Nita's bronchial tubes were constricted and she was beginning to suffocate. A prison officer reported that Nita was weeping and demanding an ambulance.

The duty nursing sister gave her a brief examination and didn't think her condition warranted medical attention. Eventually, they decided to act, but the prison van was slow to arrive. When it did arrive, there was disagreement about her security rating and how many officers should be escorting her. While they dithered, Nita's condition was getting worse. "The deceased was hysterical and probably hypoxic by that time," the report says.

When the van arrived they asked her to walk to the front gate, but they realised she was too ill to walk any distance, so an officer went to fetch a wheelchair from the infirmary. But that was locked and there was yet another delay. By now Nita was becoming incontinent so they had to wait while she went to the toilet. Eventually, they got her into the prison van, but the driver didn't know the way to the hospital and missed a turn.

As they drove, they heard Nita in the back of the van say "hurry". Then she went quiet.

When they arrived at the rear of the surgery, they unlocked the van and found Nita slumped in a coma. Amid the kerfuffle, she'd been transported in a prison van rather than an ambulance, which would be fully equipped for such an emergency. The doctor on duty at the time checked for signs of life and could not find any. The report describes the scene.

> One could reasonably expect that a medical practitioner would have attempted to resuscitate the deceased, but that did not occur. The explanation that Dr Hughes gave was that he did not attempt resuscitation because the deceased was "clinically dead". However, he made no enquiry to discover how recently any sign of life had been observed and his own assessment was that she had only been dead for a very few minutes.
>
> He described the conditions in which he examined the deceased as far from ideal. Unfortunately, they were some distance from the doctor's surgery, which was exceptionally well equipped and possessed a full range of resuscitation equipment, including a defibrillator.

The final report of the royal commissioners was tabled in April 1991, running to five volumes and 339 recommendations. The major reason for the number of Aboriginal deaths, it concluded, was the "grossly disproportionate" rate at which they were custody—in the order of more than 20 times the rate for non-Aboriginals.

Twenty-five years after the royal commission, various commentators have catalogued ways in which the situation has actually become worse, but Kate is pragmatic about what they were able to achieve. "We're never happy with what happens after a royal commission because governments don't do what you really wanted them to do." The royal commission was extensively covered by the media, and for a while there were almost daily revelations. Despite its many flaws, one Indigenous person described the report as "compulsory reading". Another called it the "biggest history lesson in Australia", and Kate says that Patrick Dodson's report is highly significant because it was the first ever to give Aboriginal people a voice who otherwise would have none.[46]

The royal commission is a big part of Kate's story, but when talked about it I could feel we were diving down a rabbit hole. We could fill an entire book, bigger than *Fragile Planet,* with these stories, so it was with some trepidation that I asked her: *Why are Indigenous people over-represented in the prison population*? Why do they do so poorly on so many social indicators such as health and unemployment?

She paused, with a look that said, "Where do I start?" It's a big question, she says, but let's also remember it's not all bad news. "It's not every community. Seventy percent of Aboriginal people are not drinkers."

Kate launched into a description of the spiralling cascade of events that can lead to an Aboriginal person landing in custody. It can begin in a relatively minor way with a traffic offence. Those who live in remote communities, where there probably isn't any public transport, drive when they "shouldn't" because they don't have a licence. "Then if you get caught, you have an automatic

---

46   This has been clearly demonstrated by two royal commissions that have been in progress as I write—one into child sex abuse and the other into banking.

disqualification for three months. And then your next penalty is nine months, but it's cumulative and soon you have 12 months. It adds up and each time there's also a fine."

"If you don't have much income, you're not going to pay the fine. Lots of people were in gaol for fine defaults when I was the Kalgoorlie magistrate."

"It's cascading and it's brutal," she says. "It's far too easy to gaol people in Western Australia. Aboriginal people are uniquely exposed because of where they live, because of their family and other obligations, and because there is no work."

In April 1991, the royal commission had been running for four years and occupied three years of Kate's life. The report was now ready. The last year had been particularly tough because they had to travel across the vast territory of Western Australia. They were running conferences with people they didn't know. They were meeting with people who'd lived on a mission and been belted through school, or talking to JPs[47] in Carnarvon who were of the view that Aboriginal people should be flogged to get them to understand what they had to do. It was a very compressed timeframe, and in the last six weeks they had the massive task of writing it up.

Eventually, the report was done, and now Kate can look back on what they achieved. "I was very pleased with Pat's report. It tells all those Aboriginal stories. It became a template for other reports including the Stolen Generation and The Little Children Are Sacred."

It had been exhausting, and with that behind her, it was time to return to university to feed what she calls her "education habit". When she saw an opening at Deakin University, she knew this would be an opportunity for a change of pace. The job was to build a course in "Environmental Heritage and Interpretation" for postgraduate

---

47   Justice of the Peace.

Indigenous and non-Indigenous students where they studied a blend of history, landscapes, and culture. It was unusual because it was co-designed with the help of students who'd contribute their own extensive knowledge of the environment and their heritage. They focused on the south-east of Australia because those regions have been most disrupted by European settlement. It countered the notion that Aboriginal people only come from Cape York or the Northern Territory. Unfortunately, it also meant that much of the material was difficult to find.

Designing and running the course took a lot of effort, but they were encouraged by comments from the students, who said things like "I never knew this stuff, and the course has been a revelation", and "This is the best thing I've done to understand my country."

Kalgoorlie

In 2004 Western Australian Attorney-General Jim McGinty recruited Kate to set up an Aboriginal sentencing system in Kalgoorlie. It would, she thought, be an opportunity to make a difference in a troubled community. But when she got there she found the work would simply not be viable without another magistrate. When she explained that to McGinty, he said they didn't have the budget—so she quit. To his credit, the Attorney-General saw the need to meet the demand, and after a little time he found the funds and appointed a third magistrate. That was enough, and Kate withdrew her resignation.

When she did start, it became clear that the work was going to be difficult. Kalgoorlie, she says, has the reputation for being the most racist town in Australia. "A well-used term is nigger nigger nigger." She looked pained as she repeated the offensive words. "It's a terrible place for Aboriginal people for a range of reasons." Despite the huge gold mines and tourist potential in the town, there was high unemployment and crime rates among the Aboriginal people.

But there was a good side too. With her experience of the royal commission still fresh, she could directly address some of the issues within her jurisdiction. Often it was simple, pragmatic things such as making sure that a magistrate was available for Saturday morning hearings. That would immediately reduce the number of people in detention on weekends who'd been picked up on a Friday.

There were good people, she says. "No doubt about that. Great, strong Aboriginal people." There were also good non-Indigenous people from Rotary wanting a community court, which meant that elders who sat with the magistrate really backed up that work.

"There were fantastically committed, very senior Aboriginal people doing wonderful work for their community, but they struggled because they needed to be a bridge for their culture and non-Indigenous culture. They were operating in circumstances where everything is judged more critically than in a non-Indigenous place."

They worked on getting kids into school because without it they have no hope; they need to get skills that will lift them out of poverty because school is a place where they get bullied. They talked to mining executives about getting people into apprenticeships.

Sometimes real progress seems forever distant, but there are high points. In 2008, Prime Minister Kevin Rudd delivered a heartfelt apology for the treatment of people described in the Stolen Generation Royal Commission. I remember the day well because it finally closed years of wrangling by the previous government who refused to use the word "sorry". At work, we all left our desks for an hour and clustered around the TV to watch the broadcast. It's hard to know what practical difference it made, but at last the nation was acknowledging misdeeds.

Still, Kate laments that there is no treaty and we should have a serious discussion with Aboriginal people about their treatment because "some of what occurred was pretty bloody brutal".

In May 2017, over 250 Aboriginal and Torres Strait Islander leaders met in Central Australia on the lands of the Anangu people and produced the Uluru Statement that calls for constitutional recognition for their people. We should be looking at the Uluru Statement, Kate says. "How come New Zealand has a treaty and we don't? How come?"

"They were here before us and they did have a culture."

After four years, it was time to move on. "Going into this job, I was looking for another challenge. Kalgoorlie and the western desert certainly provided that." Now it was time for the next challenge, but this one would be of a very different sort.

Interference

In July 2009, Adam Morton wrote in the *Sydney Morning Herald* what would prove to be a prescient observation: "Victoria's new environmental watchdog reckons some people would describe her as 'very blunt.'"

"This could sound fairly ominous for the state government, given it has just appointed Auty to a five-year term in a completely different, but perhaps just as combative, position."

Kate's office was to produce a pair of reports that would be delivered to the Victorian Parliament. The first was a "public participation" report[48] and, as with the Deaths in Custody Royal Commission, it was an opportunity to encourage public participation and help build momentum toward change. She and her team travelled across Victoria, collecting comments and ideas from people. They had many conversations that were one-to-one or one-to-many. Anybody who wanted to talk was invited. They found there were "many publics" because every town had its own issues. People described what they were doing for the environment.

---

48   Titled: *Many Publics Report: Participation, inventiveness and change.*

"I'm interested in the little people," Kate says, "and people who have the ability to make change. The report I wrote about this fieldwork was the most important report my office produced."

As they pushed to complete the next report (*State of the Environment*), things were getting hectic. There was a flurry of publishing details to be sorted, proofreading, final edits, and the artwork and signoffs all had to be done before it could go to the printers. That would be okay, Kate had seen it before. That was part of the job, but it couldn't have come at a worse time in her personal life.

While this was happening, her brother Peter was dying of pancreas cancer. He didn't have other family, and Kate spent the last week with him in a small regional Victorian hospital as he slowly and excruciatingly died 16 days before the extensive environment report was due. Two months later, Kate's father died. It was just days after the report was tabled in parliament.

In telling me this, Kate became visibly upset. "The toughest thing I've ever had to do was look after my family, but at the same time continue the job and be professional. But yeah, you get through it."

And then she added a surprising twist. "It gave me some sort of idea of how difficult sometimes it is for Aboriginal people who have buried lots more family members than I have."

In spite of it all, Kate says she's proud of what her team achieved. It's a different setting, but it reminded me of Simon Sheikh and the GetUp movement who were also mobilising people who are otherwise disengaged from politics. Whatever one's political persuasion they're both antidotes during a dangerous time for democracy when so many people are so disillusioned and disconnected. Widespread apathy in a nation eventually slides into anger, which becomes an invitation to dangerous populist demagogues.

The report, which led to the most challenging engagement

with the then conservative state government, was to be the *Climate Change Foundation Paper,* which looked at how climate change was—and already is—affecting Victoria. What would happen as temperatures ratchet beyond the 0.9°C already experienced? How should people and the government respond?

And should we be concerned about a few warmer days? If we get a longer summer and a few more days at the beach, that doesn't sound too bad. If only it were that simple, but it isn't because the warming is turning the heat up on the kitchen stove. Any cook knows how a small change in temperature can make or wreck a meal, but that's a simplistic analogy. The climate change paper catalogued a disturbing array of consequences of various warming scenarios, from manageable to disastrous. It included water security, food ecosystems, and threats to infrastructure.

The climate change paper takes pains to explain that it's based on the best available science and warns of the dire consequences to Australia, which is particularly vulnerable. This was borne out by the catastrophic drought, followed by fire then floods during early 2020. As the report says, "In Victoria our seaboard, our biodiversity, our infrastructure are all at risk. Native species and agricultural production are both exposed. The risk of extreme events is elevated."

The climate change paper had been commissioned during the term of a Labor government, but before the report could be completed, Labor was ousted by the Coalition led by Denis Napthine. It might've looked promising when Napthine appointed Ryan Smith as the Minister for Environment and Climate Change. That made him the only minister with "climate change" in his title, but any hope soon evaporated. *The Guardian* newspaper commented, "… Smith mentioned climate change not once in parliament this year. His website reveals no speeches or statements on climate change in 2014. Nor has he released a single media release on that part of his portfolio this year."

Things were not looking good for Kate's office when she started getting hints about the new attitude to climate change. Staff at the Victorian EPA were told to drop any work on the topic. Word got around that the new government was giving the public service instructions to avoid the words "climate change". Now they must say "climate variability". That would be less threatening, more palatable.

The next indication of their attitude wasn't even a hint. It was a hammer.

The report was well underway when Kate's office took a call from the minister. She was told to front up at his office to discuss—what, he didn't say other than it was about the climate change report, so when she and a staff member arrived, they could only guess.

"I had no inkling of what I was going to be confronted with," Kate says.

It was one of those defining events that she remembers in vivid detail. The Victorian Parliament House is built in the neoclassical style with an imposing edifice. Their meeting was to be downstairs in a small dark room, just big enough to squeeze in five people. When the minister appeared, he was accompanied by his chief of staff and his environment adviser. Already this was looking like a statement about power. "There were three of them, and two of us," Kate remembers. The minister stood at the door so he could exit if he was called back to parliament, which he did a couple of times before they were finished.

The minister didn't wait to raise his concerns about the *Climate Change Foundation Paper*. When the moment came, he revealed why he'd summoned her.

What can I do if I don't like it?

Kate Auty is not a person usually lost for words, but at this point she says she was speechless. "I was somewhat perplexed by that question." When she did gather herself, her reply was blunt: *There's nothing you can do if you didn't like it.*

She told him that the report was based on climate change science. It would be rigorous, it would be robust, and it would be peer-reviewed.

The story still rankles with Kate, but there was also a sense of pride that she'd refused to be cowed. And why—why would he object to work that was backed up by the best available evidence?

"I struggled to understand why or what there was not to like about a report that was subject to so much scrutiny," she says. "It's ideological. And of course, we're all familiar with what science is telling us about what burning coal is doing to the climate. There are big powerful interests in this, and they are exercising that power. Clearly, they don't want to see their interests undermined."

"I struggled with the ideological nature of that direction. It was not proper process, it was political interference."

I imagined what it would be like to be in Kate's position on that day. On one hand she was hearing the dire warnings about climate change, and on the other was a government minister saying we should ignore it. A truck is bearing down on us, but according to that thinking, the best solution is to pretend it isn't there. It got me thinking about how someone like Ryan Smith might react if ever they realised what climate change really means, and they obstructed people trying to avert it. What would they say then? Oops?

"What was the personal impact on you?" I asked. Her answer was interesting, because at first she deflected attention from herself, saying, "It was tough for my team." And then she put it into the wider context. "It was tough for me because we knew that we were struggling against what we saw as an ideological tide, both in Victoria and federally.[49] We knew that we were a small office standing out against that."

The minister didn't get the answer he was looking for, but he

---

49   Around this time the Coalition Federal Government was unravelling the carbon pricing mechanism.

wasn't done yet. Kate says he would have closed the office if he could. That was beyond his powers so he did the next best thing. He starved them of discretionary funding, leaving them without money to pay people on contract. Some of those people had been contracted for three years, and Kate's office refused to sack them. In the face of her resistance, their salaries continued to be paid, but it provided the conservative government with the opportunity at the end of her term to say she had "overspent".

Despite that, the report went ahead. "We produced the report, we published the report, we circulated the report, and it now has a life across Victoria. It was received well by the community and by scientists. I'm very pleased that we were responsible enough to do that." Even years later, she says, people are still referring to it.

It was deeply ideological to be pressured to ignore the climate change science, she says. Not long after the report was published, she resigned—but not without a parting shot. We only need to read to page four of the report to find these two quotes (my emphasis):

The warming around Australia is consistent with the global pattern and cannot be explained by *natural variability* alone.[50]

And ...

Victoria's climate is naturally variable and severe weather events such as bushfires and floods have occurred throughout history. [But] ... consistent with scientific understanding of conditions that may be more likely in a warmer world, compared to *natural variability* alone.[51]

---

50 *State of the Climate 2012*, CSIRO and the Australian Bureau of Meteorology.
51 *Report on Climate Change and Greenhouse Gas Emissions in Victoria*, Victorian Government Department of Sustainability and Environment Melbourne, March 2012.

I couldn't let that one pass. "So that wasn't an accident, was it?" She laughed. I thought not.

Meeting Kate Auty for the first time was mostly luck. I'd just started writing *Fragile Planet* when I visited an open day at Daylesford, Victoria, where they have a community-owned wind farm. In a paddock not far out of town, they constructed a pair of turbines. Gale and Gusto, they call them. It would be good, I thought, to see the work that's become a model for other community energy projects. And importantly for the book, I was hoping to meet someone with a strong story I could write. Once the formalities were over, I tried to sidle up to a person who might be a promising subject. His dad knew my dad, so that was a start, but it seemed there were a few other people who also wanted his time. That left me staring vacantly into space with what my wife Anne would call a gormless look. What I didn't notice was that my friend Lynda had collared Kate.

"Talk to Rod," she said. "He does community radio and is writing a book."

A moment later, Lynda and Kate appeared, and now I had an introduction. The fact I was unknown didn't seem to matter; she'd talk to me anyway, and a few weeks later we recorded our first interview. Now I see that her willingness to talk feeds into her engagement with the community. It's the ordinary[52] people that matter, not just the stars. Unprompted during one interview, she would tell me, "Sitting here, having this conversation with you, I don't really want this chapter to be about me."

"There's so much good stuff happening, so many brave people, but we never say, 'gee that was amazing.'"

---

52   In the early days of planning the book, a friend suggested I should include Peter Garret, but I made a deliberate decision that instead I should write about people who are not celebrities. While they're fun and often worthy, celebrities are not people "like us".

Community seems such a warm, slightly fluffy term with a slightly dangerously socialist edge, but community is the core of democracy and the foundation of society. We don't have to like our neighbours, but unless we can figure out ways to build toward our common good, we have no hope. Living in a harsh environment, Aboriginal people know this because if they don't cooperate, they'd perish. Community, Kate says, is the place where you find ideas. It's where you get action because it's local and things happen on a manageable scale.

"Think globally, act locally."

If that's the good side, communities can also be a barrier. They can be obstructive and resistant to change. It goes both ways, Kate says. It tests your capacity to think on your feet, and sometimes you don't get it right.

Today,[53] Kate Auty is the ACT Commissioner for Sustainability and Environment, where she spends much of her time stirring people into action. Often it's people who might otherwise be disengaged, and often they're obscure. The key, she says, is to start where you are, consider your place, your strengths and weaknesses. Where do we want to go?

Then we take the next step. That may seem obvious, but at a time when humanity is facing momentous challenges, we can feel powerless, like rabbits in the headlights until it's too late. The next step is never momentous. It's a single stride in the thousand-mile march, eating the chocolate elephant one bite at a time.

And along the way, we must celebrate our successes because, with that, we tell ourselves and everyone we touch that we are not powerless.

---

53   Kate's tenure ended in February 2020. She's now returned to her roots in northern Victoria, where she remains active in community environmental issues.

The Lady with a Laser
Monica Oliphant

Sometimes in life, our most profound decisions occur in the middle of the most mundane circumstances. Monica Oliphant was listening to the radio while washing the dishes when she caught an idea that would change her life.

The Middle East was in the grip of war, plunging the world into an oil crisis. Then, as now, nations would support dictators and inflict chaos to secure supplies.

But what if we didn't need the stuff? Nobody would go to war over solar energy. It sealed her decision and she's spent every year of her life since then in the pursuit of renewable energy.

Writing a book like *Fragile Planet* invariably means contacting people you've never met. Often they are high-profile, or in the case of Monica Oliphant, have names that are giants in science history. So when a friend suggested I call her, it might have been intimidating. I needn't have worried, because almost as soon as we began our conversation, we felt like old friends. She replies to my emails with *Dear Rod*, and in our first phone call we chatted for over an hour.

A few weeks later, I drove to her modest house on the edge of Adelaide. The suburbs are being swallowed by the city as it creeps

across the surrounding countryside, and getting to her house
meant navigating the roadworks of
yet another freeway development.
When Monica welcomed me
inside, I saw shelves lined with
family photos and ornaments from
her travels around the world. And
as I might've guessed, there were
books about history, energy, and
the environment. Later she'd show
me the biography of her famous
father-in-law, Sir Mark.

Soon she'd be speaking at an international conference in
Sweden, then not long after in Germany and Mali. Clearly, I'm not
the only person who wanted to talk to Monica, and being in her late
70s hasn't slowed her down. Even then, she wasn't much interested
in talking about her various awards. It wasn't false modesty, but
that she doesn't connect the idea of herself with celebrity. "How I
got an Order of Australia is beyond me," she told me.

In wartime Britain, Monica Oliphant was what they called a
"latchkey kid". Like so many others of her time, she'd find her way
home from school wearing a door key strung around her neck
while her parents were occupied by the war. Even if the war was a
horrendous experience, it instilled a sense of independence that has
stayed with Monica.

When the German bombers flew overhead and the air raid sirens
howled, families would scramble downstairs to their Morrison
Shelter. They would huddle in the sturdy steel frame that looked
like a pet cage, about the size of a dining table. Monica's earliest
memories are of climbing over the rubble and into the crater of
a neighbour's house where she could pick flowers. Sometimes she

thinks about her relative who refused to shelter because he'd been a German soldier who'd killed another man in the previous war. Burdened with shame, he seemed to feel there would be some justice if he was killed by a German bomb.

Monica's parents, Franz and Olga Kammer, thought they'd escaped the Nazi persecution of Jews in Austria, but now Franz was considered an enemy alien, and even though his radio engineering skills would be useful to the war effort, he found himself in an internment camp. He joined thousands of Germans, Italians, and Austrians in temporary quarters on racecourses and housing estates, while a large number were sent to the Isle of Man. A great many were Jewish refugees and almost certainly not sympathetic to the Nazis, but they were interned anyway. As the camps became overcrowded, Britain began deporting the detainees overseas, mostly to Canada and Australia.

In 1939, the government requisitioned the Blue Star Line ship *SS Arandora Star*. What had been a luxury cruiser became a troop ship and the means to ferry the burgeoning detainee population. At about 6am on 2 July 1940, the *Arandora Star* was only a day out of port when it was torpedoed by a U-boat—and with it 865 lives. A British newspaper reported that *only one torpedo was fired, but it must have ripped the ship open, as she began to settle very rapidly,* and went on to describe the desperate scramble of passengers onto lifeboats. The German High Command exploited the sinking with a communiqué using language that dehumanised the enemy while overlooking the fact that many of their nationals were on board.

The survivors presented a pathetic sight. Some of them were clad only in pyjamas, while others were wearing only thin singlets and trousers. Others had oddly assorted garments, many of which had been supplied by the crew of the rescuing warship. A large number were barefooted.

When Olga received the news, she was in hospital, just a few days before the birth of Monica. Then Monica was born and she was told that her new baby had Down Syndrome. Olga now thought she was a single mother with a disabled child.

It was alarming news, but neither proved to be true. Her father had in fact, not been on the *Arandora Star*, and Monica was a normal, healthy baby.

In 1949, Monica was aged nine when her family sailed by ship to Adelaide. In her childish world view, she imagined they'd be living among kangaroos and she'd ride to school on a horse. Instead, when they arrived at their shared rented house, they found they were in an industrial area with dense traffic. There were definitely no kangaroos.

Monica was a motivated student and wanted to be at the top of the class, but one day when she was walking past a classroom she overheard a couple of teachers talking. They mentioned her name, and then her IQ results. "They weren't very good," she says. "Ever since I thought I was stupid. I thought I was really not very bright." It might have been discouraging, but instead it spurred her to try harder. "I tried to show myself ever since that perhaps I am brighter than my IQ." Despite being "not very bright", she was top of the class. Then at university, she studied physics and applied mathematics, which apparently "wasn't very difficult".

"I was the only female in my class in 1960, but I never felt I was any different to anyone else," she says. Later, she'd encounter a similar situation at the Electricity Trust of South Australia (ETSA), when people would ask her, "Are you a receptionist?"

In researching *Fragile Planet*, I'd developed a method where we'd record two interviews for each chapter. The first would be a general chat about the person's background to establish a sense of their character and their history. In the second, we'd focus on their stories.

At the end of my first interview with Monica Oliphant, I explained that our readers would want to hear the anecdotes, the quirky people, and the struggles they faced. We didn't want long, dry technical dissertations on how solar panels or the electricity grid operates.

The universal human story is adversity, and how we overcome. Monica listened intently, and when we met a couple of days later, she clearly had been thinking it over. She started to launch into a story, but I deflected her so we could clear up some other questions. With that done, she started again. "I just wanted to say …" but she hesitated and her voice began to waver. "My parents were Jewish and that coloured things for me. It's funny … I can't … I find it hard to say … that's why I don't tell people." She began to weep, and I realised she was telling me what happened to her parents' families during the Nazi holocaust.

Her parents had escaped, but her father's brother died in Auschwitz. Her mother's sister and brother both got out. Medical experiments were performed on Monica's mother, but she died of multiple sclerosis soon after she got out.

Her uncles escaped on a boat to Israel, but it wasn't allowed to land, so instead it sailed to Cyprus. Meanwhile, her cousin, grandparents, and her mother's older sister were in a Budapest ghetto. Each day they took more people to the concentration camps, but then the war ended. They were some of the lucky ones to escape the gas chambers.

The experience left a deep mark and she says, "It made me think that wars are pretty awful." It also changed her attitude toward religion. "I'm not Jewish really. I'm just anti-religion because it creates so many problems." Her mother didn't want her to be Jewish because she didn't want Monica to have problems like she'd had, but she did suggest that her daughter go to religious instruction in the Church of England. Monica did, until one of the priests said, "All Jews are clots." So she left and never went back.

Monica says her mother wanted to be a doctor. "She would have been really good." But in Hungary, Jewish people, and especially girls, weren't allowed to go to university. Instead, she worked with her parents in their business making cucumber and tomato preserves.

Monica's description of the plight of her Jewish relatives was brief but harrowing. Then, without pausing, she went on to talk about her early career as a research scientist. Her first job was at the Weapons Research Establishment, where she got a job in the newly formed Laser Lab. It was exciting times after the first laser had just been built by the Hughes Research Laboratories.

Today you can buy a cheap compact laser over the internet, but in the early 1960s they were hand-built. These were highly specialised devices, and big enough to fill an entire room. Using Dr Gordon Troup's design, they constructed what was probably the first laser in Australia. It was such a new idea that constructing such a device had to be done from first principles and there were no Ikea instruction manuals. It took Monica, her supervisor Dr Fred Thonemann, and a technician months to get it working.

Monica gave me a somewhat technical description of how they did it:

We made the laser from scratch using a ruby rod about 6 inches long that had been donated by another lab. We made our own polished elliptical cavity with the ruby rod at one focus and a Xenon flash lamp at the other. Then external Fabry Perot mirrors with multi-layer dielectric mirrors were made, tuned to 694.3 nanometres (dark red) to let laser light out, and a nearby screen to see whether the system was in fact lasing. Then, of course, there were the capacitor banks and electronics to discharge high voltage pulses into the flash tube. (This was quite a long time ago—about 56 years so my memory is a bit hazy).

The core was a ruby rod about 10 centimetres long in a polished cavity with mirrors at the end. Punching the light out required an enormous current that was well beyond what was available from mains power. That meant they needed a very large condenser (now called a "capacitor"), which would accumulate charge that could be released in an instant. Charging the condenser was like inflating an enormous balloon, taking a lot of huffing and blowing, and releasing it with a bang.

And bang it did. The first time they powered it up, the electronics hummed while it built up energy. Monica hid behind equipment when her colleague hit the button, but the laser didn't fire. So they waited for it to cool down and recharge. They tried again, and this time it went off with a tremendous noise. "I remember being very excited when a small spot of red light showed up on the screen and rushing off to tell my boss," she says.

While Monica was investigating lasers, her husband Michael was working in the Weapons Research Establishment computing labs that had emerged during the Cold War. It was interesting and challenging, but they really wanted to return to England to advance their research careers. After a short search, Michael found a job at Ferranti Computer Systems, and Monica picked work where she could continue her research into lasers. With the amount of hardware now orbiting the Earth, tracking satellites with lasers was becoming increasingly important. Her work was more esoteric, even by her standards—plasma diagnostics and Thomson scattering of laser beams off electrons.[54]

The work kept them busy, and by nights they both began master's degrees. Then after a couple of months, Monica found she was pregnant with their first child Katherine. Five years later, the time

---

54   That's also obscure to me as science writer. Even after reading the Wikipedia entry, I'm not sure what "Thompson scattering" is.

had come to return to Australia and show off their child to their grandparents. It felt good to be home, but it wasn't long after that Michael's health declined. He'd always suffered ulcerative colitis, and now it flared up again. The disease causes inflammation of the large intestine and probably triggered his cancer. By the time it was discovered, it had become malignant. It was tough and they were both finishing writing their master's theses, Michael was struggling with cancer, and Monica was again pregnant.

In 1971, they knew he was dying, but he hadn't completed his degree. Even with the cancer, he'd managed to write his thesis, but they didn't think he'd live long enough to be awarded his master's. Monica sent a letter to their supervisor, Dr Houldin, to ask if it could be accelerated. It gave Michael great pleasure when Dr Houldin agreed. He died soon after, aged 35.

Ten weeks later, Monica gave birth to their second daughter Michele. Now she was a single mother with two young girls and living in Melbourne with a mortgage while coping with Michael's death. For a while, she worked part-time marking maths papers. It helped pay the bills, but it left the question of what to do with her career. She felt she was done with lasers, so the question loomed until the oil crises of the early 1970s tipped the world into recession.

Monica sold her house in Melbourne and moved to Adelaide, where she picked up a part-time job at Adelaide University, again working on lasers. That gave her time to begin applying for other jobs. She was still a single mother, and in the early 1970s, childcare was difficult to find. On one occasion she went to an interview with her young daughter in tow. There were no toilet facilities and Monica was horrified to discover her daughter left a puddle on the floor.

Looking back on that time, Monica says with a hint of guilt that she probably would not have achieved what she has today if Michael's illness had not struck. Being thrown onto her own resources motivated her to push her career.

Then, in early 1973, there was a moment that would change the course of her life. It was one of those curious blends of the profound and the mundane, looking out the kitchen window while washing the dishes and listening to the radio. The world's economic and political environment was being rocked by events in the Middle East triggered by the oil crisis. McFarlane Burnett was saying that if the world relied on solar energy instead of oil, there'd be no war. As she wiped food scraps off the dinner plates, she made a life-changing decision. It was a bold decision, because back then solar energy was little more than a niche technology that had barely made it out of the labs.

The oil crisis began when the OPEC oil cartel imposed an embargo in response to United States' support for Israel during the Yom Kippur War. By October 1973, the price of oil was US$3 per barrel, and by March 1974, most countries were paying nearly $12 globally. It shook global economies and political leaders into realising that oil is a Jesus Bolt,[55] because if supply was cut off, civilisation would literally choke.

When it happened again in 1979, I remember long queues at the petrol station when fuel was rationed to odd/even days. That was bad, but the worst-case scenario is frightening. In NSW alone, there are 14 million cases delivered each week through 25,000 truck trips to retail outlets. If Australia's supply was cut off, shops would be running out within three to four days.

It was the trigger that set Monica on the renewable energy path—a brave decision because her background was in physics and lasers rather than renewable energy. Still, as she told her story, she seemed unfazed. Perhaps it shouldn't be surprising given that she'd already launched into the exclusively male domain of physics.

It was also a brave move because at that time renewable energy

---

55   The Jesus Bolt gets its name from the last words uttered by a pilot when they notice that one critical bolt is loose.

was very much on the fringe. The emerging technologies were still a long way from competing with fossil fuels on cost and reliability. Solar PV cells were extremely inefficient and expensive, and only used in niche applications such as satellites. The best wind turbines were the small but reliable Dunlite machines, used mostly on farms. They produced a tiny amount of power compared to the systems used today. In Monica's home state of South Australia, there wasn't a single turbine feeding into the grid.

Sir Mark

When Monica met Michael she was immediately aware of his father, not just because of their developing relationship, but because Sir Mark Oliphant was already a famous figure. *The Bulletin* magazine ran a story with a picture of him on the front and titled "White Oliphant". He had a reputation for being outspoken, and when she met him for the first time, she was nervous. She needn't have worried, because he gave her a warm welcome. "He was always very kind to me. He took us to the shops to help us buy an engagement ring."

No doubt he was also charmed and intrigued by the physicist who'd been the only woman in her university honours course. A 1960 photo shows a pretty, young Monica with Michael, and Sir Mark with his characteristic shock of white hair.

Monica had been described to me as a formidable person, a trait he probably noticed. Another *Fragile Planet* character, Leonard Cohen had encountered this while they were working on a project together, and he says he had made remarks that she then politely and surgically demolished. In his colourful way, Leonard says she's "a battleship disguised as a tugboat", conceding that he was outclassed. He had, as we say, been hit with a velvet brick.

Having a famous father-in-law might have caused her to retreat, but instead her reaction was the same as when she'd overheard her teacher saying she had an average IQ. It was a spur that she says, "Made me strive to do something of my own life so people wouldn't just say I was an Oliphant."

Sir Mark had started his career in 1927 at the great Cavendish Laboratory with Sir Ernest Rutherford, unpicking the structure of the atom.

As World War II grew desperate, the British became concerned that they should build the bomb before the Germans did. The US had been providing substantial support, but the Japanese attack on Pearl Harbour was still some months away, and they were not formally at war. Oliphant was a member of the MAUD committee, which had been looking at the possibility of an atomic weapon, and in August 1941 he was sent to convince the Americans that they should make it an urgent priority.

When he arrived in the US, Oliphant's first encounter was with an American bureaucrat who he later described as an "inarticulate and unimpressive man". He did what bureaucrats do best: filing the papers and burying the proposal in process. Oliphant had more success when he met Samuel Allison, who later said, "Oliphant came to a meeting and said 'bomb' in no uncertain terms. He told us we must concentrate every effort on the bomb, and said we had no right to work on power plants or anything but the bomb."

At this point, the bomb was only a theoretical possibility, and Oliphant and his colleagues might not have appreciated what it would really mean until it was used to obliterate the cities of Hiroshima and Nagasaki. When they did see it, they were horrified. Oliphant said it was the army and the politicians who'd asked for it, but it was the scientists who delivered it, and they felt responsible. Monica says, "They wanted to get there before Hitler did, but later they realised what this thing actually meant."

The ensuing nuclear arms race alarmed many scientists internationally, and in 1957 Oliphant joined them in founding the

Pugwash peace movement. Years later, one observer[56] commented, "As a South Australian, I had the privilege of hearing Mark speak and can confirm his 'belligerent pacifism'. For a time he was the governor of our state, but even in this official capacity as the Queen's representative in our state, he eloquently and passionately argued for environmental issues, and vehemently campaigned against nuclear weapons."

To many Australians, the name Oliphant is fading, but in South Australia it is prominent. There's an Oliphant Avenue in Adelaide, Mark Oliphant Conservation Park, and Mount Oliphant in Arkaroola. He was knighted in 1959, and was governor of South Australia from 1971 to 1976.

In later years, he'd visit his wife Rosa in the nursing home each day, and sit by her bedside holding her hand and reading. Monica says, "In her final years, Mark was a wonderful companion to her. He said that for over 60 years she had looked after him and now it was his turn to look after her—and he did." She died in 1987.

The Right to Die

Mark Oliphant was known for being outspoken, and as he aged, a topic that weighed on him was euthanasia. In an interview he told Ellen Fanning:

> The realisation by the old that they're losing their marbles, as it were, and that they forget, and do silly things. It's time then for the active man—for the active man or the woman who has led an active life—to be assisted to die. It's foremost in my mind now.

56   Darren Holden, "How an Australian scientist tried to stop the US plan to monopolise the nuclear arms race", *The Conversation*, 15 May 2018, www.theconversation.com/how-an-australian-scientist-tried-to-stop-the-us-plan-to-monopolise-the-nuclear-arms-race-96539

I realise my days are numbered and I do not want to go into a home and just be one of those being looked after and kept alive unnecessarily.

He could also be provocative:

Oliphant: There's a great scientist that I know in Cambridge who should be dead and he's not—he just loves to be alive. He's just a nuisance to all his friends and relatives.
Fanning: And that's his right too, isn't it?
Oliphant: No I don't think he is … he's cluttering up the world and he should not.

Monica also recalls his attitude, saying, "My father-in-law said he would do the same thing, but he gradually faded away as he approached his late nineties. He couldn't do it because he didn't know he was in that condition. He wouldn't have liked what was happening to him." He died a few months before his 99th birthday.

It was the same question that confronted Monica and her mother who was in her late eighties when she developed cancer, and as it began to spread, she was forced into surgery. As the pain became intolerable she was taking stronger doses of morphine, and she knew it was only a matter of time before she'd have to leave her home. Monica remembers that she was an independent person who did not want to go into a nursing home.

I could see the memories were still difficult for Monica. She paused then added, "That would have been terrible for her."

When it was clear she wasn't going to get better, she bought a copy of *Final Exit: The Practicalities of Self-Deliverance and Assisted Suicide for the Dying*. The book by Derek Humphry, which catalogues ways to commit suicide, remains controversial and has been banned in France. Olga read about the ways to end her life.

Her first thought was to gas herself in her car, and she asked Monica to go out and buy some tubing.

Understandably, Monica said she couldn't, so Olga went out and bought some herself. She tried, but her hands were too weak to attach the hose to the exhaust.

If Monica was concerned before, now she became alarmed and would ring her mother every day to see if she was okay. When her mother didn't answer, she raced to her house. Monica found her mother sitting in a chair, still breathing. She'd left a note saying she'd taken a large vodka and a large dose of morphine used for pain relief. The note said that she should be allowed to die. But the ambulance came and they resuscitated her. "She was not very happy about that," Monica recalls with obvious pain.

About a month later it happened again. In the end, it took three attempts and though it was a painful episode, it was a final release. "Her quality of life was pretty bad and she wanted to go," Monica says. "My mother took control of her own life by committing suicide." It firmed Monica's own attitude to euthanasia, that it should be a personal choice. "When the time comes I would like to be able to be in control when I go. If you don't own your own life, then what do you own?"

It was a deeply distressing time for Monica. Her family had moved away and she was left on her own. Looking back, she recalls, "My behaviour was quite strange." To compensate, she threw herself into her work on solar energy.

The Renewable Journey
McFarlane Burnett could not have known that a few simple words[57] in the early 1970s would be the inspiration that launched Monica

---

57   Andrew Blakers was also inspired by the idea that no country would go to war over solar energy.

Oliphant's 40-year journey into renewable energy. A small ripple travels further than we can imagine.

Though Monica's father-in-law had loomed taller than any wind turbine and been a proponent of nuclear energy, she never considered going into the field herself. She'd enjoyed a short course on the subject in her honours year, but there were no opportunities in Adelaide so she gave it no further thought.

In any event, Sir Mark's view on nuclear power changed. Initially, he'd been in favour of its use for peaceful purposes, but later he said, "I suddenly realised that anybody who has a nuclear reactor can extract the plutonium from the reactor ... and I, right from the beginning, have been terribly worried by the existence of nuclear weapons and very much against their use."[58] He then became an advocate of solar energy.

Monica decided she wanted to devote herself to renewable energy, but realised how little she knew. She needed to learn fast and began buying every book she could find on solar energy and applying for research positions. At the time, solar PV was expensive and inefficient, so her first work was with solar hot water and concentrating solar systems.

Solar hot water is a simple idea, but the sun beams down at only about a kilowatt on a square metre. To really crank it up, a concentrating solar system focuses sunlight onto a small patch.[59] For a while, she worked in the emerging field of concentrated solar thermal heating.

Ironically, researchers found it difficult to source funding for solar research because the Middle East crisis had passed and oil prices dropped, leaving renewable energy uncompetitive. Since

---

58 Moyal, Ann, *Portraits in Science*, National Library of Australia, 1994, p. 31
59 There's a lot of energy in sunlight. At school we used to fry ants and burn our initials into timber fences with a magnifying glass, which meant we were getting temperatures of over 230°C.

then, the economics have changed, and electricity from renewable sources is cheaper than fossil fuels, but for transport oil still dominates. Renewables have had to meet the hurdles of an emerging technology as it builds maturity and economies of scale.

As the price of oil returned to normal, money for research was tight at Flinders, and so Monica moved on in 1981 to join the then vertically integrated Electricity Trust of South Australia. It kept her employed, but she was about to learn what life in a bureaucracy can be like. At university, she'd been accustomed to just asking someone if she needed information, but in the bureaucracy everything has a process and there's a hierarchy. That, she says, got her into "big trouble".

Still, that did not slow her down. Later she told the *Guardian*, "I reckon I was the employee from hell, but I wanted to do these things and if it wasn't in the work plan, I would say, 'maybe I can get funding'. I would do what I wanted, and they let me. Then I would get funding, so they couldn't stop me. They thought it was easier to let me go and I probably wouldn't do much harm."

She'd been told to keep a watching brief on new developments in renewable energy, but got bored with that, so she wrote a report showing the areas where she thought renewable energy would work first. Her report showed, unsurprisingly, that a good start would be in off-grid locations that were receiving large diesel subsidies. She did that on her own initiative, but when she showed it to her boss, he said, "Why are you doing that? Are you trying to take my job?"

Then Monica added wryly, "… and he never read the report!"

That was a clue that her job in this part of ETSA was leading nowhere, so she transferred to another department where she could turn her attention to energy efficiency.

Solar panels and wind turbines are the sexier part of the story, so it's easy to overlook the other side of the equation: demand. Just on its own, population growth has meant we need 1-2% more energy every year, and a huge amount is wasted every day in leaky buildings and inefficient appliances.

In a single year, Australia uses about 4,075 petajoules of energy.[60] It's hard to grasp that sort of number other than it's stupendously large. What it means, however, is that it's an opportunity because saving even a few percent is a lot of energy.

Monica would travel around South Australia, looking at ways to improve the efficiency of houses. Then, for someone whose work had been technically oriented, she took an unusual step when she realised that human aspects are at least as important. There's no point buying energy-efficient appliances if the residents crank their heating up to tropical levels and don't bother switching off lights. She sought help from a social psychologist who suggested that householders would be more sensitive to their energy use if they were getting feedback on their consumption. That gave her the idea to install displays showing how much electricity a house was using at any given moment.

She continued with this theme in the early 1990s with the South Australian Housing Trust, where she found other people also eager to find ways to help tenants. They knew that energy efficiency and education could help make houses more affordable and liveable for low-income families, but the question was how? To fill the gaps, Monica led a study that looked at things as simple as how roof colour affects a house. They monitored what happened when householders installed rooftop solar systems.

Her approach was ahead of the times because back then the residential sector was regarded as too diverse and small to be looked at. Monitoring household energy use became mainstreamed shortly afterward.

In the early 1990s, solar hot water systems were appearing on

---

60   "Energy consumption", Department of Industry, Science, Energy and Re-
      sources, https://www.energy.gov.au/data/energy-consumption.

houses, but Monica soon learned they had a serious opponent: gas. The gas companies were in a hurry to sign up new customers, especially in new housing developments where they'd invested a lot of money in new pipelines and needed to recoup their costs. Lines were laid along miles of residential streets, and it would be a lot cheaper to connect houses while their work crews were already in a suburb. By 2017 there'd be 37,000 kilometres of natural gas pipelines across the nation. In the new housing developments, they were offering builders free gas water heaters and cookers if they connected a new house to the mains. It was a "loss leader" that would grab customers who'd stay connected long after the gas was installed. Even today it costs money to be taken off the grid.

Seeing this, Monica says she became "anti-natural gas", and even had a bit of a vendetta against it. An all-electric home with solar panels should be cheaper to run and have lower emissions. Free appliances and cheap supplies offered by the gas companies drew in many customers, stifling competition and squeezing out solar systems. The irony is that by 2016 Australia would be selling its gas reserves on the international market, and prices began to escalate to the point where it's now expensive.

Although gas is cleaner than coal, it still generates CO_2 while the need to reduce emissions grows ever more urgent. And it's not just the products of combustion, because gas networks leak, especially around the old cast iron pipe, and methane is a much more potent greenhouse gas.

Many years later Monica laments that, despite the fact that renewable technologies have proven themselves, there are conservative politicians who resent anything that looks like government meddling in the economy and the response to climate change has been hijacked by people who treat the science as if it were a socialist plot. In spite of them, renewables are now becoming cheaper than fossil fuels. Still, if that's how people think, then the pragmatic might be to shift the debate away from the science and focus on how climate change is already affecting the economy.

If technology can be difficult, people can be perplexing, and Monica had an air of frustration as we talked about how the grid had failed in South Australia. She was dismayed, she said, by claims that the blackouts were caused by unreliable wind farms. It was ludicrous, blatant distortion when the problems were actually caused by poor management.

"I don't understand the misinformation about wind and solar. Why do these people cling to belief when overwhelming evidence shows that global warming is occurring due to human influence?"

Like me, she's struck by the emergence of Donald Trump, saying, "I'm really struggling with how to deal with fake news." How do we deal with a person whose rules of engagement revolves around winners and losers rather than evidence?

A clue perhaps is in Anna Rose's book *Madlands*, where the author tries to get behind the logic of climate change denialist Nick Minchin, who, it's said, "considered the issue a plot by the 'extreme left' to 'deindustrialise the world.'"[61] It's a telling comment because it's all about ideology and nothing about science.

Monica is especially disappointed with how her South Australia has been treated in spite of its renewable energy leadership.

"If we had bipartisan political support—especially federally—on energy issues and there was pride in what is happening in South Australia, and a willingness to help make us world best practice instead of putting us down—that would be a great accomplishment."

"What is gratifying, however, is that since the recent change in government from Labor to Liberal in SA, the trend toward a reliable

---

61   Graham Readfearn, "United states of denial: forces behind Trump have run Australia's climate policy for years", *The Guardian*, 15 December 2016, www.theguardian.com/environment/planet-oz/2016/dec/16/united-states-of-denial-forces-behind-trump-have-run-australias-climate-policy-for-years.

and cost-effective electricity grid with high-penetration variable renewables is continuing."

In 2015 and 2016, the last two coal power stations closed in South Australia, which, in 2017, was generating 45% of its electricity from wind turbines. Meanwhile, electricity prices have been climbing steadily, giving the opportunity for the anti-renewable lobby to claim that renewable energy was to blame. It's an unfortunate muddle that was proven untrue by analysis showing prices has more to do with gas and not much to do wind power.[62]

When I met Monica, she was about to travel to Darwin to visit her family, and then on to Sweden where she was to address an international conference on renewable energy. Though not far off 80 years old, she still has a lot of stamina. Rather than slowing down, she's cramming in her overseas trips while she can.

I saw a glimpse of her energy during one of our conversations when she leapt to her feet, saying, "Have a look at these slides." She flicked on her computer to show me graphs depicting gas and electricity prices in South Australia. The slides were showing how gas prices were around $5,[63] and then some months later it was $20. The cause? Australia is now selling much of its gas on the volatile international market.

She described how, on a winter's day in July 2016, wind speeds were low in South Australia, and while the grid connection to Victoria was down for maintenance, electricity supply was under stress. Meanwhile, in reserve, the Pelican Point gas plant was on hand. It could've been started, except that with high gas prices the electricity company decided to leave it offline. With a shortage of supply, the electricity spot price shot up. It was a good day for the electricity company, which made a killing while the gas generator sat idle.

---

62   Hugh Saddler, reported by Peter Martin, 13 July 2017.
63   Price per gigajoule.

That day wasn't an isolated event. Monica's other slides show a regular heartbeat of prices dancing between $50 and over $10,000. At one moment, the generators would bid electricity supply at $50 a megawatt-hour. Five minutes later, they'd withdraw supply to artificially create a shortage.

Then they'd rebid at $10,000 a megawatt-hour. Then, for the next few hours, prices oscillated wildly, peaking up to $14,000. A nice little earner, as they say, and by the time it'd settled, they'd earned a tidy $178 million.

Even though, strictly speaking, the company hadn't broken any rules, their behaviour attracted attention, triggering a review by the market regulator. Meanwhile, consumers are left wondering why electricity is expensive.

Still, it's not all bad news, and even with a change of government, South Australia is now being hailed as a world leader on the path to renewable energy.[64] They have a thermal solar energy plant under construction at Port Augusta, and the so-called lithium "Big Battery" helping to stabilise the grid.

Looking Back

In the late 1990s, the owners of the Wilpena Pound tourist resort in the Flinders Ranges needed a reliable power supply, but they were miles from the nearest grid. An obvious answer was solar power, which would greatly reduce the high cost of transporting fuel. The question then was, who could advise on such a solution? Back then, solar electricity was still an immature technology and few people had any expertise. Luckily they were able to find Monica, who was keen to work with the team at ETSA.

---

64   Giles Parkinson, "Why South Australia energy transition is seen as model of success around the world", *Renew Economy*, 5 December 2018, www.reneweconomy.com.au/why-south-australia-energy-transition-is-seen-as-model-of-success-around-the-world-83079/.

To back up the solar panels, they'd need an auxiliary diesel generator because batteries of the day weren't viable. The problem then was where to install them within the fragile landscape? Wilpena Pound is nestled in the ancient, arid Flinders Ranges and holds many precious Aboriginal heritage sites. After a bit of work, they found a suitable location and the work could proceed. By today's standards, 100 kilowatts is tiny, but then it was the largest solar/diesel generator in the southern hemisphere.

Monica has warm memories of the occasion, saying, "It was one of the big things in my career, to go around with an Aboriginal elder. He showed me the campsites and burial grounds. He didn't want the plant to be seen from various peaks. He tried really hard to find a good site for us."

In later years, Monica has been recognised with the highest awards. She was named Senior South Australian of the Year 2016, granted an honorary doctorate, and in June 2015 she was given an Office of the Order of Australia. Her citation reads: *For distinguished service to the renewable energy sector as a research scientist, particularly through pioneering roles in solar photovoltaics and power generation …*

She says winning the Order of Australia was joyful, but even more joyful was becoming president of the International Solar Energy Association in 2008.

Now Doctor Monica Oliphant has been well recognised for her success, but how, I asked, did her technical skills combine with her ability to engage people?

The tone of her reply didn't surprise me. "I'm not trying to be modest, but I'd say I'm not particularly good at either."

"Just a belief of what should happen, and keep plucking away at that."

A Question of Hope
Dr Siwan Lovett

"You can pick up the pieces," he said.

At first, Siwan Lovett couldn't figure out what that meant. Then as he addressed the environment seminar, it became clear. Humans have launched the planet into a new geological epoch, with devastating consequences. Climate change is fundamentally disrupting the Earth system. Food, water and sea levels, among other things, are out of kilter.

A pall of gloom fell over the audience. Siwan was the next speaker. What do you tell people at a time like this? What does it mean to have hope?

It reminded me of the blockbuster tagline: Catastrophe is looming, and only one man can save us.

By my own perverse logic, this tired *One Man* cliché encapsulates two of the most important things I've learned about Dr Siwan Lovett. The tagline on countless books and movies, usually from the US, is the inverse of Siwan. She's definitely feminine and she does not work alone. She says we have the environment and we have science, but it's nothing without people. It's *people* who have damaged the environment and it's *people* who must repair it.

Luckily she also has a sense of humour because when I told her this was how I'd open her chapter, she gave a hearty laugh. "That's not true, no way! No way, it's the network! You need other people to feel that they've got a gift, something to give."

Siwan[65] remembers the environmental awareness in her family and their strong connection to the land. Her mother grew up on a farm in Wales and met her father when he moved to Bangor to study agriculture, a course in which she was also enrolled. After finishing their degrees in Australia, they were drawn to research and teaching roles at the University of New England. Her mother researched blue-green algae before becoming a science teacher, and later a public servant. Her father worked in both the university and private sector including the Grains Research and Development Corporation.

At home, Siwan's family would have lively conversations. "You're green, Mum," she'd say, "but Dad, your workplace could be a bit less brown and a bit more green." Later, she came to appreciate that it's hard for people to think "green" while they are "in the red". Over time their property in Murrumbateman was becoming increasingly covered in trees and areas were fenced off to protect shelterbelts and swampy meadows.

Siwan's path toward river restoration was more a series of chances rather than something she'd planned. In the 1980s, boys were encouraged to study science and maths, but girls were not. She thrived at the Presbyterian Ladies College in Armidale, where girls were given a strong, rounded education. It was helped by the fact that her mother was head of the science department, and Siwan remembers she "would make it really alive and entertaining". Even then she didn't head toward a science career. After leaving school, she worked as a horse groom, takeaway waitress, and secretary in an engineering firm. It was, she says, a lot of fun, but after 18

---

65   In welsh 'Si' is 'Sh', so Siwan is pronounced Shuwan.

months she needed to move on so she enrolled at university where she majored in sociology and organisation theory.

For her honours thesis, she wanted to study AIDS, but there were ethical issues and the hospital refused access because of the complications of being around wards where there were blood products. Instead, she went to Plan B, which was to write about how R&D is done in Australia.

It didn't take long after graduating for Siwan to show her interest in people, which meant delving straight into some of the more troubled parts of society. It began with two years in the Tasmanian prison system and mental health institutions that cared for people with a range of disabilities. These experiences, she says, exposed her to the realities of life for some of the most vulnerable people. It was tough but rewarding work. Then she saw an opportunity to study for a PhD at the Australian National University where she could combine her interests in organisational change and rural R&D. She was fascinated by the idea that a few key people can change an organisation by being in the right place at the right time. This, Siwan says, taught her about the power people she describes as "tuned-in".

I got to know Siwan because somehow I'd signed up for a newsletter from the Australian River Restoration Centre (ARRC). Like most people who get a lot of this stuff, my usual response was either to delete the emails or move them to Spam. But for some reason, I started to read them and was enjoying the short, pithy articles. They had an optimistic tone, describing work that was being done to restore degraded waterways. Sometimes they were humorous, like this one: "... research undertaken in the United Kingdom that shows, somewhat horrifyingly, that cattle defecate (poo) five times more when standing in the river than out on land (ewwww)!"

Siwan and the ARRC team host site visits to rural properties where they can demonstrate how they work with landowners to protect and restore waterways for economic and environmental benefits. One damp day I travelled about an hour north from Canberra to a small farming town called Breadalbane. In the community hall, there were about 30 people, mostly local farmers, who were keen to talk about restoring watercourses on their properties. The surrounding countryside is like much of Australia, with vast tracts of lightly treed paddock. Running through many of them are the ugly scars where water has ripped away the topsoil, leaving deeply eroded gullies. It's unsightly, but to the farmers this damaged land also represents lost income. On a later trip, I would meet Margie, who owns a property on the north edge of Lake George, and she described how landowners feel more than just the economic cost when they see their land degraded. Being part of the country is central to their life and seeing gouges dug across their land affects them personally.

Breadalbane wetlands. Siwan is on the left side, looking toward the right (photo by Rod Taylor).

We huddled out of the rain in the small Breadalbane community hall to hear a range of speakers. Wally Bell is a local Aboriginal man who gave us a ceremony they call Welcome to Country. He told us how his people don't think of land as something that is "owned". Instead, they see themselves and the land as deeply entwined, each belonging to the other. We should be "custodians", he said. We live for a short time, but the land is forever. One day, maybe, we'll stop thinking that land is nothing more than a commodity to be bought and sold, and begin to recognise that without land we have nothing. We can only hope.

Then we met a researcher who studies the complicated migration of birds across eastern Australia. She showed us the tracks followed by the birds. They looked a bit haphazard, but there was definitely a logic to how the birds sought out their next feeding site. That birds can do this over great distances shows how remarkably adapted they are to Australia's highly variable climate.

About half[66] of Australia's land area is used by agriculture, which is a stupendous figure when you consider the amount of land that is desert. It means, of course, that the way land is managed makes a huge difference to the survival not just of birds, but of most of our fauna and flora.

The Breadalbane event reminded me of the "and only one man" quote because I was seeing an example of what happens when people cooperate. Great things become possible theatre far beyond what the lone hero can do. We—and especially Hollywood culture—celebrate the lone hero, but it's people like Siwan and her team that bring together a group of people with a common cause. Each of those people then carries the ideas into their communities, which becomes a widening circle of change.

Siwan started the day with a short talk, then, after introducing the speakers, stepped aside. She'd watch them attentively, with a

---

66   "Australia – Agricultural Land (% Of Land Area)", *Trading Economics*, www.tradingeconomics.com/australia/agricultural-land-percent-of-land-area-wb-data.html

half-grin and a subtle nodding gesture. For her, it was less about being the centre of attention and more about seeing the energy that other people could contribute—not just the other speakers, but the people who'd travelled to see them.

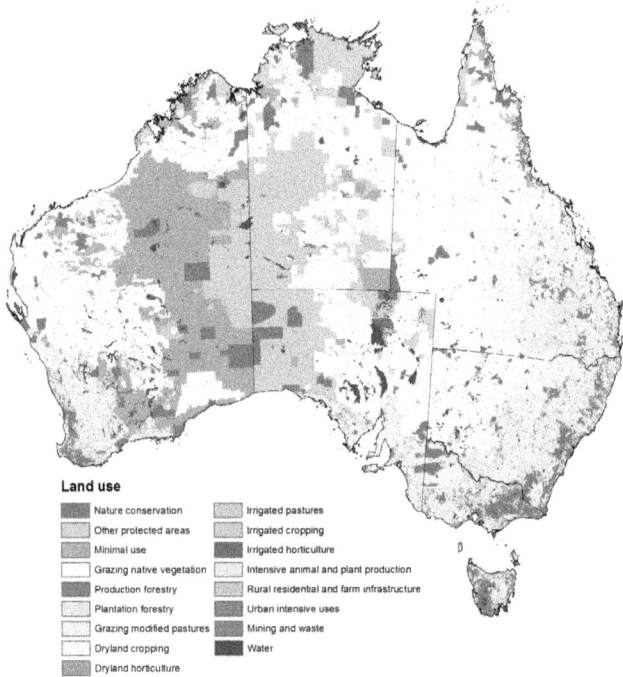

Land use

Nature conservation	Irrigated pastures
Other protected areas	Irrigated cropping
Minimal use	Irrigated horticulture
Grazing native vegetation	Intensive animal and plant production
Production forestry	Rural residential and farm infrastructure
Plantation forestry	Urban intensive uses
Grazing modified pastures	Mining and waste
Dryland cropping	Water
Dryland horticulture	

National scale land use 2010-11.[67]

Siwan's parents had both had careers that were connected to land management, but it was not something she'd ever seriously considered. Her PhD was based in social science, and during her research she'd interviewed Dr Phil Price, an executive with the Land and Water Resources R&D Corporation. When a position came up at Land and Water Australia, Dr Price called her to suggest she apply. Why would he do that? It seemed strange, she says. "I was a social researcher. I didn't know anything about water!"

---

67   "Land Use", Department of Agriculture, www.agriculture.gov.au/abares/ aclump/land-use.

It was a calculated move because Dr Price could see it wasn't the science that was lacking—it was the people. Looking after the land must be guided by science, but it's futile if it's not used. All the knowledge gained is useless while it remains hidden in the minds of boffins and fusty journals that are only read by academics. Phil Price knew he needed someone like Siwan to connect science with the people who could make it real.

Siwan soon found she'd hit a steep learning curve, and not just because she hadn't studied the science. She was just 30 at the time and was working with men who were ten years older. These were men who'd spent years doing science and were eminent in their field. Or sceptical farmers who knew what it meant to make a living from the land and could spot ignorance from 50 paces. At least her "Dr" title meant they'd take her seriously, but what they didn't know was that her doctorate was in social science, not water. That might be enough to get the conversation started, but still it wasn't always easy. "I felt like an impostor," she says.

It was a difficult start, but over time the balance shifted. Her confidence grew as it became clearer that her skills complemented the science so that now she could say, "I thought you [the scientist] might say that, but it's not resonating over here." She no longer feels the need to justify her role of "being an undercover social scientist". Seeing the landowners and scientists coming together at Breadalbane was evidence of that.

Blue Green

Siwan's mother was researching blue-green algae before it became a big problem and, like so many scientists, the next funding grant was always hard to find. It's a universal problem for scientists whose work hangs on funding and they typically spent a large portion of their time just writing the next grant application. The research money ran dry and Siwan's mother became a science teacher, which is unfortunate because blue-green algae has become a serious problem. It's not uncommon for people in Canberra to find their urban lakes are closed due to algal blooms. During summers it can affect long stretches of the Murray and other rivers.

Being around an algal bloom is not a pleasant experience. The water turns a sickly green, which is where the name Cyanobacteria comes from and why it is commonly called blue-green algae. It is actually a bacteria rather than an algae, and it exudes a dank, putrid odour. Birds swimming through it look like they're wading through sludge. There's a long list of reasons why you don't want too much contact with afflicted waters. Toxins from some species can cause liver damage, stomach upsets, nervous system disorders, and skin and eye irritations. It produces a range of toxins and it can kill livestock, wildlife, and pets. I can't say I've tried it, but apparently it doesn't taste good either.

Siwan told me that when she sees an algal bloom, "I always think about being suffocated. I get the feeling that the algae traps in-stream plants and animals so they have nowhere to go, and my reaction is to want to clean up the algae so the river can breathe again."

Even then, algae is part of the natural system and it isn't always out of place because sometimes it drives the food-webs in riverine ecosystems. She says the problem is "when you see the long stretches of stream with no vegetation, warm water, and covered in sticky, cloying algae, you know that the system is out of kilter and that something needs to be done". In that sense, it's a little like the crown-of-thorns starfish on the Great Barrier Reef. They've always been there, but when the ecology is disrupted, their numbers grow out of proportion.

In 2009,[68] a severe outbreak hit large parts of the Murray

---

68 Simon Lauder, "'Potentially toxic' algae bloom threatens Murray-Darling", *ABC News*, 28 March 2009, www.abc.net.au/news/2009-03-28/potentially-toxic-algae-bloom-threatens-murray/1633630.

River from Lake Hume east of Albury-Wodonga to Barham, 600 kilometres away.[69] The bloom started in Lake Hume, which was nearly empty, and from there propagated, downstream. It came during the Millennium Drought that had hit south-eastern Australia. This was the same drought that had driven the Prells to the edge of bankruptcy.

People living downstream were affected, with one resident in western Victoria complaining that "the water that comes out of my hose stinks to high heaven". Having it in your local river is bad enough, but imagine it coming out of your tap. It could be unpleasant, but it also has economic impacts, with towns such as Corowa having to invest in charcoal filters for its water treatment plant.

Cyanobacteria is natural in the environment, but a bloom is the sign of a system out of balance. Decades of agricultural and urban runoff have accumulated in reservoirs and, combined with warmer waters, made outbreaks more common. With so little water flowing down the Murray, the nutrients weren't being flushed, and in 2009, low water levels in Lake Hume exposed those nutrients in the bottom layers to light, and the Cyanobacteria bloomed.

The link to climate change is complex, but blooms are linked with El Niño. Evidence is now showing that as the world warms by 1.5°C, severe events will become twice as common.[70] Researchers are becoming increasingly convinced that global warming is driving an ominous mix of hotter and drier weather.[71] Southwest Australia

---

69   And in January 2019, another. This time parts of the Murray-Darling system have experienced devastating fish kills.

70   "Expert Reaction: Extreme El Niños twice as common in a 1.5C warmer world", *scimex*, 25 July 2017, www.scimex.org/newsfeed/extreme-el-ninos-twice-as-common-with-1.5c-rise-in-global-temperature.

71   "Climate change stealing rain from Australia by shifting winds towards Antarctica", *Canberra Times*, 1 October 2016, quoting ANU researcher Professor Abram.

has lost one-fifth of its rainfall since the 1970s. One expert noted a series of blooms in 2007, 2009, 2010 and 2016, prompting him to write, "Are toxic algal blooms the new normal for Australia's major rivers?"[72]

The Drain and Anxiety

Knowing Siwan's attitude to creeks and rivers, I thought it'd be a good idea to show her a photo from near my home. "I brought you a photo of our creek," I told her before handing over a tablet so she could see it.

"Oh." She laughed and then she frowned, but I was unsure if she was bemused or dismayed.

Did I say "creek"? I fibbed. I should have said "drain"—that's the engineering word for "creek"—or at least it was when this thing was built. According to the engineers who built it, water is a problem that requires perfectly a formed concrete structure to whisk water away as fast as possible. Forty years ago, they cleared the vegetation, straightened the creek, and bulldozed the ponds and obstacles. Now along the edges, we have mown grass while the nearest trees are five metres away. What was a meandering, messy watercourse is now an efficient drain.

In the fully engineered world, trees, people, and water have an assigned place, but Siwan says this leaves us disconnected. "When walking alongside that drain you would feel remote. You wouldn't feel or smell the water. It's not the same connection you'd have if the concrete was removed and there was a mix of mud and birds and fish."

"That drain is about certainty, control, and fear," she said. "It's protecting those things we hold important like cars and houses." We

---

72   Darren Baldwin, "Are toxic algal blooms the new normal for Australia's major rivers?", *The Conversation*, 18 May 2016, www.theconversation.com/are-toxic-algal-blooms-the-new-normal-for-australias-major-rivers-59526.

can't control the creeks, so we turn them into drains. "We don't get the same emotional response being near a drain. When you're on or near water, your shoulders go down and you start to feel connected. You can't connect with concrete." The world is a messy place, she says, and we should learn to accept that. As she speaks, she may also be telling herself because it contradicts her impulses. Earlier she had told me, "I never liked uncertainty. I always like to control things—always like to be in control of my world. So I get anxious when I can't be in control of my world."

There'd been a trauma early in her life, which she didn't want to discuss, but it had contributed to panic attacks for several years. "It's a very lonely existence," she says, "because so much to do with mental health is internal. I have been really successful at work and have a great life, but I still have this worry about something happening. So why do I feel anxious?" Eventually, she went to a psychologist who helped her "to accept things rather than trying to push away feelings".

This was becoming a common story among the people I'd met writing *Fragile Planet*. A few had told me how they suffer from anxiety or depression, which got me wondering if that's normal. One in four Australians will experience anxiety and about one in seven experience depression. Why would the people in the book be any different? It's hard to say, but each of the people I'm writing about has achieved remarkable things. I was mulling this over when I heard a researcher say that often it's the negative emotions that motivate. Maybe success and anxiety are almost necessary companions.

I asked my environmental activist friend, Jenny Goldie, how she deals with the relentless bad news about the state of the planet. She looked glum and admitted she finds it difficult. Yet somehow she copes and soldiers on. She told me about her friend who finds it overwhelming and is diagnosed as clinically depressed.

Learning to accept her fears has been an important step for Siwan. Whether the anxiety is justified or not, the feeling is real. That validation is the starting point for improvement. One year she had a bad episode over Christmas and read a book called *I Had a Black Dog*. "The dog is always by your side. Sometimes it's enormous and other times it is sitting behind you, but it never leaves," she said. She learned to accept that the dog will always be a part of her life. Sometimes large, sometimes small.

Siwan's connection with people has been another key. "The best way to deal with uncertainty is to connect with other people. Surround yourself with people who believe a lot of what you believe. I don't really see the point of going to talk to someone who doesn't want to talk to you."

The feeling of hope is essential, she told me. "I couldn't get up in the morning without hope." It's a difficult problem when calamity looms. How should we respond to news of uncontrolled population growth and global warming? It's a question that weighs heavily and, by chance, it was something I'd arranged to discuss with Clive Hamilton that very afternoon.

In Siwan's case, she was preparing to give a talk about climate change where she and Clive were the first speakers. They chatted for a moment, then Clive told her she "could pick up the pieces".

"That made no sense until he started his talk. The apocalyptic future he mapped out was scary and overwhelming. He presented it clinically and factually and at the end of his 15 minutes, the despair in the room was palpable."

Clive Hamilton is the author of books with ominous titles such as *Requiem for a Species*, and Siwan's description of what happened at his presentation rings true. Clive tweets gloomy lines such as "The great climate silence: we are on the edge of the abyss, but we ignore it."

Clive's latest book, *Defiant Earth: The Fate of Humans in the Anthropocene*, explores the impact that humans have had on the planet. It now seems the effects of global warming will be enough to prevent the next ice age and probably the one after that too. The impact of humans has been deep enough to profoundly disrupt the way the Earth functions. And worse, for the past hundred years humanity has been systematically dismantling the planet's life support systems.

Throughout human history, the Earth has been sufficiently large and robust that the effect of people has been local. The scale of impact has been limited to a geographical area such as a bay or a rainforest. Now that balance has changed and the activities of humans are so large that the functioning of the planet itself has been altered. Until now, humans were actors on an unchanging stage, but with the Anthropocene, the entire stage is no longer stable. The future of humans and the future of the planet have been loosely coupled, but Clive says now the two have become entwined. He uses the term "rupture". It's a violent, unsettling notion.

The significance of the Anthropocene is hard to overstate.[73] Climate scientists are saying that the planet is sliding toward instability, replacing the geological epoch known as the Holocene. For the past 10,000 years, the Earth system has been extraordinarily stable, without the earlier wild swings between cold and hot, wet and dry that were dominant in earlier times. It has allowed humans to flourish and spread across the globe. Almost every human system such as agriculture and industry relies on a reasonably predictable future. Our civilisation has been made possible by the stability of the Holocene.

In *Defiant Earth,* Clive presents another sobering fact. If we could weigh all vertebrates on Earth, humans would account for 30% and domesticated animals 67%. The total mass of all wild animals on Earth is less than 3%.

---

73   Paul Crutzen published significant early work, including: Crutzen, P.J. 2002, "Geology of mankind", *Nature*, No. 415, p. 23.

Paul Crutzen and Paul Stoermer coined the term Anthropocene in 2000, but the idea has been creeping up on us for some time.[74] Take, for example, this description by Nick Middleton in his book *Surviving Extremes*. Greenland, he writes, is "... wild and untamed, a primeval wilderness seemingly untouched by man". If you think about that for a moment, it's jarring that we find it noteworthy that there are still places on the planet not touched by humans. Our domination of the Earth is the new normal.

Clive was describing a disaster for all of humanity, so it's not surprising if he cast a pall of gloom across the auditorium. If the scale of this story is so far beyond the individual, then what then does it mean to have "hope"? Do we just give up because it's futile?

With Siwan's comments that morning fresh in my mind, I tackled Clive about how such dire words would affect people. Would they fall into despair, an ocean of hopelessness? Would people retreat into denial or worse, toxic tribalism? It's not a new question to Clive, who'd given a presentation after launching *Requiem for a Species*. "A lot of people were in shock, and I was *rebuked*, vigorously, by an ecologist. He took me aside and *lectured* me about how I was *irresponsible* to write this book and I should be giving people *hope*." Even now when I think back on it, I can hear the dismal tone of Clive's voice as he said *hope*.

Clive continued, "I said 'So we should *lie* to people?', and he said, 'Oh no no no, I don't believe that.' Well then let's treat people as adults, let's treat them as though they can deal with the truth. And if the truth means we grieve, so be it."

---

74   If you find that depressing news, here's a lighter facet of the Anthropocene. It's now being said that a marker of this era will be ... chickens. There are now 21 billion chooks around the world—three for every person on the planet, which means future palaeontologists may be digging up drumstick fossils. Carys E Bennett, et al, "The broiler chicken as a signal of a human reconfigured biosphere", 12 December 2018, www.royalsocietypublishing. org/lookup/doi/10.1098/rsos.180325.

"I do know people who have, and they've become immobilised. I don't blame them for that. We all respond to these things differently. I'm more worried about the people who deny it, close it off as if everything is all right. I don't think that's a responsible way to respond to the facts."

As Clive recounted this story, the pitch of his voice changed, sounding, I thought—anxious. His inflexion rose as he said *rebuked*, carrying tinges of resentment and frustration. He might be capable of delivering a "clinical and factual" presentation on the topic, but reliving the moment was not easy.

Clive describes the large-scale predicament facing humanity, but what toll has it taken on him? When I asked, he paused, sighed, and then looked at his watch. "Ohhh, what day is it today? When I wrote *Requiem for a Species,* it was after I'd written a paper that set it out so clearly, so *brutally*, that it sent me into a very deep depression. That was the natural response, but I came out of it just enough to write the book. That year, and the next couple of years, I was deeply disturbed. And at one level, I still am."

It is, he says, like the stages of grieving: Denial, Anger, Bargaining, Depression, Acceptance. "One comes out of it, and you get with it, and you can become effective, and passionate, but not become absorbed in it. The Earth is changing, but we can slow it down, which is why we must not sink into the slough of despair, and not come out."

I asked how he thought his writing might affect people. What message should he give younger generations? He frowned, then paused before he answered. I can still hear the edge of desperation in his voice. "I ask myself, 'How do I talk to my grandchildren about this?' I don't know the answer to that. *I don't want to talk to them about this.*"

I had similar thoughts a few days later when I joined my co-producer Eleanor in the studio to broadcast the interview. Eleanor was close to finishing her Chemistry PhD and was contemplating her future life. How did she feel about this? She's not a person who looks to be prone to negativity, but after hearing Clive she said, "That was really depressing." Her peers are of an age where they're making plans, getting married, buying houses, and having kids.

In my youth, there was talk of nuclear war and the possibility that our world would be consumed by the insane strategy of Mutually Assured Destruction. To us it was a theoretical proposition, a disaster that *could* happen. We had the possibility of calamity, but climate change is different because it *is actually* happening. In my lifetime it's gone from just being a possibility to us seeing glimpses of what a disrupted global climate system looks like. Nuclear weapons and global warming aren't going away. Humanity is doing a poor job on both fronts.

I felt sorry. Sorry for being one of the generations that have inflicted this on our children, sorry for exposing Eleanor to such gloom. I apologised before launching into a short impassioned speech to her and our radio audience that whatever comes, whatever the odds, we must do our best.

My response to Clive Hamilton's depressing story was similar to Siwan's. After his talk at the conference, her opening words were: "Well, Clive said to me that it was my job to pick up the pieces, and that is what I am going to do." Hers was a call to action, but are we really just fiddling?

"I still feel that locally we can do so much to create environments that are able to shelter humans and ecology from the negative impacts of climate change," she said.

Rivers of Carbon

The Rivers of Carbon program provides funding and works with landowners to repair degraded waterways. Siwan points out that a degraded river stores less than 2% of the carbon that a pristine river does, and the difference is visible in the drain I'd shown her earlier. The concrete base has a sad, thin layer of algae and not much else. The occasional yabbies and feral weather-loach make their way upstream, but compared to its natural state, it's barren.

At Australind: Margie Fitzpatrick (far right), with Siwan Lovett and other members of the team (photo by Rod Taylor).

Downstream, the concrete gives way to a creek that is closer to what was once there. It's still a boggy, messy creek, and the main difference is the assortment of weed plants and pest fish. The muddy puddles are thick with redfin and fat, ponderous European carp. The carp are filter feeders that churn up the sediment, making the water murky. Swarms of mosquito fish were introduced in Australia in 1925 to reduce swarms of mosquitoes—which is ironic because they also eat frog larvae that would otherwise reduce mosquitoes. Collectively, the feral fish have effectively eliminated native fish from our creek, and yabbies are uncommon. The flow of water is also very different, with urban runoff and changed flow patterns from upstream where the city has grown enormously.

The creek may be seriously degraded, but it's far better than the drain upstream. Returning this waterway to its natural condition may be technically possible, but it's not viable. It has been forever altered, and now the job is to nurture it so that it remains a vibrant waterway. For all its flaws, the creek is a reasonably attractive part of the landscape where people walk to appreciate nature. It retains a vital role as a filtering system to trap sediment and urban runoff. Further down, it runs into the Molonglo River, and then into one of the world's great river systems, the Murrumbidgee.

Our drain is now about 40 years old and we've since learned something about the value of wetlands, with some of those concrete drains being ripped up and converted into semi-natural ponds. The builders of the drain may have done long-term damage, but they did construct a concrete sediment trap just before it flows into a pond. It shows at least they had some idea of the function of a creek.

Riding my bicycle to visit Siwan one morning, I was thinking about rivers when I came across a bizarre and frightening scene. I had to cross a busy intersection with four lanes of traffic in each direction. On the far side was a grey-haired man holding a walking cane in one hand and a sonic guide in the other. It's a difficult crossing even if you're fit and have good eyes, but he didn't seem to want assistance so I rode on. I presume he made it safely because I haven't seen any news with the headline, "Bystander Watches as Blind Man Hit by Car".

Twenty minutes later I met Siwan and she told me about the Rivers of Carbon approach to rivers. She says we should *mess it up and slow it down*. It's an approach that reverses our natural inclination to make things tidy by removing obstacles. Straighten up that messy river, get rid of the water weeds and the fallen trees. Siwan says healthy rivers "are complex and messy. They retain water, nutrients, and carbon."

The old-school land management practices say we should

"clear our paddocks, pick up wood and natural 'litter'. Straighten our streams and get water flowing as quickly as possible." Just like that road and just like our drain, I thought—fast and efficient, but unfriendly to life. Another sterile construction built for a single purpose, swift and tidy designed to channel stuff—water or cars—as fast as possible. Fast roads are dangerous for people, and modified fast rivers strip away topsoil and biodiversity. They might be neat, but they're both sad, depleted environments, hostile to life. Concrete drains and motorways are among the ugliest constructions ever conceived by humans.

The Great Barrier Reef

In April 2017, reports appeared with more news of how humans are affecting the oceans. An ABC story showed great white slabs of dead coral. "Great Barrier Reef: Severe coral bleaching hits two-thirds of reef, aerial surveys show."[75] At 2,300 kilometres long, the reef is considered the largest living thing on Earth. The main culprit is warming, but another is runoff from agriculture. Along the Queensland coast, the sugarcane farmers are under scrutiny.

It might be tempting to drop into the blame cycle, but farmers apply fertiliser to their crops to improve productivity—to grow food that we then eat. They're as concerned about the Great Barrier Reef as anyone. One told the *Huffington Post*, "I don't think any cane farmer goes out there to actively wreck the reef."[76] Saving the reef means improving farming practices, but Siwan's approach is to support them, not attack them.

---

75   "Great Barrier Reef: Severe coral bleaching hits two-thirds of reef, aerial surveys show", *ABC News*, 10 April 2017, www.abc.net.au/news/2017-04-10/great-barrier-reef-severe-coral-bleaching-hits-two-thirds/8429662.

76   Cayla Dengate, "How Your Sugar And The Great Barrier Reef Are Inextricably Connected", *Huffington Post*, 6 February 2017, https://www.huffingtonpost.com.au/2017/02/03/how-your-sugar-and-the-great-barrier-reef-are-inextricably-conne_a_21602809/.

On one trip, Siwan and Phil Price were visiting a sugarcane farmer in Innisfail, in the heart of Queensland sugarcane country. A local farmer, Tom, was held up as a champion of riparian management in the community because of how he'd adapted his land to trap sediment. He'd planted hardwood trees that he would later harvest. Tom and his wife drove Siwan and Phil across the paddocks to show off the work, but when they arrived, they were speechless. "We hopped out and, I kid you not, in front of us behind these tall waving fields of sugarcane was this most beautiful park landscape. The trees had been mown around it. It was like walking through Windsor Castle, or a Japanese garden. Tom was so proud, so proud!"

Phil and Siwan looked at each other and kept quiet. Tom had got it wrong, and somehow they'd need to break the news without offending him. The riparian zone was beautiful, but it wasn't trapping much at all because the short grass wasn't doing anything to slow the water. Siwan was wondering how to respond when she remembered she had an edition of their magazine *RipRap*, which included an article on sediments. So she left Tom with a copy and made arrangements to return the next day. She recounts what happened next.

We were bumping along in a ute across the back of the paddock going to look at a wetland in the neighbour's paddock and he said to me, "You've got lovely teeth. Where did you get your teeth?"

I didn't know what to say. So I said, "That's good. From my parents I guess." Anyway, we drove along a bit and he said, "I had a look about *RipRap* last night," and I said, "Did you find it interesting?"

He said, "Yes, I was reading this article, and it was saying you have to keep the grass a bit longer to trap the sediment."

And I said, "Well, yes you do."

Tom said, "I'm cutting my grass too short, aren't I?"

I said, "Yes, you are. If you could let that grass grow a bit longer, that would trap sediment from going into the river."

He'd been mowing around the edges because that says they're good farmers, and it's nice and neat. But what we're actually telling them is it's gotta be messier.

She described another occasion when she and her colleagues were visiting a property and she heard one of them remark, "Well, this is a shit piece of stream." She remembers thinking "No one is going to invite us back here again. You're trampling all over the place, and all over their identity." If they'd spoken that way when they were visiting Tom's, it would never have worked; he wouldn't have listened and he'd still be showing off his neatly trimmed grass.

Their investment of time and energy building relationships gave them the foundation to develop guidelines for the sugar industry. "That's the power of empathy and emotional intelligence," she says. "It's what I've noticed over the years when you start listening."

The Sheep Farmer

Margie Fitzpatrick's sheep station, north-east of Canberra, has been occupied by her family since the mid-1800s. In the shearing shed is a large aerial photograph of the land as it was 10 years ago. It's a bleak scene, showing the damage inflicted since Australind was converted into a farm. The low ridges are lightly treed, but the land around the watercourses is badly degraded. Sheet erosion has stripped large areas of soil, leaving ugly white scars. Parts of the creek have cut gullies into what was once productive land

The early settlers arriving from Europe had no idea how to manage land in the Australian environment where the soils are poor and rains are unpredictable. In Britain, farms are covered with rich, thick grass, and there is no El Niño to flick weather between extremes of wet and dry. These farmers were told to clear vegetation as quickly as possible, to recreate "British" farms. For many years, Australia's soldier-settler schemes subsidised the clearing. They chopped and ring-barked trees at a furious rate because they were seen as an obstacle to good farming. My grandfather was a mild man (born 1904), and one of my few memories of him ever showing anger was when he described how the Mallee country was treated. Axes and chainsaws weren't fast enough, so they'd dragged a chain between two bulldozers.

The results were disastrous, and within a few decades soils and rivers suffered lasting damage. In the good years, they heavily stocked their paddocks so that when drought came there was nothing to protect the soil. Margie recalls what it was like at Australind: "I can remember coming down here and seeing all the erosion, and thinking how horrible it all was and I couldn't imagine what we were going to do about it."

The loss of soil is yet another daunting problem. There's evidence that the collapse of the Roman Empire was connected to the way they allowed their soils to degrade. Soil also goes by the name dirt. It's a disparaging term, but the equation is simple: soil equals food. We have a long way to go to feed a growing population.

Like the Prells, Margie's story is of people on the land struggling through the Millennium Drought. She describes what it was like: "When the drought came in the nineties, it wore a really big hole in my husband. Two weeks after we moved here he was diagnosed with advanced cancer. I remember digging in the garden one day and I was really cranky because he was going to leave us. I decided I really want to live here, I really want to live this life. I'm going to live here with you or without you. I was cranky and I didn't want him to die."

Margie Fitzpatrick packs a lot of energy into her small frame.

She decided that she was going to restore Australind but, she says, she "had no idea how to repair anything", so she started working with local Landcare groups and Greening Australia and later the Rivers of Carbon team. With their help, she completed several projects and now she's a Rivers of Carbon champion and member of the team. Siwan says it's connections like these that show the power of the network.

The first thing they did was put in fencing to keep stock away from the edges of the streams and the badly eroded areas. They planted trees and shrubs, and they constructed rock pools to get the water safely down rather than eroding. They were reversing the misguided practices of the first farmers who'd believed the best way was to tidy up their paddocks and move water quickly through the land. Instead, they were messing it up and slowing it down.

Where the small gullies started to form along the valleys, they arranged rocks into a rough interlocking pattern that would slow the water and trap sediment and vegetation before it washed into the creek. Over time these will gather silt, allowing grasses and shrubs to take root. The sadly degraded hills will slowly revert to productive pasture. The trees provide shade for the soil as well as the grass, and on hot summer days it gives refuge to stock and wildlife.

The work with Margie and other landowners shows what can happen when people are motivated. It's not something that can be imposed from outside. Siwan is clear: "We never go anywhere unless we're invited." It happens when landowners see a benefit, whether it's economic, environmental, or aesthetics.

Siwan's focus is on people, but people are complicated and their motives can be different. What happens, I asked, if a landowner disagrees? What if they have different priorities? That sparked a response. Siwan told me firmly, but gently, "We don't have those conversations."

Undeterred, I ploughed on. "Do you ever find you have

differences of opinion on, say, whether to increase stock numbers?" Okay, dumb question.

Her response was firmer this time, but still gentle. "When they have a strong, emotionally based belief, we don't have those conversations. Sometimes you disagree. We don't make progress by being adversarial. It's much better if we win people over. If we can do that we'll have a true advocate." That makes sense, I thought. You'll have no greater ally than a sceptic converted.

Margie Fitzpatrick (far right) showing us around Australind
(photo by Rod Taylor).

Siwan and the Rivers of Carbon team had organised a field day to celebrate the transformation that was occurring at Australind. I arrived on a cold and foggy morning to find a crowd assembled at Margie's shearing shed. People stood around a small fire, drinking coffee served by the catering van. The road there required a few complicated turns, but each intersection had been carefully marked by large, helpful signs. Soon everyone was ushered inside to hear the Australind story. The audience was enthusiastic and engaged, but what they didn't know was that Siwan had been fretting all week.

"I thought no one was going to come. I was getting all negative," she said.

She began her presentation with a PowerPoint slide, highlighting Rivers of Carbon's achievements:

Revegetated 994.6 hectares, Sowed 36.7 kilograms of seed
Planted 136,060 tubestock
Protected 110.5 hectares remnant vegetation
Enhanced 376.4 hectares of remnant vegetation
Controlled weeds on 478 hectares
Fenced 145 kilometres

Then she flicked the side aside and told the audience, "That's the management stuff, but if you ask the Rivers of Carbon team what really matters":

Working with 103 landholders, 1843 volunteers
Indigenous and Green Army partnerships
45 events
Reaching thousands through social media

In other words, by harnessing the energy of people, the successes on Australind can be amplified many times.

After the presentations, Margie took us down to show us the results of the hard work. Her enthusiasm was contagious as she showed us with obvious pride what they'd achieved. Improving the land on Australind still has a long way to go, but we saw plant life returning to the valleys. The creek has developed pools with rich growth of reeds and sedges, and what looked like clean water. It was slow, messy, and to my untrained eye, it's a healthy system.

Margie's satisfaction shows. "It's taken this long since I was 16 and I'm way past that," she says, "but now I'm finally doing something about it."

Across Australia, the effects of climate change are starting to show, and science is highlighting the need to make land resilient. As temperatures increase and rainfall becomes more sporadic, the job of nurturing water and vegetation is becoming urgent. Healthy ground cover will help to constrain soil temperature and retain water. The messy pools on Australind have become hotspots of biodiversity, refuges that allow life to return when conditions improve.

Margie's farm still needs a lot of work, but she can see the results. "The watercourse is now incredible," she says. "The life is vibrant. There is shade and a lot of green. There's biodiversity of plants and different species."

"It's tremendous, it makes me get up and keep going. When I look down at the river, I see how beautiful it is. I love to sit down there and think wow, this is beautiful."

"That's a piece of cake at the end of the day."

Paris 2015

Going into the Paris climate talks of 2015, Clive Hamilton wasn't optimistic. He'd seen attempts to get international agreement on global warming, saying, "Copenhagen in 2009 is when everything collapsed. It was a disaster from every point of view." He'd witnessed promises that turned to failure. "I believed, or at least half-believed, that when BP rebranded itself as Beyond Petroleum, I thought this was something really important."

"But what a fool I was. BP started drilling in the Arctic and buying up every oil well they could. It was a cynical exercise by BP."

The prospects for the Paris summit were not looking good. "What

I saw at Paris was this dreadful shadow of Copenhagen hanging over us and the prospect of catastrophic failure." He went with low expectations, but he says there was a glimmer. "Environment activists went into a deep depression, but they learned lessons of how to build consensus."

He says a combination of economics and the skill of the French organisers changed the dynamics of what happened next. "Mark Carney [Governor of the Bank of England] was talking about the way in which the central bankers of the world were worried that the switch out of fossil fuel energy may be so abrupt that there would be many stranded fossil fuel assets—and that it will spark a global financial crisis. So they commissioned a report on how to manage the transition to a zero-emissions economy."

Given the right circumstances, he thinks change is possible. "I've never seen anything like that at a conference in the past." At another event, there were institutional investors. "These are the big picture people. These guys don't talk about billions per day. They talk in *trillions*. All they were talking about was how they were going to move toward renewable energy and away from fossil fuels because they recognise the risk."

I've never come remotely close to knowing a global investment banker and the idea of someone who can sign off on a billion dollars before breakfast is completely alien. It's hard to imagine a group of people further removed from someone like Margie Fitzpatrick raising sheep on a modest farm. And yet they have something in common. In the end, they are just people doing their best. Whether it's shifting money or shifting livestock, they have families and friends, they care about their health, and they want the people around them to thrive. Nobody wants to destroy the planet.

Making stupendous amounts of money isn't something that interests me (well, not much), but it'd be pointless to expect everyone to think the same way. A human flaw is to project our own logic onto someone else. Their life situation and history may be nothing like yours. We don't change people's motivations, and if we want to affect their behaviour we need to work with how they think. Clive saw an element of this in Paris. He said their interest in renewable energy was "not because they had an ethical epiphany, that they looked into their grandchildren's eyes and said, 'I've got to become a good person and get out of fossil fuels.' They could see a hard business case for change."

Siwan Lovett understands this and uses the same principles to engage landowners. Start with the person's concerns, learn what their needs are, and work with that. Leadership begins with the question: Why? Why change, why spend time and energy doing something? Until that's established, there's not much point in talking about the What or the How.

My encounters with Siwan Lovett and Clive Hamilton left me wondering about the role of hope. If we have no hope, why even try? Give up and sink into despair. Or party. Blitz the back yard. But then I get Clive's point: why pretend? When we're facing a crisis, let's call it what it is. Goodness knows we're already paying the price for denialism from those who say it's our God-given right to do whatever we want. Grow, consume as fast as we can, and hang the consequences.

I must confess to feeling deeply pessimistic, but then hope is not a binary condition because there are shades and no matter how bad things get we can always do better. If ever it seems futile, there's one thing I know. We could easily fail, but doing nothing will *definitely* fail.[77]

---

77   I'm reminded of this advertisement posted by Ernest Shackleton before embarking on an expedition to Antarctica: "Men wanted for hazardous journey. Small wages, bitter cold, long months of complete darkness, constant danger, safe return doubtful. Honour and recognition in case of success."

The vast majority of humanity has neither the knowledge nor the ability to solve problems of this scale. Most people are fully occupied just trying to get by. Feed the kids, pay the rent, look after Grandma. Everybody has some role to play, but the readers of *Fragile Planet* have a vital role to play. We occupy a special place in history, and what we do is critical. Surely that's something to hope for.

Epilogue
Houston, I Have a Plan

Did I say a plan? Actually, I don't have a plan, but I do have a dream. I have a dream that we will change our attitude to the planet, and stop treating it like a Magic Pudding—that no matter how much you take, there's always more. I dream that we will let go of the notion that prosperity relies on consuming as much as we can, as fast as we can. I dream that we will learn to nurture our fragile planet, not just because it's a beautiful place, but because we have no choice.

The genius of Martin Luther King's speech was not that he told us about a plan, but that he explained *why*. Why should anybody want to do anything—what's the point? It's the essential first step because the boldest, most beautiful plan will rot in a desk drawer if nobody's interested.

If there's one defining attribute shared by the people in this book, it's motivation—these are people who understand *why* we need to act. Each has seized upon the idea that there is something important; that there's something they can do for the environment and for the community. The people in *Fragile Planet* are fiercely driven to avert the worst of climate change.

Their motivation is coupled with the sense that they are not helpless. They are not simply passengers in the back of the aeroplane going wherever the pilot takes them and then complaining when they're going somewhere they don't like. They can see what needs to be done, and get out of their seat and do it. Even though Inez Harker-Schuch was raised by dysfunctional parents, she realised early in life that she was able to care for her siblings and her mother who suffered multiple sclerosis. She saw a goal, and her life experiences showed her that she could do something.

Simon Sheikh acquired a strong sense of social justice from his parents. And like Inez, he cared for his parents during his early years when his father had a heart attack and his mother suffered mental illness. He began his activism while at high school by writing a letter to the editor. He joined the Australian Youth Climate Coalition, and later took over leadership of GetUp. His motivation to drive these causes was paired with a realisation that he could influence the things that matter to him. This, combined with exceptional intelligence, taught him what he could do.

If each person started with motivation, what came next is as diverse as any ten characters might be. Susan Jeanes chose politics. Andrew Blakers toiled for years in a lab to learn how to make better solar cells. Leonard Cohen found ways to plant trees. Siwan Lovett studied social science, which she applied to restoring river landscapes. Kate Auty's career in law gave her the power to work toward social justice and, in particular, to help the plight of Aboriginal people and the environment.

Where their motivation comes from is hard to say. Partly it's in their bones—something nature put there—and partly it's circumstance that nurtured it. Almost all the people I met spoke of others who inspired them. Every time I met Kate Auty, she made glowing references to one person or another who'd shaped her thinking. Monica Oliphant was listening to the radio when she heard McFarlane Burnett saying that unlike oil, no country ever went to war over renewable energy. Siwan Lovett was mentored by Phil Price, who steered her toward work in the environment where she could connect with landowners and rural communities. Leonard Cohen spoke of how he was motivated by his mother and Gael Rudwick, who gave him ideas about *why* we need to save the environment. In that sense, those people were leaders to him, which then inspired his own leadership in planting trees. This gives a clue to the next defining attribute of the people in *Fragile Planet*.

Each person's life was influenced by another person who showed leadership, and, in turn, they became leaders. It's this thread of leadership that drives the ripple of change that we need. In some ways, this seems like a contradiction because much of the news we hear is focused on science and technology, while leadership sits quietly in the background. Yet the most wondrous piece of technology is worthless without the will to use it. It's not technology that's lacking, it's leadership.

Charlie Prell saw opportunities for wind energy, which he's combined with his heritage in farming and rural communities. His approachable, no-nonsense manner is something that connects with other landowners. Now he devotes much of his time to promoting renewable energy and advocating for farmers who are facing the disastrous effects of climate change.

Olympia Yarger is also driven by a love of agriculture and has seen how maggots can convert mountains of food waste into high-quality animal feed. She's as happy lugging around bins of stale vegetables as she is presenting to a room of venture capitalists. Using her pragmatic skills, she's creating an innovative business that will earn a profit while solving an environmental problem.

Monica Oliphant and Andrew Blakers have seen how renewable energy can transform the old smoke-stack systems used to generate electricity. They both spoke of how these technologies will lead us away from polluting oil that has triggered so much destruction. They have doggedly pursued their goals in their own ways. Monica Oliphant travelled across the country, helping town councils reduce their energy costs by managing their demand and using renewable alternatives. Andrew Blakers pioneered solar technology and is now promoting pumped hydro energy storage.

Susan Jeanes is unusual, even within this group of unusual people, because she saw how politics shapes Australia's response to the big questions of social justice and climate change. Australians are rightly cynical about the failure of politics to address urgent issues. Yet, as a member of parliament, Jeanes's presence was significant during the John Howard term of government when the first renewable energy target was formulated. Those targets gave a critical boost to the work of people such as Monica Oliphant and Andrew Blakers.

Jeanes shows that even within conservative politics there are some who understand the urgency of climate change. Since then, conservative politics has been captured by people who believe that the goal of humanity is materialistic individualism. They have scuppered attempts to address climate change because they can't tolerate the idea of a government intervening in the economy. The approach is doomed because if we don't change the economy, physics will do it for us. We're beginning to see the early signs of vast economic impacts inflicted by more serious droughts and violent storms, and we have not yet reached 1.5 degrees warming. This thinking is also driving moderate voices away from the conservative side and as it does so, politics is sinking into polarised, partisan debates about whether climate change is even real.

The political split over environmental issues in Australia and the US is an unmitigated disaster. In both countries, the right-wing of politics has come to view climate change as a socialist conspiracy to undermine capitalism. While Al Gore made a powerful pair of documentaries, *The Inconvenient Truth*, an unfortunate side effect has been to exacerbate the divide, swinging many Republicans into climate change denialism.

For people concerned about climate change, politics is a depressing place because it's the compost bin where science goes to die. The bin is littered with the mouldering corpses of one report after another that pressed for urgent action, which were then skewered by ideology. The Garnaut and Finkel reviews were pragmatic attempts to balance economic and environmental concerns with political reality. Both failed.

The problem is that science and politics don't play by the same rules. Politics is largely the art of convincing people that you are right and that your opponent is not just wrong, but that they are weak, incompetent, or even corrupt. Too often, they resort to distortion, obfuscation, and outright lies because winning is more important than the truth. They do it because politics relies on the ability to persuade people with the force of argument, which is why so many politicians come from law backgrounds.

That might work in parliament, but the Earth's climate system isn't listening. To connect with political thinking, scientists must learn how to be *climate whisperers*—don't change the science, but understand the logic of why politicians behave as they do. Most want to do the right thing but they are deeply constrained in the fishbowl of public attention where appearance means everything, and where they are forced to compromise by the bargaining of one goal or one constituency against another.

Does that sound excessively pessimistic? Maybe it is because Jeanes and a few politicians I have met seemed to me to be genuine people. Part of the problem, of course, is that the media feasts on a good stoush, and that makes them all look bad. The media loves conflict and adores finding a politician who's caught out for one reason or another. Added to that is the relentless bias of some major media players. The Murdoch press is relentlessly antagonistic, running headlines during the 2019 federal election such as "Priceless: Shorten's climate change cost". This is all part of the environment they inhabit. If you've ever endured a toxic work culture, you'll know how that can drive even the best people to behave like monsters. While there are a few lamentable characters in politics, much of their behaviour can be explained by a sick political landscape.

Science, then, is another trait that unites the people in this book. Each accepts the evidence-based critical thinking that is the core of science, and even where they don't have first-hand expertise, they know that on balance it can be trusted. Simon Sheikh's training may be in economics, but he knows what climate change is doing to our planet. Seeing the devastation of Cyclone Tracy, Inez Harker-Schuch chose the difficult path from a successful modelling career to studying science, and now she's building a climate computer game. Olympia Yarger has the help of taxonomist Dr Bryan Lessard to find the best insects to process food waste. At her plant, she monitors qualities such as protein in the animal feed they produce.

While these are examples of science in the western tradition, Aboriginal people have had 60,000 years to observe the ecology of the Australian landscape. Scientists are now starting to learn from the first Australians, but sadly an enormous amount of their knowledge has been lost, particularly in the southern and eastern parts of the country. Just over 200 years of European occupation has been devastating to indigenous people and their culture, and they continue to suffer disadvantage.

Kate Auty has dedicated much of her professional life to redressing this disadvantage. But it's more than that because she's helping to restore a sense of pride and to celebrate what Aboriginal people have achieved. Kate Auty's story is central to this book because she builds the link between the environment and people. The irony is that a modern technological civilisation has so much to learn from people who were once viewed as primitive. We might learn, not simply for some notion of cultural equality, but because our situation is urgent. Aboriginal people understand that the environment is not just another resource to be exploited until it's gone.

Siwan Lovett, too, is an exemplar of the link between people, science, and the environment. Her focus has been to bring people together to solve difficult problems. She and the other people in this book are helping with the critical work of strengthening the community. They know that the most important hurdle is not technology or science, it's people. Technology is easy, people are hard.

A large part of science is simple curiosity. There's a fundamental, innate joy in learning about nature and how to manipulate it. Olympia Yarger made an interesting observation about her success when she said, "Don't pretend you know something when you don't, just ask the right people and you'll keep learning." Susan Jeanes said something similar when she was invited to be interviewed by Stan Zemanek. She realised that she knew nothing about the radio talk show host, so she asked for advice. It was a clever move because Zemanek was an acerbic character who enjoyed trapping unwary guests. Armed with that knowledge, she was able to beat Zemanek at his own game.

In these stories, we can see strength in our ability to ask questions. The art of the question is our most powerful tool—for it is through questioning that we uncover the truth. It is the question that reveals what other people think, what they care about, and what they can do. The unspoken message in a question is that we value the person we are talking to, and that is an essence of leadership.

One thing I did not discuss much with the people in the book, but cannot let pass, is the question of population growth. The impact of this is almost completely ignored, and political parties such as the Greens seem terrified to mention it because of connotations of racism. However, there's nothing racist about helping people of all ethnic groups across the world to control their population growth. Right now Australia is running a near-suicidal rate of growth that is damaging not just the environment, but stretching infrastructure to the point of breaking. My own town of Canberra used to be a "town" but now it's becoming yet another bloated city with the skies full of construction cranes. Every problem is more difficult to solve with this rate of growth.

I began *Fragile Planet* fretting about the rise of Donald Trump. A year later it's no surprise that he and his cohort are inflicting enormous damage. His concerted attack on science and anything related to the environment has generated ripples of despair. What hope do we have when the world's most powerful nation elects him as president?

That raises the question of hope. Should we shroud ourselves with some sort of "hopey gloss" as Clive Hamilton puts it? It's tricky because there's a fine line between a tough problem and an impossible one. Do we collapse into the pit of doom because it's all too difficult?

The ten people in *Fragile Planet* say otherwise. They have not given up, they have not surrendered. Each of them has persevered, often through great adversity on a journey that parallels our global challenge.

While climate scientists talk about tipping points, perhaps we're also seeing social tipping points. The Berlin Wall is a famous example of how, almost overnight, a society can rapidly flip into a new state. As I write in 2019, there are signs that attitudes are changing in Australia and elsewhere. People are realising that climate change is a dire threat, and they are demanding action.

Maybe, then, I do have a plan. I shall write a book that tells the story of ten remarkable Australians, which you shall read, and perhaps you too shall feel inspired.

Afterword

It's now April 2020, and we've decided to delay publishing until October. Amid the global pandemic, we felt the launch would get lost among all the other news.

In all, it's been a horrendous start to the year, almost beyond comprehension. Australia has recorded its worst-ever drought, followed by the worst-ever bushfires. Vast areas of the country have been devastated. Before the current lockdown rules, we travelled to the NSW coast, down to Victoria. We'd all seen the images in the media, but to see it first-hand was heart-breaking.

By the time you read this, the US election will probably be over. I began this book fretting about the election of Donald Trump. It might've been worse, but some of my worst fears have come to pass because he and his cohort have inflicted vast damage, not just to the environment, but to the foundations of democracy. Trust in institutions, science—and truth in general—has been eroded toward a culture that promotes emotional, sometimes violent responses. Meanwhile, our government in Australia is at the whim of the vested interests of corporations such as coal miners.

On the brighter side, I hear snippets from the people in this book. Monica Oliphant, despite her senior years, remains a powerhouse, driving renewable energy through numerous forums. Charlie Prell has become a force behind Farmers for Climate action, making their presence felt in political circles. Conservative politicians are being forced to notice the changing attitudes of their traditional base. Olympia Yarger's business, Goterra, has just received a major cash injection and is making waves with their modular food-waste processing systems.

Also on a brighter note, Anne and I have recently become grandparents. Rowan's blue eyes stare at us with curiosity and a piercing intelligence. While the year 2100 seems a long way off, he could live to that age. I wonder what the world will look like then? It reminds me daily, whatever the odds, we cannot give up now.

The themes in *Fragile Planet* are more urgent than ever, as is the heroic work by people whose stories it tells. A startling and encouraging sign we're witnessing is conservative governments who have blithely ignored scientists about global threats suddenly taking notice and acting on their advice. We even have neoliberal-thinking governments spending huge sums of money to keep economies and communities afloat.

We are fortunate they have realised the only way forward is through concerted collective action, while unfettered self-interest will lead to disaster. Maybe some of this will signal a longer-term change of culture. We can only hope.

Rod Taylor
October 2020

Acknowledgments

Thinking about writing a book? Writing a collection of biographies is far more difficult than I knew. Don't even start until you have people around you like those who've helped me.

For starters, people who knew nothing about me had to share with me—and you—their very personal and sometimes harrowing stories. That's a level of trust I've found almost daunting. I cannot begin to thank enough each of the people who allowed me to write about them. They are a remarkable collection of people showing dedication in the face of what could be a terrifying future. They give me hope that we can make a difference.

The next time you watch a movie, notice the long list of credits showing just how many people are behind a production. Visible on the front cover of *Fragile Planet* is my name, and inside are the people whose stories we read. What you don't see are those who have supported me through this project. It's taken over three years, which is a long time to see a result. Sustaining that effort is not easy, and I cannot say strongly enough that the encouragement of many people has kept me going. Staring for hours at a wobbly manuscript grinds you down. I've been buoyed and excited by people who've done nothing more than show an interest. Maybe it's just "I can't wait to read your book", or "How's it going, Rod?" I can't list them all, but I assure you, we wouldn't be here without them. Not least among those people is Jenny Goldie, who is always helpful, always encouraging.

A key person who got me started was Heather Smith, who I met at the Community Energy Congress in 2017. We did a "speed dating" event and, through her, I met Leonard Cohen, Monica Oliphant, and Susan Jeanes. They are great characters, thank you! And, Dear Reader, keep your eyes out for Heather and the next Community Energy Congress. I'm not good with large gatherings, but I don't think I've ever been to an event that was so busy with the most wonderful, optimistic people.

Then having written a manuscript, there's the huge, challenging job of looking in an unbiased way at your own work. For that, I'm eternally grateful to Madeleine Parker and Dr Rebecca Colvin. Mads and Bec went through each chapter in detail, suggesting where I could improve the story. Their insights have been crucial— not just to make it better, but to motivate me. Both are adept at the shit-sandwich method of criticism that goes like this: "Rod, I really enjoyed this chapter, but what you could improve is ..." This would be a far poorer book without their help.

Other surprising people who helped popped up along the way. I went to a really excellent talk by Mark Reed, a professor visiting from the UK. His work revolves around making research "impactful". A key, he says, is empathy. That's empathy to understand the needs and motivations of others. His ideas are things we could take through all facets of life, not just academic fields. Look him up at www.profmarkreed.com.

After his talk, I approached Mark to ask if he'd be willing to give me feedback on my book, and even though he'd never heard of me, he agreed! A few weeks later, he sent me very thoughtful comments on how to improve it. That was most generous, given it's the only time we've ever met.

On the same evening, I met Savanah McGuirk, who encouraged

me to talk to Mark. And then she offered to help review the manuscript. That she did, while on a holiday to the UK! Savanah duly sent me back her edits, picking up a bunch of things that I had missed (it can happen).

If ever you've written biography, you'll know one of the mind-numbing, tedious jobs is transcribing interviews. Even harder for me, because I am severely hearing-impaired. For each chapter, I had five hours or more of recorded interviews. Well, how about that—by chance, I was doing some community work with Polly Templeton, whose day job happened to be transcribing parliamentary speeches for Hansard. Thank you, Polly.

Writing a book can be a family affair, as it was with this one. I liked the idea of getting my mum and my sister Alison to help me de-mangle my words. The Grammar Gorillas provided, shall we say, fearless feedback on my sometimes garbled writing.

In my household, there are differing opinions on who came up with the idea of writing an environment book that focuses on people. My daughter Katie reckons she said, "Write about people." Well, that's her story anyway. Katie is herself an accomplished fiction author and does highly professional manuscript assessment. Look her up on KJTaylor.com.

Having survived all that, the next thing was to find a publisher. In that, a huge help to me was Laurine Croasdale from the Australian Society of Authors (asauthors.org). I highly recommend ASA to any aspiring author.

The publisher turned out to be Michelle Lovi from Odyssey Books. Thank you, Michelle, for your trust. And then, for gently but doggedly rescuing my prose from those places where the cat walked across my keyboard.

Finally, if you've ever lived with a person writing a book, you'll know we can be really tedious. Even when we're not writing, we're thinking about writing, so that when prompted, we'll talk for hours. For putting up with me, I am eternally grateful to my wife Anne. Anne humoured me, made meaningful suggestions, and encouraged me all the way through. And then she'd skilfully change the topic because there are other things in our world beyond me and my book.

About the Author

As a boy, Rod Taylor watched with fascination the moon landing. That sparked an interest in science that has never faded. An offhand remark by his father around the same time was his first environmental awareness, which has progressed from interest, to concern, and now to alarm.

Today, Rod is a Canberra-based science writer. Rod's science columns have appeared in the *Canberra Times* newspaper and other publications for over 10 years. He broadcasts a weekly science show and has appeared on ABC local radio, Radio National, and the BBC.

Aside from media, his other background is in IT and business systems. He rides a unicycle and an off-road motorcycle—and has fallen off both.

He has recently completed his book: *The Edge of Silence: A sometimes grumpy, often quirky, always curious exploration of going deaf in a world of sound.*

He is currently co-editing a compilation of major writers on the Green New Deal.